# KEY IDEAS in PSYCHOLOGY

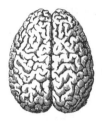

## Matt Jarvis    Julia Russell

First published in 2002 by:
Nelson Thornes Ltd
Delta Place
27 Bath Road
CHELTENHAM
GL53 7TH
United Kingdom

02 03 04 05 06 / 10 9 8 7 6 5 4 3 2 1

A catalogue record for this book is available from the British Library

ISBN 0-7487-6564-6

Illustrations by Oxford Designers and Illustrators and Florence Production Ltd
Page make-up by Florence Production Ltd

Printed and bound in Spain by GraphyCems

# Contents

# Dedications

To my son Sam, who has already enriched life beyond all expectations. MJ

To my brother Mike, for all his 'good ideas'! JR

# Introduction

PSYCHOLOGY has been shaped by a set of key ideas, some of them theories and others more general topics or specific concepts. The aim of this book is to review a selection of these key ideas and discuss how each fits into modern psychology. We have chosen a range of ideas that span the major branches of the discipline; social psychology, cognitive psychology, developmental psychology, individual differences and biological and comparative psychology.

Some of the ideas, such as evolutionary psychology and social constructionism, are relatively new, and you may not see much written about them in traditional psychology texts. Others, for example classical conditioning and Freudian psychoanalysis, have been around as long as psychology itself, but you may be surprised at how much psychologists have discovered about them in recent years, and how important they remain in contemporary psychology.

For both new and more traditional ideas we have aimed to produce a 'state of the art' account. We have broken down each key idea into small, manageable chunks, reviewed the latest research findings in the area and discussed ways in which psychologists in real-life settings have applied the idea. *Key ideas in psychology* is a handbook, intended as a helpful accompaniment to other psychology text books.

# Acknowledgements

❀

We would like to thank everyone who has helped with this venture. Rick, Carolyn, Louise and Emily at Nelson Thornes have been, as always, helpful and supportive. Thanks as well to Maggie Linnell for her helpful comments.

Photo credits

- ❀ Albert Bandura (p.106)
- ❀ Bettman/Corbis (p.52, 58, 64, 90, 122)
- ❀ Corel 136 (NT) (p.43)
- ❀ Corel 638 (NT) (p.19)
- ❀ Corel 752 (NT) (p.83)
- ❀ Image 100 22 (NT) (p.1)
- ❀ Pfizer Inc. (p.111)
- ❀ Photofusion/Paul Mattsson (p.12)
- ❀ Robert Harding Picture Library (p.129)
- ❀ Science Photo Library (p.24)
- ❀ Stanley Milgram © 1965 (p.96)
- ❀ Wellcome Library (p.31)

# Attachment theory

❦

## The Idea

A TTACHMENT THEORY WAS FIRST DEVELOPED IN THE 1950s by psychiatrist and psychoanalyst John Bowlby. Bowlby was interested in children's emotional development and looked particularly at the impact of an infant's first relationship – that with their mother or other main carer – on their later development. He proposed that humans have evolved the need to form a close relationship in infancy, and that failure to form such a relationship harms a child's development. Mary Ainsworth contributed to our understanding of attachment by devising a system for classifying attachment types and by looking into factors affecting attachment type and the consequences of attachment type.

- ❀ Maternal deprivation
- ❀ Social releasers
- ❀ Internal working models
- ❀ Classifying attachment types
- ❀ Sensitive responsiveness and competence hypotheses

## Maternal deprivation

BOWLBY considered forming an attachment to be an essential part of a child's development, and that disruption to the attachment could be harmful. In his early work Bowlby (1951) identified two particularly serious consequences of the failure to form an attachment or serious disruption to the attachment during the sensitive period (for example, prolonged separation from the primary carer).

- *Affectionless psychopathy*. This is the inability to experience guilt or deep feelings for others. This interferes enormously with one's relationships in later life. It is also associated with criminality, as affectionless psychopaths find it difficult to appreciate the feelings of their victims and so lack remorse.

- *Developmental retardation*. Bowlby proposed that there is a critical period for intellectual development and that if children are deprived of a maternal relationship for too long they could suffer retardation (abnormally low intelligence).

## Social releasers

BOWLBY noted that infants are born with a set of instinctive behaviours including smiling, sucking, gesturing and crying. He proposed that these have evolved in order to maximise the chances of being well looked after and hence surviving. Bowlby called these behaviours *social releasers*. Their function is to elicit instinctive parenting responses from adults. The interplay between social releasers and parenting responses is the process that builds the attachment between infant and carer. Failure on the part of the carer to provide the appropriate parenting response to the child's social releasers leads to psychological damage. This is a crucial aspect of Bowlby's theory as it suggests that the most important factor in a child's development is the effort and skill of their primary carer. In a classic demonstration of the importance of social releasers Brazleton et al. (1975) systematically observed mothers and babies during their interactions and noted that both mothers and babies imitated each other's movements and took turns to initiate a new movement. They called this *interactional synchrony*. The researchers also tried asking the mothers to ignore their babies' signals. The babies quickly became concerned and some curled up and became motionless.

## Internal working models

THIS is one of the most important aspects of Bowlby's theory (Bowlby, 1969). Bowlby proposed that the developing child formed a mental representation of their first attachment relationship and that this would have profound effects on their later relationships and on their own success as a parent. He called this mental representation an *internal working model*. If the child internalises a working model of attachment as kind and reliable, they will tend to bring these qualities to their future relationships. If, however, they are neglected or abused, there is a chance that they will reproduce these patterns. Bowlby believed that patterns of behaviour were transmitted down through families by the formation of internal working models as well as by passing on genes.

## Classifying attachment types

IN a naturalistic observation study, based in family homes, Ainsworth (1967) observed children's behaviour with caregivers and strangers. She suggested that different attachment types could be seen, based on the independence shown by playing infants, the anxiety they displayed when left alone or with a stranger and their response to being reunited with the primary carer. Based closely on this observational study, Ainsworth and Wittig (1969) developed a laboratory procedure to classify attachment types. This is called the *strange situation*, and it is still the most popular procedure for classifying attachments. The rationale behind the strange situation is that infants left in an unfamiliar room display different behaviour towards the primary caregiver and towards strangers according to the security of their attachments. Based on the strange situation, Ainsworth et al. (1978) proposed three types of attachment:

- *Type A – avoidant.* These children play independently and do not show distress when the mother leaves or make contact when she returns. Between 20 and 25% of British 12–18-month-old children are classified as type A.

- *Type B – securely attached.* These children play independently and do not show much distress in episodes 3 and 4. They greet the carer positively when she returns. They are likely to be distressed when left alone. Most (60–75%) British 12–18-month-old children are classified as type B.

- *Type C – resistant (or ambivalent).* These children explore less when playing than others. They are very distressed on being left with a stranger, but, although they rush to the carer on her return they do not readily accept comforting. Around 3% of British and 15% of American infants are classified as type C.

## Sensitive responsiveness and competence hypotheses

LIKE Bowlby, Ainsworth believed that the major determinant of the quality of a child–parent attachment was the quality of care provided by the primary carer. She saw the crucial ingredient of successful parenting as *sensitive responsiveness* – i.e. how successfully the parent detects and responds to the child's signals. Tracy and Ainsworth (1981) tested whether there was an association between mothers who displayed low levels of sensitive responsiveness and babies who developed insecure attachments. They observed mothers interacting with their babies in their own homes and rated them on a scale of sensitivity. The babies were meanwhile given an attachment classification based on the strange situation. The mothers of insecurely attached children (types A and C) tended to be less responsive to the child and to cuddle them less than did mothers of the type B children, supporting the idea that responsiveness is important in the development of secure attachments.

Ainsworth also proposed the *competence hypothesis*. This is the idea that securely attached infants are advantaged in their later development, especially in their ability to form successful relationships, by having a secure attachment.

# The Idea Today

MANY ASPECTS OF ATTACHMENT THEORY ARE WELL SUPPORTED BY CONTEMPORARY research – there is, for example, evidence to support the idea that patterns of relationships are passed from one generation to the next by internal working models.

Fonagy et al. (1993) assessed pregnant women's internal working models using a standard interview called the Adult Attachment Interview (AAI). They then measured how securely attached their babies were at 12 and 18 months. Mothers who reported insecure attachments with their own parents tended to be those whose babies displayed insecure attachment towards them. This strong association between mothers' reports of their own maternal attachment and their attachment with their own babies is powerful evidence for the importance of internal working models.

There is a substantial body of evidence for the idea that we are advantaged by secure attachments. McCarthy (1999) investigated the friendships and romantic relationships of 40 women. He found that those with type B attachments were more likely to have successful relationships of both types. Type As had the greatest difficulties with romantic relationships and type Cs had the poorest friendships. Myron-Wilson and Smith (1998) demonstrated the significance of attachment type in children's peer relationships in 196 children aged 7–11 from South London. Type Bs had virtually no involvement in bullying, type Cs were most commonly the bullies whilst the victims tended to be type As. Research has also demonstrated that securely attached children are advantaged in their cognitive development. Meins (1997) performed a series of studies comparing securely and insecurely attached children on a variety of cognitive tasks. In one study mothers of 30 securely attached and 18 insecurely attached 12–13-month-old infants were trained to record the children's use of language. At 19 months the records were analysed. Children are classified as 'faster' in language acquisition if they have a vocabulary of 25 words or more at 19 months and 'slower' if their vocabulary is less than 25 words. The majority of the securely attached group (77%) were classified as 'faster' in their development of language, as opposed to only 12% of the insecurely attached group.

Ainsworth's sensitive responsiveness hypothesis has received partial support from contemporary studies, although it appears that she did not take sufficient account of individual differences in the *temperament* (the genetically influenced personality) of children and the contribution this can make to attachment type. Children with type B attachments come from the complete spectrum of temperament types (Sroufe, 1985), but it seems that type A attachments are associated with both controlling and rejecting parenting (Vondra et al, 1995), *and* with a temperament characterised by low sociability and low emotional reactivity (Fox et al, 1991). Similarly, type C attachments are associated with both under-stimulating and unresponsive parenting (Vondra et al, 1995) *and* an irritable temperament (Goldsmith and Alansky, 1987). It thus seems that sensitive responsiveness is one important influence on attachment type but is not the whole story.

## Current status of the idea

THE major ideas of attachment theory are largely supported by modern research, and attachment is an important area of research and practice in current child psychology. There are, however, important criticisms of the approach. As we have seen, in its classic form attachment theory neglects the importance of temperament for children's development, and can thus be said to be *reductionist*, focusing on one aspect of development at the expense of others. Attachment theory has also been criticised by feminists (e.g. Burman, 1994) because it lays the blame for anything that goes wrong in children's development at the door of their primary carer, who is usually a woman. The idea of sensitive responsiveness places great pressure on mothers to 'get it right' and so to focus on childcare at the expense of other aspects of their lives, such as their career.

## The Idea in Action

ATTACHMENT THEORY HAS A NUMBER OF PRACTICAL APPLICATIONS IN WORKING WITH young children. Bowlby's work resulted in huge changes to standard practices in nurseries and children's wards. Before the recognition of the importance of attachment, nursery nurses were typically not permitted to form relationships with children in their care and hospitals did not permit parents to stay with sick children. This has now changed, and it is generally recognised that children benefit from the presence of attachment figures in times of stress and from having substitute attachment figures around when primary carers are not available. Fonagy's research into internal working models (Fonagy et al., 1993) has shown that we can identify mothers who are likely to have difficulty as parents because of their own parenting, meaning that they can be offered support before they get into difficulties. It is also possible to train parents in sensitive responsiveness in order to increase the chances of their child forming a secure attachment. Juffer et al. (1997) demonstrated the effectiveness of this approach in helping adoptive parents form an attachment with infants. Thirty families received training in sensitive responsiveness, which involved being filmed and being given feedback on their responses to the infants. After three sessions these families had significantly higher scores in sensitive responsiveness than a control group who had not received the training. In a similar study Van den Boom (1994) demonstrated that training parents in sensitive responsiveness increased the number of children with difficult temperaments that managed to form secure attachments to their primary carers.

## Further Reading

GROSS, R. (1997) Attachment theory, extensions and applications. *Psychology Review* 4, 10–13.

HOLMES, J. (1993) *John Bowlby*. London, Routledge.

JARVIS, M. (2001) *Angles on child psychology*. Cheltenham, Nelson Thornes.

MARRONE, M. (1999) *Attachment and interaction*. London, Jessica Kingsley.

SCHAFFER, H.R. (1996) *Social development*. Oxford, Blackwell.

# Attribution theory

## The Idea

ONE OF THE THINGS WE CONSTANTLY DO WHEN WE ARE INTERACTING WITH OTHER people is make judgements about why they are behaving as they are. This process is called *attribution*. The main decision we have to make in the attribution process is whether a person's actions are a result of the situation or of their character. We make an *external attribution* if we judge that the behaviour is a result of the situation and an *internal attribution* if we judge it to be a product of the person's character. Heider (1958) suggested that we make attributions as a way of making the social environment more comprehensible, predictable and safe. Attribution theory is the collective term for the various explanations that have been proposed to explain how we make internal and external attributions.

* Correspondent inferences
* Covariation
* Causal schemata
* Attribution biases
* Stages of attribution

## Correspondent inferences

JONES and Davis (1965) developed their correspondent inference theory to explain the circumstances under which we will make internal attributions – when we attribute people's behaviour to their character. Three criteria must be met for us to make *correspondent inferences* (to infer that a person's actions correspond to their character):

1 *Actions must be deliberate.* We cannot make judgements about someone based on accidents or situations in which they have no choice as to how to act.

2 *Actions must have distinct effects.* If a behaviour has a distinct effect we can make a judgement about why the person acted that way. If a behaviour has multiple consequences it becomes much less clear why they did what they did.

3 *Actions should be relatively low in social desirability.* Behaviour that simply follows social conventions reveals little about a person's character. However, when people do something unexpected or less socially acceptable that can be quite revealing.

A real-life example of how we make correspondent inferences is in judging violent criminals. If someone has attacked someone else then they have deliberately behaved in a way that is socially undesirable and has distinctive effects, and we would tend to make a correspondent inference and judgement about their character.

## Covariation

CORRESPONDENT inference theory describes the basis on which we make attributions on isolated actions, but Kelley (1967) proposed an explanation for the way we make attributions when we have information about the person's past behaviour and about how other people behave in the same situation. Given this information we can judge how an action *covaries* with our own behaviour and that of others based on three criteria:

1 *Consensus.* Whether other people also act in the same way in the same situation.

2 *Consistency.* Whether the person we are judging always acts that way in that situation.

3 *Distinctiveness.* Whether the person behaves similarly across a range of situations.

A real-life example of the covariation process takes place when teachers make judgements about students based on punctuality at lessons. If Lucy is always late (high consistency) to all lessons (low distinctiveness), and other students are generally on time (low consensus), then a teacher is likely to attribute her lateness to Lucy's character. If, however, all students are late to one teacher's lessons (high consensus) but on time to those given by other teachers (high distinctiveness) then it is likely to be the situation (i.e. this teacher's lessons!) that has led to the problem.

## Causal schemata

KELLEY (1972) has pointed out that sometimes we have to make attributions based on a single, isolated behaviour, without the necessary background information to make correspondent inferences or judgements about how the behaviour covaries with the usual behaviour of the person and others. In these cases we rely on *causal schemata*. A causal schema is the body of knowledge we can draw on to explain the typical reasons for an action. For example, if a stranger falls in the street in front of us we are likely to draw on our memory of other people falling, and might judge that the person collapsed because they were drunk. Of course, there might be particular circumstances at the time of the collapse – for example, slippery ice on the pavement. In this case we tend to attribute the fall to the ice and discount our usual explanation for falls. This tendency to only attribute behaviour to the most obvious cause is called the *discounting principle*.

## Attribution biases

IN reality we are not always as logical as correspondent inference and covariation theories would predict – there are a number of common errors or biases in the attribution process. The most common is the *fundamental attribution error*, our tendency to overemphasise the character of the person and de-emphasise the situation, which leads to incorrect internal attributions. For example, if we saw someone in a fight in the street we would probably make the attribution that they were a violent individual, and not take account of the circumstances that led to the fight.

Another attribution bias is the *actor–observer effect*, where the person behaving in a certain way tends not to make the same attributions as observers. *Actors* tend to make external attributions when their behaviour is low in social desirability and internal attributions when it is high in desirability. *Observers* tend to do the reverse. We are also influenced in our attributions by the consequences of someone's actions, so we are likely to make a particularly harsh internal attribution where a person's behaviour causes death or serious injury.

## Stages of attribution

A limitation of early theories is that, although they describe the logical rules we use to make attributions, they do not describe the process. A further problem is that they do not easily explain why we make so many errors in attribution. Both these points were addressed by Gilbert et al. (1988), who proposed that attribution takes place in three stages:

1 *Categorisation*. First the behaviour is identified.
2 *Characterisation*. Next, we make a judgement about the character of the person based on their behaviour.
3 *Correction*. Finally we assess the situation and judge whether the person might actually be responding to the situation.

A real-life example of these stages in the attribution process would be when we see a motorist humbly apologising to a police officer by the roadside. We would categorise the behaviour as apologetic, characterise the motorist's personality as meek and humble, then consider the situation and perhaps conclude that their behaviour was actually very sensible under the circumstances and make an external rather than an internal attribution. Gilbert et al.'s model neatly explains the fundamental attribution error by saying that we first make an internal attribution, then if we are distracted or overloaded by other information we do not complete the third stage, and are left with our incorrect initial judgement that a person's behaviour is attributable to their personality.

# The Idea Today

RECENT STUDIES HAVE ENHANCED OUR UNDERSTANDING OF THE PROCESSES OF correspondent inference and covariation. Wittenbaum and Stasser (1995) investigated the role of conversation in making inferences. In their study 336 undergraduate students were given information about the person who had written an essay arguing either for or against the legalisation of cannabis. This information was either irrelevant to the writer's view on cannabis, supported or contradicted their stance. Participants then estimated the writer's attitude to cannabis legalisation before and after a three-way conversation. Before the conversation the participants made strong correspondent inferences (they attributed the views on cannabis to the character of the writer). However, when the conversation was preceded by irrelevant information about the writer or information counter to the view expressed in the essay, conversation considerably weakened the tendency to make correspondent inferences. Vonk and Konst (1998) tested whether the tendency to make correspondent inferences is affected by in-group favouritism. They read 149 employees in an organisation descriptions of either positive or negative behaviour by a fellow employee, and gave them information to suggest that either the situation or the character of the person involved affected their behaviour. When the target person was an in-group member, participants were more likely to make external attributions for negative behaviour and internal attributions for positive behaviour. The opposite effect was found for out-group members. This out-group effect appears to operate between men and women, and affects perceptions of the victims of crime committed by the opposite sex. Workman and Freeburg (1999) carried out a study in which 638 students read a story about a date rape, saw photographs of the victim and were asked to attribute responsibility to the victim, the perpetrator or the situation. Men were more likely to attribute responsibility to the victim, although interestingly this effect was sharply reduced if the victim was someone they knew.

There appear to be some cultural differences in the tendency to make internal and external positive and negative attributions. In a study by Stander et al. (2001) Chinese couples made more relationship-enhancing attributions (i.e. internal attributions for positive behaviour and external attributions for negative behaviour) to their spouses than did American couples. Pfeffer et al. (1998) compared attributions for crime in British and Nigerian 7–10-year-old children. Interestingly, the British children made more internal attributions, suggesting that people committed crime because of their character, whereas the Nigerian children tended to make external attributions, blaming crime on factors like poverty. These differences are important because we cannot tackle crime or aid people in their marriages without understanding their cultural attitudes to those issues.

## Current status of the idea

ATTRIBUTION remains a well-researched topic in social psychology, with the bulk of research taking place in America. There is relatively little controversy surrounding attribution theory. Clearly we do make correspondent inferences and use covariation information. We are not, however, as logical as early theories suggested and our understanding of attribution biases has been particularly useful to understanding real-life situations.

WE CAN IMMEDIATELY SEE PRACTICAL APPLICATIONS IN THE RESEARCH DISCUSSED IN the previous section. Clearly, understanding the attributional norms of different cultures in relation to crime and marriage enhances our ability to tackle criminal behaviour and failing relationships. An understanding of the fact that men tend to blame female victims of crime has been used to modernise police practices.

An understanding of attribution has proved particularly helpful in clinical settings, for example in working with depressed people, in whom both correspondent inference and covariation processes appear to work slightly differently. Yost and Weary (1996) compared depressed and non-depressed students on a standard correspondent inference task like those used in the Wittenbaum and Stasser and Vonk and Konst studies. They found that the depressed students had much less of a tendency to make correspondent inferences. Wall and Hayes (2000) assessed depression and attributions in 160 clients of a university counselling service. They found that depressed patients tended to make internal attributions for anything that went wrong in their lives – they blamed any failures on their own shortcomings. This understanding of cognition in depressed patients has enhanced the ability of cognitive behavioural therapists to treat depression (see p.36 for a discussion of cognitive-behavioural therapy).

There are other clinical applications of attribution theory. Seneviratne and Saunders (2000) compared the attributions of alcohol-dependent patients for their own and other patients' relapses. In keeping with the actor–observer effect, the patients had a tendency to blame their own relapses on the situation and those of other patients on personal weakness. Substance-abusing patients, like alcohol-dependents, appear to be particularly judged with internal attributions. Holleman et al. (2000) surveyed 55 GPs and 315 medical students to establish their attributions concerning the reasons for drug abuse: half blamed the substance abuse on the personal shortcomings of the patients. This is profoundly unsympathetic compared with attitudes to other patient groups – and unjustified, given the large amount of research linking substance abuse to traumatic life events.

 Further Reading

BARON, R. AND BYRNE, D. (1998) *Social psychology*. New York, Allyn and Bacon.

GROSS, R. (2001) *Psychology, the science of mind and behaviour*. London, Hodder and Stoughton.

PENNINGTON, D. (2000) *Essential social psychology*, 2nd edition. London, Arnold.

# Authoritarian personality

❀

## The Idea

FOLLOWING THE HOLOCAUST THE AMERICAN JEWISH Committee commissioned a large body of research into the roots of anti-Semitism. A number of theories emerged from this research, but one of the most influential has been that of the authoritarian personality, proposed by Adorno et al. (1950). They suggested that one important factor in the development of prejudice was the existence of a personality type they called *authoritarian*, the product of harsh parenting. Authoritarians are particularly susceptible to acquiring extreme and unreasonable beliefs from propaganda such as the anti-Semitism of Nazi Germany. Adorno's authoritarian personality is characterised by political and economic conservatism, hostility, rigid morality, strong racial in-group favouritism (ethnocentrism) and intolerance of disobedience or non-conformity.

❀ Measuring authoritarianism: the AS, E, PEC and F scales

❀ The childhood roots of authoritarianism

❀ Case example: Mack

❀ Further characteristics of authoritarians

❀ Altemeyer's right-wing authoritarianism

## Measuring authoritarianism: the AS, E, PEC and F scales

THE starting point for Adorno's research was the collection of questionnaire data from several thousand participants, initially students but also factory workers and officers in the armed forces. Participants answered questions that allowed Adorno to assess anti-Semitism, ethnocentrism, political conservatism and fascism. The anti-Semitism (AS) scale assessed attitudes towards Jewish people, including statements like 'In order to maintain a nice residential neighbourhood it is best to prevent Jews living in it.' The ethnocentrism (E) scale included items relating specifically to Jewish and Black people, and more general items to assess in-group favouritism, for example 'America may not be perfect, but the American Way has brought us about as close as human beings can get to a perfect society.' The political–economic conservatism (PEC) scale assessed the conservatism of social attitudes, using items such as 'Young people sometimes get rebellious ideas, but as they grow up they should get over them and settle down.'

Adorno et al. found a strong relationship between anti-Semitism, ethnocentrism and conservatism, i.e. people scoring highly in one also tend to score highly in the others although, interestingly, people tended to score more highly on conservatism. This suggests that someone can be fairly conservative without being ethnocentric, but that extremely conservative individuals tend to be ethnocentric. Ethnocentrism is thus a more extreme attitude than conservatism. Adorno et al. also assessed a variable that they named *fascism* after the political ideology of the Nazis. Fascism is the tendency to submit to authority and to punish those who do not conform, to be highly rigid and conventional in ideas, and to be preoccupied with strength and power. The F-scale measured fascism by assessing these variables. Authoritarians scored high on the F scale as well as the AS, E and PEC scales.

## The childhood roots of authoritarianism

ADORNO et al. conducted interviews with a number of the questionnaire respondents. One factor that emerged strongly from these interviews was the childhood experiences of authoritarians. These individuals had had extremely strict parents who tolerated no disagreement or expression of anger from children. These children were left with a residue of anger, which they dared not express. Adorno explained the link between these experiences and the development of an authoritarian adult personality using Freud's model of the mind (see p.66). The anger resulting from the unfair treatment by their parents is *repressed* so that the child becomes unaware of it and identifies strongly with their strict, uncompromising parents. This means that, in Freud's terms, they develop a powerful and punishing superego. This makes them highly conformist and obedient to authority. The rigidity of thinking in the authoritarian is the result of maintaining the repression of their early anger – resistance to thinking about new ideas reduces the risk of rediscovering the anger.

---

### Case example: Mack

Adorno et al. used case examples to illustrate their theory. One case of a typical (rather than extreme) authoritarian was that of Mack, a 24 year-old student who had recently been discharged from the army on medical grounds and who hoped to become a corporate lawyer. Mack scored very high on the AS, E, PEC and F scales. When speaking of ethnic or political groups other than his own Mack displayed stereotyped views and hostility. His account of out-groups was dominated by

---

concerns about their gaining power over him, for example that Jews would become too powerful in business. He was anti-trade union and highly supportive of the government, except he did not believe that governments should regulate business on ethical grounds. He condemned homosexuality and believed that a woman's place is in the home. Interestingly, in view of Adorno's explanation for authoritarianism, Mack was also extremely hostile to people who did not show proper respect for their parents.

Mack described his childhood, in which his mother had died and he and his sister had been brought up by their father. Although there is no evidence of violence or abuse by Mack's father he appeared to be rigid and highly moralistic, and to have been restrictive of Mack's activities, for example not allowing him to have a part-time job. Adorno interpreted Mack's adult characteristics in terms of emotional responses to his childhood. Thus his hostility against out-groups can be understood as the result of repressed anger towards his father. Mack's great respect for powerful figures, for example the government, and his lack of empathy with weaker people, can be seen as resulting from his identification with a harsh father and the absence of a more loving second parent.

## Further characteristics of authoritarians

WE have already established that authoritarians are ethnocentric, intolerant, hostile, rigid and conservative. In further research Adorno et al. uncovered more specific information – for example, prejudice is not based merely on ethnic or political differences. They found that authoritarians were also found to be highly sexist and homophobic. It was also interesting to note that racial prejudice was least against ethnic groups whose stereotypical characteristics were most acceptable to authoritarians. Irish people, who were stereotyped in the USA during the 1940s as strong, assertive and quick-tempered, did not arouse the same hostility in authoritarians as Black and Jewish people. There was also a relationship between authoritarianism and religious behaviour. Church attendees were more likely to be authoritarian than non-attendees, although attendees whose parents were from different religious backgrounds were less authoritarian than those from a single religious background.

## Altemeyer's right-wing authoritarianism

THERE have been many attempts to refine the concept of authoritarianism. One of the difficulties with Adorno's research was the number of different personality factors associated with authoritarianism – nine in the F scale alone. Altemeyer (1988) developed a scale of right-wing authoritarianism (RWA) to measure the three characteristics most reliably associated with the authoritarian personality: conventionalism, submission to authority and aggression. Altemeyer agreed with Adorno about the childhood roots of authoritarianism but preferred to use the language of observational learning (see p.105) rather than Freudian psychoanalysis to describe the process of becoming an authoritarian. Thus children acquire their social attitudes through imitation of adult role models, and if those role models display intolerance, rigidity and submission to authority so will the children who identify with them.

# The Idea Today

MOST CONTEMPORARY RESEARCH INTO AUTHORITARIANISM USES ALTEMEYER'S RWA scale. Many studies have supported the early findings of Adorno et al. about the characteristics of authoritarians. Rubinstein (1995) investigated the relationship between authoritarianism, religiosity and gender attitudes in 165 Jewish students. People high in authoritarianism tended to be more religious and have more traditional attitudes to gender than those lower in authoritarianism. Recent studies have also supported the idea that authoritarians show greater prejudice than others. Whitley and Lee (2000) assessed attitudes to homosexuality in 216 American students along with a number of personality variables. The variable that was most strongly associated with homophobia was right-wing authoritarianism. Authoritarianism seems to be linked to a range of conservative attitudes to sex. Katz et al. (2000) assessed authoritarianism in 135 Israeli students using the F scale, along with attitudes to sex in relation to paraplegic people and people with learning difficulties. Authoritarians expressed generally negative attitudes towards sexual activity in people suffering both paraplegia and learning difficulties, particularly the latter group.

Although many of the fundamentals of Adorno's theory are supported by modern research, recent studies have revealed that some aspects of his work were oversimplified or closely linked to the culture of his time. For example, given that Adorno was essentially investigating the Nazis it is not surprising that he associated authoritarianism with right-wing politics. However, it seems that in societies where extreme left-wing politics are the 'establishment' authoritarians favour the left. For instance, McFarland et al. (1996) investigated authoritarianism and social and political attitudes in post-Communist Russia and found that those scoring highest on a translated version of the RWA scale tended to support Communism and dislike Capitalism, although in other ways they were typically authoritarian – religious, rigid and prejudiced. Given the political and historical context in which Adorno and his colleagues were working it is also unsurprising that anti-Semitism was associated with authoritarianism in 1950. This association appears to have weakened in the last 50 years: in a survey of 1119 White non-Jewish Americans, Raden (1999) found only a weak association between anti-Semitism and authoritarianism.

Another way in which ideas in psychology have changed since Adorno's time is the recognition that genes, as well as environment, affect the development of personality. McCourt et al. (1999) performed a twin study on authoritarianism, using the RWA scale, with identical and fraternal twins reared together and apart. There was greater similarity in the authoritarianism of identical twins than fraternal twins, and twins reared together were more similar than those raised apart. This suggests that both genes and family environment are important in the development of the authoritarian. McCourt et al. calculated that environment and genes each accounted for 50% of the variance in authoritarianism.

## Current status of the idea

THE emphasis in social psychology has shifted since Adorno's time, away from individual differences in social attitudes and behaviour in favour of a greater understanding of the social processes underlying phenomena such as prejudice. Thus most social psychologists would place more emphasis on social identity (p.140) and social representations (p.145) than authoritarianism in understanding prejudice. However, the principle that there is a personality type particularly prone to acquiring prejudice is thoroughly supported by contemporary research, and Adorno et al. appear to have been right about both the typical background and the social attitudes of such individuals. There are now valid measures of authoritarianism such as the RWA scale, and assessing authoritarianism has practical applications in predicting behaviour in situations such as jury service. Thus, in spite of the unfashionable nature of theories of individual differences in social psychology, authoritarianism remains an important concept.

The Idea in Action

ALTHOUGH THE AUTHORITARIAN PERSONALITY IS NOT – AND WAS NEVER INTENDED TO be – a complete explanation of prejudice, it has proved helpful in understanding why some people are particularly prone to acquiring prejudices. Whilst this has not allowed us to eliminate prejudice it has allowed us to identify people prone to developing prejudices and predict their behaviour. This has proved useful, for example, in the legal system, where authoritarians display distinctive attitudes towards defendants. In a study by Feather and Oberdan (2000) 170 Australian students completed the RWA scale and were shown scenarios in which a White or Asian person who deliberately imported drugs to Australia, or who was tricked into doing so, was caught and sentenced. Authoritarians differed from other participants in making little distinction between whether the offence was deliberate or the result of being tricked. They also displayed more pleasure when the Asian person was punished, unlike more liberal participants. In a related study Feather et al. (2001) assessed authoritarianism in 241 participants and presented them with a scenario in which a company distributed contaminated meat that caused widespread food poisoning. In different conditions participants received differing information on whether the company was aware of the risk and on how free individuals were to take action to prevent the meat being distributed. Authoritarians made judgements on the guilt of the employees on a different basis than the other participants. They generally ignored information about whether the employees had known about the risk to the public. They were, however, more sympathetic than non-authoritarians towards employees who had been constrained in their actions by their employers. Feather's research has important implications for key aspects of the legal system. Authoritarian and liberal jurors will not be sympathetic to the same circumstances or swayed by the same arguments, therefore authoritarianism will be important in jury selection and for the best tactics for the prosecution and defence to take in a trial.

 Further Reading

ADORNO, T.W., FRENKEL-BRUNSWICK, E., LEVINSON, D.J. AND SANFORD, R.N. (1950) *The authoritarian personality*. New York, Harper and Row.

HAYES, N. (2000) *Foundations of psychology*. London, ITP.

WETHERALL, M. (1996) *Identities, groups and social issues*. London, Sage.

# Behavioural genetics

The Idea

BEHAVIOURAL GENETICS IS THE STUDY OF THE ROLE OF GENES AND ENVIRONMENT IN determining individual differences between people. Genes and environment are sometimes called 'nature' and 'nurture', respectively, because our genetic make-up is biological (hence nature), but our environment is a product of people (hence nurture). Although there are still debates in some areas of psychology about the relative effects of genes and environment on our behaviour and characteristics, most psychologists now accept the importance of both factors. Behavioural geneticists are interested in studying both genes and environment. Behavioural genetics is *not* a theoretical position emphasising the importance of genes, but an area of research.

 Inheritance and heritability

* Twin studies

* Adoption studies

* Molecular genetics

* Shared and non-shared environment

## Inheritance and heritability

*INHERITANCE* is the passing on of genetic material (*genes*) from one generation to the next. This genetic material provides the template for physical development of the individual. It is easy to understand how a characteristic like eye colour can be under the control of genes because eye colour is obviously physical in nature, but the way genes might affect psychological characteristics is more complex. It appears that genetic differences between individuals produce biological differences between people (sometimes very subtle) that, in combination with our environment, lead us to develop into unique individuals. Psychological characteristics that are affected by genetically influenced biological differences are said to be *heritable*. The more powerful the effect of genetic differences on a psychological characteristic the more heritable it is said to be. Some aspects of personality and some mental disorders are believed to be highly heritable.

## Twin studies

WE know that identical twins (also called monozygotic (MZ) twins) share 100% of their genes. We also know that fraternal twins (also called dizygotic or DZ twins) only share 50% of their genetic material. These facts give us the basis for two types of *twin study*.

- The first type of twin study involves comparing the similarity of MZ and DZ twins who have been reared together and hence have experienced a similar environment. If MZ twins, who share more of their genes and have a similar environment, are more similar than DZ twins, this is powerful evidence for the importance of genes.

- In the second type of twin study, we can compare the similarity of MZ twins who have grown up in the same family with those who have been brought up in different environments and see whether those who have grown up together are more alike than those who grew up apart. The fact that MZ twins reared apart show more differences than those reared together demonstrates the role of the environment but the fact that even separated identical twins tend to be much more alike than two unrelated people demonstrates the importance of genes.

## Adoption studies

AN alternative way of studying inheritance involves adoption. If children are adopted into an environment different from that of their birth family then we have a naturally occurring experiment where the children have the genes of the biological parents and the environment created by the adoptive parents. Adoption studies constitute the most direct tests of heritability because they separate out the influence of genes and environment in the form of 'genetic parents' and 'environmental parents'. Any similarity between child and biological parents suggests a role for genes, whilst any similarity between child and adoptive parents suggests a role for environmental factors. The similarity of 'genetic siblings' (those who have the same biological parents) and 'environmental siblings' (who have grown up in the same family environment) can also be studied in adoption studies.

## Molecular genetics

THERE are many limitations with twin and adoption studies. For instance, separated twins and adopted children may not actually end up in families with a different environment, meaning that we have not really separated out genes and environment. Moreover, the numbers of twins that are separated and adopted have declined in recent years, and we might simply run out of participants to study.

However, technological developments have allowed a new line of research – *molecular genetics*, which looks at the association between particular genes and particular characteristics. In psychology we can use molecular genetics to look for associations between particular genes and psychological characteristics. Genetic material is extracted from individuals (or in some cases whole families) and associations are calculated between variations in particular genes and the psychological characteristics of the individuals or families. For example, we know that 40% of people suffering from *Alzheimer's disease* have a mutation in a gene coding for apolipoprotein E (only 15% of the general population have this mutation). Not everyone who has the mutation develops Alzheimer's, and not all Alzheimer's patients have the mutant gene. This tells us that the mutant apolipoprotein E gene is just one risk factor for Alzheimer's disease.

## Shared and non-shared environments

THE field of behavioural genetics has taught psychologists a great deal about the effects of people's environments as well as their genes on their development. One important lesson has been the difference between the shared and non-shared environment.

When we talk about the environment, we need to distinguish between two ideas: that growing up in the same environment will make two children similar, and that raising two children in different environments will make them different. If children grow up in different environments (*non-shared environments*) they are very likely to have different experiences, and so their environment will cause them to develop differently. However, just because two children are raised in the same (*shared*) environment – for example in the same home with the same family – this does not necessarily mean that they will have similar experiences. Parents may bring up a second child quite differently from the first, and two children with different interests and personalities may seek out different environments and end up being treated quite differently. Thus similarities in environment are less likely to produce similar children than differences in environment are likely to produce different children.

# The Idea Today

BEHAVIOURAL GENETICS RESEARCH HAS REVEALED IMPORTANT INFORMATION ABOUT THE role of both genes and environment in individual development. Particularly exciting findings have been in the area of molecular genetics. A recent study by Chorney et al. (1998) appears to have, for the first time, isolated a gene linked to intelligence. Two matched groups of children were established: a 'superbright' group (average IQ 136) and a matched group of children the same age but with an average IQ (IQ 103). DNA was taken from the two groups and their genetic makeup analysed. There was a significant difference between the two groups in the frequency of a single gene (called *IGFR2*), situated on chromosome 6 – twice as many of the 'superbrights' as control children (33% and 17% respectively) had a particular form of the gene. This suggests that *IGFR2* is one of the genes associated with cognitive ability, accounting for about 2% of the variance in intelligence. Some of the most exciting behavioural genetics research tells us as much about the importance of environment as genes. Grigorenko and Carter (1996) compared IQ in 60 pairs of MZ twins and 63 pairs of DZ twins, and found that the MZ twins were significantly more similar in IQ. They also discovered that IQ was associated with a number of environmental factors, including parenting style, level of the mother's education and the socio-economic status of the family. These results demonstrate the importance of both genes and environment.

Some aspects of personality appear to be affected by genes, whilst others are more a product of environment. Stroganova et al. (2000) assessed activity, irritability, aggression, frequency of negative emotions and sociability in 172 twins, aged 8–12 months. MZ twins were extremely similar in all factors except sociability, suggesting that sociability is environmentally determined, whilst genes play quite a powerful role in the other factors, at least in infancy. Molecular genetics studies on adults have begun to suggest which genes might be involved in personality. Two studies, by Benjamin et al. (1996) and Ebstein et al. (1995) have found associations between alleles of the gene *DRD4* and novelty-seeking behaviour. Other studies have found associations between *DRD4* and drug taking and hyperactivity, both of which could be related to a tendency for novelty seeking.

The study of mental disorder has also benefited from behavioural genetics research. Eley and Stevenson (2000) have looked at depression in MZ and DZ twins, assessing the family environments of the participants. They found that MZ twins were more likely to share depression than DZ twins, suggesting a role of genetic vulnerability. However, it was also found that sufferers of depression were significantly more likely to have experienced significant losses in childhood. This suggests an important role for both genes and environment in depression. A common finding in modern research into mental disorder is that the role of genes may be not so much to directly produce a disorder, but rather to make sufferers more vulnerable to environmental risk factors. Wahlberg et al. (1997) studied adopted children who had a biological parent who suffered from schizophrenia. They also assessed the communication styles of the adoptive parents, along with those of a control group adopted from parents without schizophrenia. Interestingly, neither having a biological parent with schizophrenia nor living with parents that use a bizarre communication style increased the risk of developing schizophrenia. However, where *both* these factors were present there was a substantially increased risk. This suggests that the genetic background of the children made them particularly vulnerable to poor communication on the part of parents.

## Current status of the idea

BEHAVIOURAL genetics research is a growth area in psychology, and its methods are enhancing our understanding of several areas, including personality, intelligence and mental disorder. However, there are controversies surrounding the approach. Although behavioural geneticists investigate both genes and environment, there is little doubt that some researchers have overestimated the importance of genes and understated the role of environmental factors. Some psychologists are concerned that this raises ethical issues as it might lead us to cease to take sufficient care over children's environments.

There are other ways in which behavioural genetics research could be misused. In 2001 legislation came into force to prevent access to genetic records by insurance companies, who could save themselves a great deal of money by refusing to insure people who, by their genetic profile, are especially likely to suffer mental disorder. As we learn more about the genes involved in personality and intelligence there is also a risk of people wanting to produce genetically enhanced ('designer') babies. This is currently illegal and barely technologically possible, but it may become a problem in the future.

OUR GREATER UNDERSTANDING OF THE ROLE OF BOTH GENES AND ENVIRONMENT IN development of individual differences can be applied in a number of ways. *Genetic counselling* involves giving information about genetic risks to adults with a family background of a genetically linked condition or to parents of children at risk of developing a genetic condition. Counselling also involves helping people come to terms with genetic risks, and on occasion aids people to make decisions, for example whether to have children and risk passing on a genetic condition. In some cases there are medical tests that can tell whether someone (an adult or an unborn child) is actually carrying the gene.

For example, phenylketonuria is a genetic condition present in 1 in 10,000 babies. Sufferers can not break down an amino acid called phenylalanine, which builds up in the body and eventually causes severe mental retardation. By identifying children with phenylketonuria at birth, doctors can prevent this retardation by prescribing a diet low in phenylalanine. As our understanding of the role of genes and environment develops, it might be possible to apply the principles currently used to treat phenylketonuria to a range of psychological problems. In principle, following the research of Wahlberg et al. (1997) we should be able to reduce the incidence of schizophrenia by making sure children carrying the predisposing genes are not exposed to the communication styles to which carriers of these genes appear to be particularly sensitive.

# Further Reading

PLOMIN, R., DEFRIES, J.C., MCCLEARN, G.E. AND RUTTER, M. (1997) *Behavioural genetics*. New York, Freeman.

TAVRIS, C. AND WADE, C. (1997) *Psychology in perspective*. New York, Longman.

# Biorhythms

MANY BEHAVIOURAL AND PHYSIOLOGICAL CHANGES IN animals are cyclical – they occur at regular intervals despite a range of circumstances. These bodily rhythms are controlled by an interaction between *endogenous* (internal physiological) and *exogenous* (dictated by external events) mechanisms. Not all rhythmical functions operate on the same time scale, and different types of cycles can be classified according to their length.

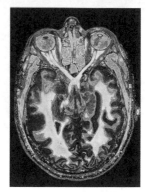

* Ultradian rhythms
* Tidal rhythms
* Circadian rhythms
* Infradian rhythms

## Ultradian rhythms

CYCLICAL changes occurring more often than daily are described as ultradian rhythms (*ultra* = 'more' (as in more often than once a) *dies* = 'day'). Heartbeat, for instance, is an ultradian rhythm and like other functions it is affected both internally by the body's pacemaker and by external factors, such as air quality or temperature. Similar rhythms can be seen in psychological functions, such as appetite and awareness.

A basic rest and activity cycle occurs throughout both our sleep and waking hours at the same rate, about every 90 minutes. This cycle affects sleep states, daydreams, hormone secretion, stomach contractions and appetite, oral behaviours such as smoking and pencil chewing, susceptibility to visual illusions and performance on spatial tasks. Some ultradian rhythms have a different time base. For instance, growth hormone shows a 3-hourly rhythm, as well as a daily one. The parallels in these biological and psychological phenomena suggest that the same internal clock controls some cycles.

## Tidal rhythms

ANIMALS living on beaches demonstrate quite different ultradian rhythms. Their behaviour is often synchronised to the tides, occurring twice a day. Limpets are predatory animals that feed when the tide is in, searching for prey on the rocks. If limpets are removed from the shore and placed in a non-tidal tank in the laboratory, they maintain their approximately 12-hourly activity cycle even in the absence of cues from the movement of the sea. Thus it seems that, although their activity rhythm is set by the tidal movements, it is maintained by an endogenous (internal) system.

A similar pattern is seen in the behaviour of fiddler crabs, which feed at low tide and retreat at high tide. In the laboratory, individual fiddler crabs will maintain their rhythmical behaviour for up to 5 weeks, suggesting the cycle is controlled by an internal system. However, in fiddler crabs living in rock pools that are not affected by the tide, the ultradian rhythm is replaced by a daily one. This evidence suggests that the rhythm can be overridden by external cues.

## Circadian rhythms

OUR most familiar behavioural rhythm is the sleep–wake cycle, that repetitive programme which insists that we go to sleep each night and wake up the next morning. Whilst we can stay up late or 'lie in', we can stay neither awake nor asleep indefinitely. Our sleeping and waking runs on a *circadian rhythm* (one which lasts *circa-dies*, 'about a day'). Other circadian rhythms include a rhythmical variation in awareness – our processing ability reaches a trough at night, as does our sensitivity to pain, manual dexterity and reaction time.

The most well studied circadian variation, the sleep–wake cycle, seems to be affected by both internal and external factors. The most obvious cue to set the cycle (such cues are called *zeitgebers* – meaning 'time-givers') is day length – the sun rises and sets every 24 hours. This cue alone is, however, is not the full explanation because even in the absence of cyclical light cues the sleep–wake cycle continues on an approximate (although slightly lengthened) circadian pattern.

## Infradian rhythms

CYCLES that operate over a period longer than a day are called *infradian* rhythms (from *infra* – 'later' (than the) *dies* – 'day'). This is a broad category, with cycles as short as a lunar month or a long as many years governed by a range of zeitgebers. The behaviour of many shore animals is regulated by the tides (governed by the lunar day) but others have true lunar cycles – i.e. they have cycles of behaviour that correspond to the lunar month. 'Spring tides', the highest high tides, occur twice each lunar month, when the moon is in line with the sun. The grunion fish (*Leuresthes tenuis*) uses this to lay eggs safely away from predators, high on the shore. They swim ashore on each spring tide to deposit sperm and eggs and are then washed back out to sea. The fertilised eggs lie in the warm, damp sand for a fortnight until the next spring tide, when the young fish are sufficiently well developed to hatch from the eggs and float into the sea. Another marine animal, the Atlantic fireworm (*Odontosyllis*) breeds once each lunar month, the females rising to the surface of the water to shed their eggs. They simultaneously produce a bright luminous substance that attracts the males to fertilise the eggs.

Circannual rhythms (those cycling approximately yearly) include migration, breeding and hibernation.

- Migration refers to the long-distance movements of groups of animals, for instance between seasonal feeding and breeding grounds. The Arctic tern (*Sterna paradisaea*) travels 22, 000 miles annually, between its two habitats.

- Synchronised breeding ensures that young are born when conditions such as weather and abundance of food will maximise survival. Differences in gestation (the length of time females are pregnant) mean that for some (mainly small) animals, mating must occur in early spring and for other (larger) animals, mating must occur in autumn.

- Hibernation offers some species a way of conserving energy during extreme winter weather and food shortages. Hibernating animals are not asleep, but in a state of inactivity and reduced body temperature (as low as $-3°C$ in the Arctic ground squirrel). During the winter hibernating animals intermittently arouse, their body temperature increases and they fall into true sleep.

# The Idea Today

RECENT EXPERIENCE HAS PROVIDED LITTLE SUPPORT FOR THE 90–MINUTE ULTRADIAN rhythm during waking. Neubauer and Freudenthaler (1995) tested 60 students every 10 minutes over 9 hours in search of rhythms with a time of between 80 and 120 minutes and found no significant cyclical changes in the students' cognitive performance, as measured by a sentence verification test, or in mood or alertness. We might expect human ultradian rhythms to be less obvious during wakefulness than sleep as our waking behaviour is constrained by social expectations, activity and interactions with others. The existence of ultradian rhythms during sleep is, however, well documented. For example, Brandenberger et al. (2001) demonstrated cyclical changes in heart rate and EEG (delta waves) varying between 80 and 120 minutes through REM and nREM sleep phases.

The concept of both psychological and physiological circadian rhythms is well supported by current research. There is ample evidence on the sleep–wake cycle, and other psychological variables have been observed. For example, Totterdell (1995) tested mood fluctuations in 30 healthy participants over 14 days, recording mood every

2 hours. He found that the participants showed a circadian variation in cheerfulness and depression.

Much research has focused on the pineal gland, which receives information about light levels from the retina and the suprachiasmatic nucleus (SCN), a clump of cells situated in the hypothalamus region of the brain, just above the crossing of the optic nerves. The role of the SCN in the sleep–wake cycle was studied by Ralph et al. (1990) in hamsters. They transplanted the SCN from fetuses of a mutant strain of hamsters with 'free-running' clocks of 20 hours into the brains of normal adult hamsters whose 25-hour cycles had been disrupted by lesions. Instead of reverting to their old 25-hour rhythm, they assumed a new 20-hour 'day'. Transplants of SCN from adults free running at 25 hours into animals of the mutant (20-hour) strain produced individuals with a new cycle of 25 hours.

The evidence for the function of the SCN and pineal gland confirms their central role in controlling circadian rhythms in mammals, but is this system the only 'body clock'? Plautz et al. (1997) studied fruit flies, which, like humans, exhibit rhythms that can be reset by bright light. This effect was believed to act, as in humans, through the eyes and nervous system. However, Plautz et al. (1977) demonstrated that (in flies at least) each cell has its own clock, encoded into a gene called *period* or *per*. They linked the part of the *per* gene that switches it on and off to a gene from firefly tails that makes a yellow fluorescent protein. The resulting flies glowed brightly and dimly as the *per* gene switched the fluorescent protein gene on and off. They concluded that the *per* gene must be regulated by photoreceptors other than the eyes, since pieces of flies that had been severed from the rest of the body continued to fluoresce rhythmically. It is possible that humans could also have intracellular clocks?

Evidence for true lunar rhythms (rather than those such as the menstrual cycle, which last around a month but are not directly affected by the moon) in humans has been elusive. However, there may be a lunar rhythm in eating and alcohol intake – De Castro and Pearcy (1995) found a small but significant increase in food intake (8%) and decrease in alcohol consumption (26%) at the time of the full moon. These differences were exhibited in the daytime as well as the evening, suggesting that an internal rhythm, rather than increased night-time illumination, was the critical factor.

## Current status of the idea

THE existence of bodily rhythms is now well established, although some controversies remain, for example regarding waking 90–minute cycles. There is little doubt that the SCN and pineal gland play central roles in the control of bodily rhythms, although the exact nature of the interplay between them and the role of hormones such as melatonin and gonadotrophin-releasing hormone are still areas of current debate. As biological techniques become more sophisticated we will learn more about the genes that control the functioning of the biological structures responsible for bodily rhythms and the mechanisms by which they act.

# The Idea in Action

THERE ARE MANY APPLICATIONS OF OUR UNDERSTANDING OF BODILY RHYTHMS. ONE such is in understanding jet-lag. During air travel around the world people rapidly cross time zones, and with each flight we have to reset our biological clock to the local zeitgeber – sunrise and sunset. This can cause fatigue, gastrointestinal complaints and shortened attention span. These effects may be due to desynchronisation of bodily functions rather than simply a lack of sleep. Travelling east to west produces fewer problems, as we 'gain' time, but the return journey presents problems. Pilots can be severely affected by changing time zones repeatedly, due to frequent and erratic exposure to the bright light of sunrise. They sleep poorly (when they *can* rest), causing tiredness when flying.

However, some research suggests that light may not be the only important zeitgeber in adjusting to new time zones. Amir and Stewart (1996) have shown that rats which receive a breeze before their light phase can reset their clocks by a change in the time of the breeze alone. For humans there may be many contingent signals that help to maintain our circadian rhythm – such as the sound of birds in the morning, the time we eat or TV programmes we watch. Whereas light schedules exist everywhere, the other aspects of our regulated lives are harder to transport, particularly if we are on holiday. These factors may contribute to the slow rate at which we adapt to new time zones. The simplest way to combat the effects of a long-haul eastbound flight is to start going to bed and getting up progressively earlier before you travel.

Seasonal Affective Disorder (SAD) is a condition experienced in the short days of winter by as much as 10% of the population (Ferenczi 1997). The symptoms of SAD include severe depression, craving for high carbohydrate foods and sleepiness. The occurrence of SAD among people in latitudes where winter nights are very long suggests that it may be related to day length. During long winter nights secretion of melatonin from the pineal gland reaches its peak, then lowers as summer approaches. This pattern has tempted psychologists to search for a link between low exposure to light, high melatonin and SAD. The relationship is partially confirmed by the effectiveness of light therapy. SAD sufferers exposed to intense artificial lighting (1000 lux or more) during the winter generally find relief from their depression. Even as little as half an hour a day is effective, lifting depression within a week. How this exposure to light affects mood is, however, unclear. Ferenczi (1997) suggests that it may either reset the circadian cycle or increase the secretion of serotonin, which is also implicated in mood disorders. Light therapy is not effective in all cases, although failure may be attributable to misdiagnosis rather than ineffectual treatment. The timing of light sessions has been the subject of much research; simulated 'early dawn' is effective but brightness and total exposure, rather than timing, appear to be the key factors.

If light therapy raises mood by affecting the pineal gland, reduced levels of melatonin would be expected following treatment. Testing the efficacy of light therapy is difficult because the participant knows whether they have been exposed to light or not! One way to overcome this may be to use an exposure technique described by Campbell and

Murphy (1998), directing the bright lights at the backs of people's knees. This was found to be effective in resetting the circadian temperature rhythm when participants' vision was screened, so demand characteristics could not be responsible for the effect. How this signal reaches the brain is not clear. It could be encoded in a change in the blood, perhaps in the haemoglobin molecule that carries oxygen, since it resembles the part of chlorophyll that absorbs light in plants. Alternatively, photoreceptors in the skin may be responsible. However, light therapy only seems to be effective in SAD characterised by sleepiness, carbohydrate craving and worsening of symptoms in the evening. For sufferers who are suicidal, insomniac and experience more severe symptoms in the morning, light therapy is ineffective (Terman et al. 1996).

 **Further Reading**

CZEISLER, C.A. AND BROWN, E.N. (1999) Commentary: models of the effect of light on the human circadian system: current state of the art. *Journal of Biological Rhythms* 14(6), 538–543.

BENTLEY, E. (1999) *Awareness*. London, Routledge.

# Classical conditioning

IVAN PETROVITCH PAVLOV TRAINED AS A MEDICAL DOCTOR AND CONDUCTED RESEARCH ON the nervous system and digestion, for which he won the Nobel Prize in 1904. He established the world's first clinic and operating theatre to be used exclusively for animals at the Russian Institute of Medicine. Here, his careful observations led to the discovery and subsequent study of the process of classical conditioning in animals. Pavlov often cared for the animals used in his experiments himself and he noticed that they would salivate to the sound of his footsteps, ahead of the arrival of their food. He realised that the dogs' responses were in anticipation of the situation and began to explore these 'conditional' responses (as he termed them). Pavlov's work on learning, for which he is now best remembered, explains how such associations are established.

- ❋ Unconditioned and conditioned stimuli
- ❋ Higher order conditioning
- ❋ Extinction and spontaneous recovery
- ❋ Generalisation and discrimination
- ❋ One-trial learning
- ❋ Contiguity and contingency

Pavlov's equipment

## Unconditioned and conditioned stimuli: the paradigm of classical conditioning

THE mechanism of classical conditioning relies upon the building of an association between a *neutral stimulus* (some aspect of the environment which does not elicit a response) and an existing *unconditioned stimulus*, which does. These two stimuli are presented until the neutral stimulus acquires the same effect as the unconditioned stimulus (the ability to elicit a response). Although this behaviour is not new, it has developed a novel association to the neutral stimulus. It is now called a *conditioned response*, and the trigger that causes it is called the *conditioned stimulus*.

Pavlov (1927) demonstrated classical conditioning in his dogs using the sound of a metronome as the neutral stimulus (NS) and a bowl of meat powder as the unconditioned stimulus (UCS). Before the experiment, the dogs would salivate (the unconditioned response or UCR) in response to the meat powder but not to the sound. During the conditioning phase the meat powder was presented at the same time as the metronome. Repeated pairings of meat and metronome resulted in *conditioning*; and the animal would salivate to the sound alone. As a result of the pairings, the NS (the sound) had become a conditioned stimulus (CS) capable of producing the behaviour (salivation) in a new situation. This behaviour triggered by the CS is called a conditioned response (CR). The acquisition of a CR may take many pairings of the NS and UCS. A summary of the learning processes is shown in the figure on p.32.

## Higher order conditioning

As Pavlov demonstrated, for a strong CS (one producing a strong CR) there appears to be little difference between the UCR and CR; they are the same response to different stimuli. Pavlov (1927) demonstrated that after a dog had learned to respond to one stimulus, this CS could be used to condition the same response to another neutral stimulus. For example, a dog conditioned to salivate to a metronome beat can be conditioned again by pairing the metronome with a new neutral stimulus such as a black square. This is *higher order conditioning*.

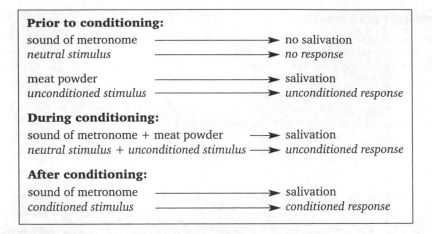

**Prior to conditioning:**

sound of metronome     ——————————————▶ no salivation
*neutral stimulus*     ——————————————▶ *no response*

meat powder     ——————————————▶ salivation
*unconditioned stimulus*   ——————————————▶ *unconditioned response*

**During conditioning:**

sound of metronome + meat powder  ——▶ salivation
*neutral stimulus + unconditioned stimulus* ——▶ *unconditioned response*

**After conditioning:**

sound of metronome     ——————————————▶ salivation
*conditioned stimulus*   ——————————————▶ *conditioned response*

## Extinction and spontaneous recovery

WHAT happens if the CS is repeatedly presented in the absence of the UCS? Over time the strength of the CR declines and eventually disappears, an effect called *extinction*. Thus if a dog was conditioned to salivate to a bell, then the bell was rung many times but no food supplied, salivation to the bell would eventually cease. However, if the bell is silent for a while, then subsequently rung again, the response may reappear. This is called *spontaneous recovery*.

## Generalisation and discrimination

HOW does an animal respond to stimuli that are similar to the CS? If the new stimulus is sufficiently like the CS, it can also trigger the CR. This is called *generalisation*. These responses may, however, be slower to appear after the presentation of the CS or they may be weaker. Pavlov demonstrated that a dog that has been conditioned to salivate to a 1000 Hz tone would also respond to tones of similar frequency (900–1200 Hz), with the greatest responses being to the most similar stimuli.

An animal can be taught to discriminate between similar stimuli by repeatedly associating one but not the other NS with a particular UCS. As a consequence only the event paired with the UCS will acquire the power to elicit a CR – the animal has thus been trained to discriminate between the two stimuli. For example, Pavlov was able to use discrimination training to condition his dogs to salivate to a 1000 Hz tone but not to a 900 Hz tone.

## One-trial learning

WHILST some responses may take hundreds of trials to become conditioned, not all conditioning is this slow. In some instances an individual can acquire a new behaviour in a single pairing of the NS and UCS; this is called *one-trial learning*. One-trial learning tends to occur when the consequences of failing to learn could be fatal, for example when we learn to avoid poisonous food that has made us sick. Perhaps festive occasions involving excessive consumption of strongly flavoured alcoholic drinks are examples of such one-trial aversion learning in humans?

## Contiguity and contingency

FOR many decades, the explanation of classical conditioning was a simple one, known as *contiguity*. If the UCS and CS appeared together, conditioning would occur. Learning arose because associations were built up between stimuli that occurred together, and the strength of those associations was dependent upon the intensity and frequency of the pairings. However, Rescorla (1966) suggested replacing the concept of contiguity with *contingency*. This means that the appearance of the CS is contingent (dependent) on the presence of the UCS. We thus learn to respond to a NS as a CS only when there is a high probability that it will appear with the UCS. Contingency has now replaced contiguity as the dominant explanation for classical conditioning.

THE RANGE OF BEHAVIOURS THAT CAN BE SHOWN TO BE CLASSICALLY CONDITIONED continues to widen. Kippin (2000) classically conditioned male rats to ejaculate to the smell of lemon or almond. The male rats were allowed to copulate with females bearing one of the two odours. Although the males initially showed no preference for a particular smell, they subsequently developed a preference to mate again with females bearing the smell that they had come to associate with ejaculation. It is believed that humans can acquire sexual preferences by classical conditioning in much the same way – early experiences of sexual arousal or orgasm can be paired with neutral stimuli (ranging from the everyday to the bizarre). This effect can be so powerful that some people are unable to achieve orgasm without the presence of such a conditioned stimulus.

Classical conditioning can also account for a range of phenomena including phobias and some medical conditions. Ferguson and Cassaday (1999) have suggested that Gulf War syndrome can be explained by classical conditioning. This syndrome is a set of symptoms including memory, sexual and sleep problems, nausea, headaches, depression, rashes and increased sensitivity to pain suffered by soldiers who saw active service in the Gulf War. Typically, each individual suffers only some of these symptoms. Ferguson and Cassaday suggested a classical conditioning model in which a sickness response has been acquired by association with a range of stimuli including oil fire fumes (present throughout the fighting) and stressful events such as witnessing injuries during the war. Following the war, exposure to any of these conditioned stimuli would produce the conditioned sickness response.

Classical conditioning is also still being actively studied in an attempt to determine how learning actually takes place. Since Pavlov developed the idea of classical conditioning psychology has developed enormously, and contemporary psychologists are seeking to understand classical conditioning from a cognitive perspective (what mental processes are involved in acquiring conditioned responses) and from a neuro-psychological perspective (i.e. what physiological processes in the brain underlie classical conditioning). Pearce and Hall (1980) have proposed a cognitive model of classical conditioning, which focuses on the importance of the *orienting response* – the attention an animal pays to a stimulus. The ability of a stimulus to elicit an orienting response will be an important determinant of the extent to which it can form associations. This theoretical approach can account for the effects of surprise on conditioning – an animal learning an association between a UCS and a CS becomes conditioned when the CS is no longer a surprise event following the UCS (i.e. when the CS acts as a reliable predictor).

So, at a cognitive level, classical conditioning seems to result from the value of the CS as a predictor of an environmentally relevant UCS. How could this be achieved at a cellular level? *Aplysia*, an invertebrate called a 'sea hare', can readily be conditioned and has simple neural circuitry. An *Aplysia* will learn to withdraw its gill in response to an innocuous stimulus associated with a shock. At a cellular level, changes occur in the release of neurotransmitter from interneurones that synapse with the motor neurone triggering gill withdrawal. In response to the shock of the sensory neurone some interneurones release substantially more neurotransmitter than others. This facilitation of neurotransmitter release is called *activity-dependent enhancement* (Glanzman 1995). In mammals, two brain areas have recently been investigated in relation to their role in classical conditioning. Findings had implicated the role of areas of the amygdala in classical conditioning, but Cahill et al. (2000) found that rats with total lesions to the relevant area were still capable of acquiring a conditioned fear response. Weninger (1999) detected cellular activity in neurones deep in the cerebellum of rabbits in response to a classically conditioned association.

## Current status of the idea

THERE is little controversy regarding the existence of classical conditioning, although as we have seen research into its cognitive and neural basis is ongoing. For a time early in the twentieth century it was widely believed that classical conditioning was the primary explanation for psychological phenomena – we could explain most or all human behaviour with reference to classical conditioning. Nowadays that seems a ludicrous idea, although classical conditioning remains important in explaining a range of human behaviours including sexual fetishism and phobias.

THE MAJOR APPLICATION OF CLASSICAL CONDITIONING IS IN CLINICAL PSYCHOLOGY. *Behaviour therapy* is the use of classical conditioning principles to alter maladaptive behaviour. The techniques employed in clinical settings include the use of *systematic desensitisation* in the treatment of phobias. In systematic desensitisation the therapist relaxes the client using progressive muscle relaxation, hypnosis or anti-anxiety drugs. The relaxed state is the UCR; during conditioning it is paired with items relating to the feared stimulus, working through a graduated sequence called an *anxiety hierarchy*. During desensitisation the UCR is maintained throughout exposure to the hierarchy of increasingly more frightening CS. *Reciprocal inhibition* prevents the client from feeling two opposite emotions at once so, by maintaining the state of relaxation, they cannot become afraid. The pairings result in the new CS becoming associated with the CR of relaxation rather than fear (see figure on p.35).

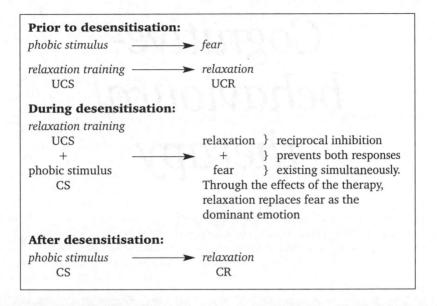

**Prior to desensitisation:**

*phobic stimulus* ⟶ *fear*

*relaxation training* ⟶ *relaxation*
    UCS                 UCR

**During desensitisation:**

*relaxation training*
    UCS                relaxation } reciprocal inhibition
    +         ⟶     +      } prevents both responses
phobic stimulus           fear     } existing simultaneously.
    CS                 Through the effects of the therapy,
                              relaxation replaces fear as the
                              dominant emotion

**After desensitisation:**

*phobic stimulus* ⟶ *relaxation*
    CS                 CR

*Aversion therapy,* which aims to eliminate maladaptive behaviour, also employs classical conditioning. An unpleasant response (the CR) is associated with the stimulus to be avoided (the CS). The resulting association causes aversion to the stimulus so the client's behaviour is altered as they avoid the unpleasant conditioned response. Electrical aversion therapy has been successfully employed by Duker and Seys (2000) to reduce self-injurious behaviours in children with learning disabilities. Aversion therapy has also been used successfully with sex offenders in eliminating conditioned responses of sexual arousal. In a study by Weinrott et al. (1997) young sex offenders listened to an audiotaped crime scenario that evoked deviant arousal and were then immediately exposed to a videotaped aversive stimulus – the negative social, emotional, physical and legal consequences of sex offences. They found significant improvement in both physiological and self-report measures of arousal following this treatment.

# Further Reading

BERGIN, A.E. AND GARFIELD, S.L. (1994) *Handbook of psychotherapy and behaviour change.* New York, Wiley.

CAVE, S. (1999) *Therapeutic approaches.* London, Routledge.

CLAMP, A.G. AND RUSSELL, J. (1998) *Comparative psychology* London, Hodder and Stoughton.

LIEBERMAN, D.A. (2000) *Learning: Behaviour and cognition.* London, Wadsworth

PEARCE, J.M. (1997) *Animal learning and cognition: An introduction.* Hove, Psychology Press.

# Cognitive-behavioural therapy

❈

IF YOU HAVE READ THE ENTRIES ON CLASSICAL AND OPERANT CONDITIONING (PP.30 AND 110, respectively) you will have heard of *behavioural therapy*; an approach to treating mental disorder and psychological distress that involves unlearning maladaptive behaviours and relearning better adapted ones. Cognitive psychology is the branch of psychology that deals with mental processes such as thinking. The cognitive-behavioural therapy (CBT) approach to treating mental disorder and psychological distress is an integration of behavioural therapy and cognitive psychology, aiming to help people learn more adaptive ways of *thinking* as well as behaving. Contemporary CBT involves combining techniques from a number of therapies, in particular Albert Ellis' rational emotive behaviour therapy and Aaron Beck's cognitive therapy.

❈  Cognitive primacy

❈  The ABC model

❈  Negative thinking

❈  Core beliefs and overt cognitions

❈  Early maladaptive schemas

## Cognitive primacy

ANY approach to improving people's mental health has the ultimate aim of making positive changes to their behaviour, feelings and thinking. Although different therapies have the same ultimate aim, they have different *mediating aims* – what they seek to directly alter. Whereas behavioural therapies have the mediating aim of changing behaviour and psychodynamic and humanistic therapies have the mediating aim of improving emotional state, the mediating aim of CBT is to alter the ways in which people think. The assumption that this will make people feel and behave differently depends on the idea of *cognitive primacy* – thinking comes before behaviour or emotion (in other words, what we are thinking determines how we feel and behave). If, for example, we think that we are a failure we are likely to feel depressed; if we think that the world is dangerous we are likely to feel anxious.

## The ABC model

ELLIS (1977) applied the principle of cognitive primacy to understanding people's responses to events. He was particularly interested in the effect of irrational beliefs on emotional responses to events, and proposed the ABC model to explain this (A = the activating event, B = beliefs, C = emotional consequences). The table below shows the ABC model applied to understanding the effects of failing an exam (from Palmer and Dryden, 1995).

| | | |
|---|---|---|
| A | Activating event | Failing exam |
| B | Beliefs | 'I should have passed' |
| | | 'I am a failure' |
| | | 'I can't bear not passing' |
| C | Consequences | Depression |

The existence of this type of irrational belief prevents people exhibiting *stoicism*, the ability to withstand the effects of adverse events. Ellis proposed that the most efficient way of helping someone to feel better was to change their irrational beliefs and make them more stoical. Abrams and Ellis (1996) identify two types of irrational belief that cause particular problems when we encounter adversity.

- *Musturbation* is the tendency to think that we *must* be perfect and successful at all times.
- *I-can't-stand-it-itis* is the belief that it is a disaster whenever something does not go smoothly.

Musturbation makes us too sensitive to failure and I-can't-stand-it-itis makes even minor problems seem disastrous.

## Negative thinking

WHEREAS Ellis was interested in the sort of irrational beliefs that contribute to stress, Beck was initially interested in the relationship between negative thinking and depression. Beck (1976) identified three types of negative thinking in depression.

The first is negative automatic thinking in the form of the *cognitive triad* of a negative view of self, negative view of the world and negative view of the future. The cognitive triad is shown in the figure below. Beck called these thoughts 'automatic' because they occur spontaneously. You can imagine that it would be at best discouraging, at worst disabling, to be plagued with hopeless and self-critical thoughts.

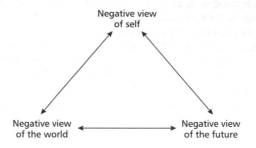

The cognitive triad

Beck also proposed that depressed people tend to selectively attend to the negative aspects of a situation and ignore the positive aspects, which means they tend to overestimate the 'downside' of any situation. We are all illogical in that we attend to some stimuli and not others, and in that we jump to conclusions. The illogic of depression is of a particularly unfortunate kind – the depressive attends to the negative and jumps to the most negative possible conclusions.

Beck's final form of negative thinking involves *negative self-schemas*. Schemas are packets of information in which our knowledge of each aspect of the world is contained. The self-schema contains all our information and beliefs concerning ourselves. Beck suggested that in childhood we acquire a negative set of beliefs about ourselves through negative experiences or critical parents. We interpret new information relevant to our beliefs about ourselves in the light of our existing self-beliefs. Any situation that requires us to examine information relevant to ourselves will activate the self-schema, and bring to mind those negative beliefs. Once we have a negative self-schema, it becomes difficult to interpret any new information about ourselves positively.

## Core beliefs and overt cognitions

A difficulty in working with the combined ideas of Beck and Ellis is that we can be left unclear about the difference between beliefs and thinking. Persons (1989) made this clearer with her *core beliefs* model, distinguishing between two levels of cognition. *Overt cognitions* include irrational beliefs and automatic thoughts but do not influence our feelings and behaviour. Instead, overt cognitions, emotions and behaviour are all products of *core beliefs*.

Our core beliefs operate across a range of situations. For example the core belief 'I am stupid' can lead to any number of overt cognitions that appear in response to specific situations, for example 'I am bound to fail' in an exam situation or 'She'll think I'm boring' on a date. Every time the overt cognition is supported, for example by failing the exam or being rejected on the date, the core belief becomes stronger. However, the opposite is also true and if by therapy we can alter situation-specific overt cognitions for the better then we can make people's core beliefs healthier.

## Early maladaptive schemas

A weakness of early CBT models is that they do not explore in sufficient depth the origins of maladaptive beliefs and styles of thinking. Young (1990) has addressed this in his theory of *early maladaptive schemas* (EMSs). EMSs are formed during social interaction with family and peers during childhood. The idea of EMSs is very similar to Bowlby's idea of internal working models (see p.2 for a discussion). Young has identified five categories of EMS.

1  Impaired autonomy – EMSs that interfere with our ability to function independently.

2  Disconnection – EMSs that interfere with the formation of intimate relationships.

3  Undesirability – EMSs that lead us to expect others to find us unattractive.

4  Restricted self-expression – EMSs that prevent us expressing feelings, either from guilt or the belief that others will not accept us as we really are.

5  Insufficient limits – EMSs that lead us to set ourselves unrealistic goals.

In adult social interactions or other high-pressure situations EMSs are activated and all events are interpreted in the light of the relevant EMS. Thus people who have had unhappy early experiences have more difficulty in adult life.

THE EFFECTIVENESS OF CBT AS A TREATMENT IS WELL DOCUMENTED AND IS CONSISTENT with, but does not in itself demonstrate the validity of, cognitive-behavioural theory (Oie and Free, 1995). However, there are now studies that provide more direct support for the principles of CBT. One line of research has been to compare the incidence of depression in people with different levels of *cognitive vulnerability* (maladaptive beliefs and thinking style). Grazioli and Terry (2000) assessed cognitive vulnerability in 65 women in the third trimester of their pregnancy and found that those with high levels of cognitive vulnerability were more likely to suffer post-natal depression.

Research has also supported Beck's notion of negative attentional bias in depression, at least in cases of major depression. Perez et al. (1999) compared sufferers of major depression with non-depressed participants in whom a sad mood had been induced by playing sad music and recalling unhappy memories on a stroop task involving unhappy stimuli. The major depressive group, but not the sad-mood participants, paid significantly more attention to unhappy words in the stroop task.

It is well documented that childhood life events are associated with adult depression (Brown and Harris, 1978; Eley and Stevenson, 2000). This is consistent with the theories of Beck and Young, but does not validate cognitive behavioural theory unless it can be demonstrated that the early experience caused cognitive vulnerability. A recent study by Parker et al. (2000) provides some support for the link between early experience and vulnerability: they interviewed 96 depressed patients, whose self-reports of their symptoms included the idea of a negative schema being activated under certain circumstances, about their early experiences. There were significant associations between reports of early experiences and the existence of maladaptive schemas that were in turn associated with the experience of depression. This suggests that early experiences do induce cognitive vulnerability and that this cognitive vulnerability may be one of the factors in depression.

## Current status of the idea

CURRENTLY CBT is the most popular model of therapy amongst psychologists who work with mental disorder and psychological distress. There is now a huge body of research showing that CBT is an effective and relatively efficient treatment for a variety of conditions. However, sound reasons have been raised for caution about the current enthusiasm for CBT. Reviews of CBT have sometimes omitted negative findings, and it is less effective than more traditional therapies in some cases (see p.41).

CBT WAS DEVELOPED PRIMARILY AS A MODEL OF TREATMENT FOR MENTAL DISORDER AND psychological distress. The practice of CBT owes much to the pioneering work of Ellis and Beck, who developed slightly different models of therapy. In Ellis' rational emotive behaviour therapy the aim of therapy is to identify irrational beliefs (such as 'musturbation' and 'I-can't-stand-it-it is'), and to challenge them by vigorous argument. Patients might be encouraged to keep a diary so that the therapist can identify evidence that the beliefs are irrational. Beck's cognitive therapy operates in a slightly different way, placing less emphasis on argument against negative beliefs and more emphasis on testing and disproving them. Patients undergoing cognitive therapy might thus be given tasks to carry out; for example a patient who said there was no point in going out with friends because they wouldn't enjoy it might be set the task of going out, and in the next session would have to admit that they had enjoyed the experience. Most contemporary cognitive-behavioural therapists use a mixture of techniques including those of Beck and Ellis.

There are a large number of studies supporting the usefulness of CBT. Typically, studies involve carefully selected participants who exhibit symptoms of one disorder only. This has meant that psychologists have been able to see that CBT is effective for the treatment of a number of disorders including depression, anxiety and even schizophrenia. For example, Fava et al. (1998) assigned 40 patients with recurrent depression to one of two conditions, drug treatment or drugs and CBT. The group receiving CBT showed greater reduction in symptoms, and 2 years later only 25% had relapsed, as opposed to 75% of the drug-treatment group. Studies have also demonstrated that CBT is effective in treating anxiety conditions – Barrett et al. (2001) followed up 52 patients who had had CBT for an anxiety condition 6 years previously and 86% were free of anxiety problems.

An exciting recent development has been in the application of CBT to treat schizophrenia and related conditions. Until recently it was widely believed that this type of disorder was not treatable by psychological therapies, but some patients' symptoms can be alleviated by CBT. Chadwick et al. (2000) tested the effectiveness of group CBT in helping patients cope with their hallucinations of hearing voices. A total of 22 participants underwent eight sessions of group CBT. At the end of this period their beliefs that these voices had power over them had significantly reduced. In another study Tarrier et al. (2001) assigned 72 patients suffering from chronic schizophrenia to three conditions: standard care, standard care and supportive counselling, standard care and CBT. Three months later the group receiving CBT showed the greatest reduction in hallucinations and delusions.

However, not all research has revealed such positive findings. Harrington et al. (1998) have pointed out that influential reviews of studies of CBT have not mentioned studies where CBT was found not to work. There are also instances where CBT has been found to be less effective than psychodynamic therapy – in a study of alcohol dependency (Sandahl et al., 1998) found that at 15–month follow-up significantly more patients were abstaining from alcohol after psychodynamic therapy than after CBT. Concerns have also been raised about the kind of research on which our understanding of CBT effectiveness is based. The vast majority of studies have focused on short-term effects on patients showing symptoms of only one condition, and we know relatively little about the long-term effects of CBT or its effects on patients with a broad range of symptoms.

# Further Reading

JARVIS, M., PUTWAIN, D. AND DWYER, D. (2002) *Angles on atypical psychology*. Cheltenham, Nelson Thornes.

PALMER, S. AND DRYDEN, W. (1996) *Stress management and counselling*. London, Cassell.

WOOLFE, R. AND DRYDEN, W. (1996) *Handbook of counselling psychology*. London, Sage.

# Cue-dependent
# forgetting

❀

## The Idea

CUE-DEPENDENT FORGETTING (ALSO CALLED *RETRIEVAL FAILURE* OR *CUE DEPENDENCY*) IS probably the most common reason for forgetting information from long-term memory. There are a number of reasons why we forget information, ranging from decay of unused memories to the forcible repression of traumatic memories. However, most of the occasions when we try and fail to recall a piece of information can be explained by cue dependency. The most obvious and dramatic example of cue dependency is the 'tip-of-the-tongue' phenomenon – we know we know something but cannot retrieve it (Brown and McNeill, 1966). Cue-dependent forgetting takes place when we have the information we are seeking in our memory but lack the necessary *cues* to access it. Cues are additional pieces of information that guide us to the information we are seeking, rather like the contents page of a book. Our understanding of the role of cues owes much to the work of Scandinavian psychologist Endel Tulving.

❀ Recall and recognition

❀ Semantic cues

❀ State-dependent forgetting

❀ Context-dependent memory

❀ Synergistic ecphory and the encoding specificity principle

## Recall and recognition

THE simplest illustration of the way in which we can have a memory but not be able to access it is the fact that we are more likely to retrieve information by recognition than by recall. Recognition involves *identifying* previously learnt information whereas recall involves actively *searching* for it. Mandler et al. (1969) demonstrated the greater ease of recognition than recall. They presented participants with 100 words five times then tested retrieval in two conditions – free recall and recognition of the words from a list of 200. Participants recalled a mean of 96% in the recognition condition but only 38% in the free recall condition. According to Tulving (1976) there is no essential difference between the processes of recall and recognition: recognition is simply easier because we have a good cue to help us locate the memory.

## Semantic cues

IN a classic experiment, Tulving and Pearlstone (1966) demonstrated that we can remember more words if we have access to the categories from which the words are taken. Participants were read lists of words, which fell into categories, for example dogs. The category names (e.g. 'dog') were included as well as a few examples of each category. In one condition the participants recalled the words without cues (free recall) and in the other they were given the category titles as cues (cued recall). In the cued condition the participants remembered more words. The category titles are a form of *semantic cue*. The word 'semantic' refers to the meaning of words, and a semantic cue is one that works because its *meaning* triggers recall.

## State-dependent forgetting

THIS occurs when cues in the form of a physiological state are missing. The particular physiological state that a person is in at the time of encoding (learning) information can act as a cue to help retrieval of that information. Emotional states can act as state cues – for example, if we are excited or afraid when we encode information we find it easier to retrieve that information if we are in the same mood. Physiological states induced by drugs can also be cues. Goodwin et al. (1969) gave participants a number of memory tasks when they were drunk or sober. They found that people who encoded information when sober recalled it better when sober and those who encoded it when drunk recalled better when drunk again.

## Context-dependent memory

JUST as information learnt in a particular physiological state is better recalled in the same state, information learnt in a particular context (a particular place or situation) is recalled better in the same context. This was demonstrated in a classic study by Godden and Baddeley (1975), who gave deep-sea divers lists of words to learn either on the beach or 15 feet under water and tested their recall in those same two situations. The divers who had learnt the words on land recalled 38% when tested on the beach and 21% when under water. Those who had learnt the words underwater recalled 21% on the beach and 32% when under water. Subjects thus recalled far better in the

presence of the context cues that were present at the encoding stage. Godden and Baddeley (1980) followed up the study with a similar procedure that tested the divers' recognition of words (as opposed to recall). This time they found no difference in the number of words recalled on land or under water – presumably because the target words themselves acted as a powerful cue and overrode the effects of the context.

## Synergistic ecphory and the encoding specificity principle

SCHACTER et al. (1978) proposed an explanation for the cueing effects of categories, state and context. At the learning stage, information is encoded as a memory trace. At this point additional information such as physiological state and aspects of the situation are encoded along with the main event or fact. When we encounter this additional information (cues) later it triggers the return to consciousness of the main fact or event. This process is called *ecphory*, after the Greek word meaning 'to be made known.' To use the Tulving and Pearlstone (1966) study as an example, the word 'dog' served as a retrieval cue for different types of dog because the category title 'dog' had been encoded along with each type of dog at the learning stage.

Tulving (1983) went on to propose the *encoding specificity principle*. This says that the greater the overlap in the information present at encoding and retrieval the greater the probability of successfully retrieving that information. This information can come in many forms, including physiological state, external context and category titles.

THERE IS A SUBSTANTIAL BODY OF RECENT RESEARCH INTO CONTEXT DEPENDENCY. THE use of smells as context cues has attracted particular attention – most of us have experienced returning to a building like our old school and having memories flood back in response to the distinctive smell associated with the place. In a study by Herz (1997) 192 undergraduates learnt words and were tested for recall 2 days later. The learning stage took place in the presence of one of several odours, and in the recall task the participants were exposed to the same or a different smell. As expected, recall of the words was best in the presence of the same odour. The effect was strongest when the odour was one the participants had not encountered before (osmanthus) or when it was particularly unusual in a psychology laboratory (pine). In another study (Pointer and Bond, 1998) 95 participants learnt a written passage in the presence of either a colour or a smell. Participants were tested for recall of the passage with or without the cue and, although the presence of a colour did not enhance recall, the smell did enhance recall considerably if present at both encoding and retrieval stages. Smells as context cues can operate over long periods. Aggleton and Waskett (1999) tested recall of participants who had visited the Jorvik Viking museum in York, a place characterised by distinctive smells. Although they had visited the museum an average of 6.73 years before the study, participants recalled details of the museum better when in the presence of the same smells.

Recent research has also supported the existence of state dependency. Duka et al. (2001) had 48 participants perform a range of memory tasks with or without alcohol at encoding and retrieval. Overall the alcohol had no effect, but those who had taken alcohol in the encoding tasks remembered better when they drank alcohol at the retrieval stage and vice versa. An exception was when the participants were given cued recall tasks, in which case there was no difference in the accuracy of recall. This is presumably because the cues given overrode the effects of the physiological state.

Sometimes it is difficult to disentangle state and context cues. For example, are smells context cues or do they work by inducing moods that in turn act as state cues? A recent study by Miles and Hardman (1998) confirms that state cues act independently of context. They had 24 participants learn word lists at rest and while pedalling hard on an exercise bike, then recall the words either at rest or pedalling. As expected in the light of past research, the words learned at rest were recalled better when at rest again and those learnt when cycling were recalled best when cycling again. Heart rates were measured at learning and retrieval stages and it was found that the more similar the heart rate at encoding and retrieval, the better the recall. This is important as it shows that it is definitely physiological state rather than the context cue of the bicycle that enhanced the recall.

## Status in contemporary psychology

THE phenomenon of cue dependency or retrieval failure is now well documented and is believed to be the most common cause of forgetting from long-term memory. It has given rise to important practical applications in situations like educational examining and police interviewing where we need to be able to maximise the amount of information people can remember. Contemporary research supports both the existence of state and context cues and the usefulness of applications that make use of them.

## The Idea in Action

GIVEN THE RANGE OF SITUATIONS IN WHICH WE NEED TO REMEMBER THINGS AND THE fact that most instances of forgetting are due to cue dependency, there should be many practical applications for our understanding of the role of cues in remembering. One area of application is in education, where both examiners and students make use of retrieval cues in the examination process. Examiners setting structured (short-answer) questions or providing quotations at the beginning of questions are deliberately giving candidates semantic cues to help them remember the information. Essay questions are recognised as harder than short-answer questions because there are fewer semantic cues in the question. Students can make use of cues in revision. One way is to revise in as similar a context as possible to that in which the exams are to be taken. In a recent experiment Grant et al. (1998) had students read an article in either silent or noisy conditions and then tested them on it in either silence or the presence of noise. Those who had studied it in silence remembered more in silence and those who had studied with noise remembered more in noisy conditions. The effect held true across multiple-choice (recognition) questions and short-answer questions (cued recall). Given that exams are always taken in silence this study suggests that students should revise in silence. The visual context (i.e. the appearance of the room) in which learning takes place can also be a context cue. Normally students do not get to take their exams in the rooms where they were given the information. However, Jerabek and Standing (1992) demonstrated that we can enhance recall by *mentally rehearsing* the environment where we learnt information. Participants were given material to learn then taken to another room for a recall task. In one condition they were asked to visualise the room in which they had learnt the information before recall; this enhanced recall. Their study suggests that students might enhance their memory on entering an exam by visualising the classroom they received the information in.

The *cognitive interview* (Fisher and Geiselman, 1988), an interview procedure increasingly being used by the British Police Force, also relies on the role of cues to aid eyewitness recall. The interview involves questions like 'how did you feel then?', which are designed to act as cues to reinstate the mood at the time of the event. Witnesses are asked to imagine as many details as possible of the setting in which the event took place in order to make use of context cues. They may also be asked to recall events from the beginning, the end and the middle in order to maximise the number of semantic cues. Research has generally supported the usefulness of the cognitive interview. Koehnken et al. (1999) performed a meta-analysis on 42 studies of the effectiveness of the cognitive interview and concluded that cognitive interviewing significantly increases the amount of accurate information recalled in interviews, although increases the accuracy of recall only slightly.

 **Further Reading**

BADDELEY, A. (1995) *Human memory, theory and application.* Hove, Lawrence Erlbaum.

EYSENCK, M.J. (2001) *Principles of cognitive psychology.* London, Taylor and Francis.

EYSENCK, M.J. AND KEANE, M. (2000) *Cognitive psychology, a student handbook.* London, Taylor and Francis.

# Diagnosis of mental disorder

IN MEDICINE, DIAGNOSIS IS THE PROCESS BY WHICH WE DETERMINE WHAT CONDITION A patient is suffering from. Diagnosis of mental disorder forms an important part of psychiatry, the branch of medicine dealing with mental disorder. There are a number of systems that we can use to classify abnormal patterns of thinking, behaviour and emotion into mental disorders. Such systems also give guidelines on how to diagnose these disorders. The two most widely used systems of classification and diagnosis are the *Diagnostic and Statistical Manual of Mental Disorder* (DSM), produced by the American Psychiatric Association, and the *International Classification of the Causes of Disease and Death* (ICD), produced by the World Health Organization.

* Historical systems of diagnosis
* The DSM-IV
* The ICD-10
* Other diagnostic systems

## Historical systems of diagnosis

HISTORICAL accounts of recognisable mental disorders go back hundreds of years. However, it is only relatively recently that mental health professionals have systematically classified sets of symptoms into mental disorders and diagnosed individuals with particular disorders on the basis of their symptoms. Early attempts to diagnose mental disorder were based as much on the social control of disadvantaged groups as on the serious understanding of mental disorder. For instance, in the nineteenth century middle-class women who were attracted to men of lower socio-economic groups were diagnosed with *nymphomania*, and women who inherited family money that male relatives would have liked themselves were likely to receive a diagnosis of *moral insanity*.

The first attempt at a comprehensive system that would classify abnormal behaviour into distinct conditions or *syndromes* came from Kraeplin (1883). However, Kraeplin's system was never universally accepted, and through the first half of the twentieth century a wide variety of ways of classifying and diagnosing mental disorder was used. In 1939 the World Health Organization added a chapter on the classification and diagnosis of mental disorder to its *International List of the Causes of Death*. In 1952 the American Psychiatric association published its first *Diagnostic and Statistical Manual*.

## The DSM-IV

THE latest version of the DSM system is the fourth edition with text revisions (i.e. changes to the structure of the classification system rather than to the classifications themselves) – DSM-IV. This was published in 1994, and the DSM-IV-TR (the fourth edition with text revisions) was published in 2000. DSM-IV contains over 200 distinct mental disorders. Each successive version of the DSM has tightened up the criteria for diagnosing disorders: newer versions, for example, tend to specify how long symptoms must last before diagnosis. Some changes have been made in the nature of disorders identified by the DSM in line with changing social norms. For example, before the publication of DSM-III in 1980, homosexuality was classified as a mental disorder, but this has now been dropped. New disorders have also been identified since the earlier versions. For example, since DSM-III the category of eating disorders has included bulimia as well as anorexia and since DSM-IV it has included binge-eating disorder.

Since the publication of DSM-III-R, diagnosis takes place on five different bases or *axes*. This approach is called *multiaxial diagnosis*.

- Axis I describes the patient's clinical condition, for example major depression or a simple phobia.
- Axis II is for chronic conditions such as retardation or personality disorders that often lie alongside Axis I disorders.
- Axis III is for medical conditions that might be important in deciding a course of treatment.
- Axis IV is for psychosocial stressors (i.e. events in the life of the patient that are of relevance to their distress). Examples include unemployment, bereavement and homelessness.
- Axis V is the *global assessment of functioning* (GAF). This is a scale from 0 to 100, which assesses how well a person is functioning overall.

Although clinicians are not obliged to use all five axes when making a diagnosis, it is widely agreed that it is helpful to do so.

## The ICD-10

CURRENTLY the ICD is in its tenth edition (hence ICD-10), published in 1992. Over successive versions the ICD and the DSM have become more alike, and the World

Health Organization and the American Psychiatric Association consulted closely when ICD-10 and DSM-IV were developed in the early 1990s. The 11 categories of mental disorder in ICD-10 resemble fairly closely those of DSM-IV-TR. ICD-10 has fewer categories and each category tends to be slightly broader. There are some differences in the language used to describe disorders and groups of disorders. The major difference between the two systems is that ICD-10 is intended primarily as a *classification* system, although it includes details of what symptoms are required for diagnosis. DSM-IV-TR, by contrast, is intended as a fully comprehensive manual for *diagnosis*, and so includes precise details of how to conduct diagnostic interviews and other tests.

## Other diagnostic systems

ALTHOUGH DSM-IV-TR and ICD-10 are the most popular diagnostic systems, there is a range of other systems that are designed to assess mental disorder in specific populations. For example, Great Ormond Street Children's Hospital in London has developed its own system for diagnosing children. Some societies are so culturally different from Europe and America that they have developed culture-specific systems of classification and diagnosis. For example, China has its own system.

# The Idea Today

FOR A DIAGNOSTIC SYSTEM LIKE ICD OR DSM TO WORK EFFECTIVELY IT MUST BE RELIABLE and valid. A system is *reliable* if people using it consistently make the same diagnoses; it is *valid* if the diagnoses identify a distinct condition that has different symptoms from other conditions and that is likely to respond to one treatment rather than another. Studies of inter-rater reliability (agreement between clinicians) reveal that some diagnostic categories are much more reliable than others, and that diagnostic procedures are more reliable for some types of patient than others. For instance, Nicholls et al. (2000) showed that neither ICD-10 nor DSM-IV demonstrates good inter-rater reliability for the diagnosis of eating disorders in children. In this study 81 children with an eating problem were classified using ICD-10, DSM-IV and a system developed especially for children by Great Ormond Street Hospital. Most of the children could not be diagnosed according to DSM criteria. Reliability of the DSM was 0.64 (64% agreement between raters), but this figure was artificially increased by the fact that most raters agreed that they couldn't make a diagnosis. Using ICD-10 criteria there was 0.36 reliability. The Great Ormond Street system emerged with much better reliability (0.88).

Validity of diagnosis can be assessed by diagnosing people using both DSM and ICD and seeing the extent to which the two systems agree. This approach is known as *criterion validity*. Of course this only tells us that ICD is valid provided that DSM is also valid (and vice versa), but it is useful to be able to tell when the two systems agree and when they differ. Andrews et al. (1999) assessed 1500 people using DSM-IV and ICD-10 and found good agreement on diagnoses of depression, substance dependence and generalised anxiety. They found moderate agreement for other anxiety disorders but there was agreement only 35% of the time on post-traumatic stress. Overall, the agreement between the systems was 68%. Generally people were more likely to receive a diagnosis according to ICD-10 than according to DSM-IV, which we would expect because the criteria for diagnosis are tighter in DSM-IV. It suggests that either DSM-IV criteria are too narrow or the ICD-10 criteria are too broad.

Some psychologists are concerned about diagnosis for other reasons than practical problems with reliability and validity of diagnostic system. Mental disorder carries a social stigma and people with a diagnosis may suffer discrimination. The media have been blamed for increasing the stigma of mental disorder by portraying patients in a negative light. This was investigated in a study by Philo et al. (1994), in which the content of local and national media in Scotland was analysed for coverage of mental health issues during April 1993. Of all the incidents (factual and fictional) covered involving mental health issues 66% involved accounts of violence. Overall only 18% of fictional and factual incidents were judged to give sympathetic coverage of mental health issues. The researchers surveyed viewer responses to the coverage of mental health issues. With the exception of those who had personal experience of people with mental health problems, for example through family or work, viewers reported negative stereotyped views of the sufferers of mental disorder.

Corrigan et al. (2000) examined in more detail what factors led to stigmatisation of mental disorder, and how the precise nature of the stigma varied from one disorder to another. They asked 152 American University students about their beliefs regarding cocaine addiction, depression, schizophrenia and mental retardation. They found that negative attitudes were related to beliefs about how controllable disorders were and to the likelihood of improvement. Cocaine addiction was judged to be the disorder in which patients had the most control and retardation was judged to have the worst prospects for improvement. Thus both these conditions were found to carry powerful stigmas, but the nature of the stigma was quite different in each case.

It seems that patients are acutely aware of the stigma attached to being diagnosed with a mental disorder and that this awareness worsens their distress. MacDonald and Morley (2001) asked 34 outpatients to complete an emotion diary in which they noted any emotion-provoking experiences and whether they had told anyone about the incident. Patients kept 68% of experiences to themselves, as opposed to a typical figure for non-patients of around 10%. When interviewed the participants said that their low levels of disclosure were because of their diagnosis – they feared that people would interpret their feelings as a result of their condition.

## Current status of the idea

DIAGNOSIS of psychological distress or maladaptive or socially unacceptable behaviour remains standard practice. In general it is felt that diagnosis allows us to target treatments to individuals that have been shown to have a good chance of success. However, even highly sophisticated systems like DSM-IV-TR and ICD-10 are limited in their reliability and validity, and some believe that the social stigma of having a diagnosis outweighs the benefits of targeted treatment. More radical thinkers look at the historical misuses of diagnosis and remain concerned that some modern diagnoses are used as tools to oppress the non-conformist. Diagnosis thus remains a controversial practice.

## The Idea in Action

NOT EVERYONE WHO RECEIVES HELP FOR A PSYCHOLOGICAL PROBLEM RECEIVES A psychiatric diagnosis. Those who visit a private psychotherapist, for example, are more likely to receive help based on their situation, personal characteristics and symptoms than on a classification of their symptoms into a particular disorder. However in the psychiatric 'system' diagnosis forms an important part of the process. There is a wide consensus that the advantage of being able to target treatment outweighs the limitations of diagnosis.

## Further Reading

DAVISON, G.C. AND NEALE, J.M. (1994) *Abnormal psychology*. New York, Wiley.

JARVIS, M., PUTWAIN, D. AND DWYER, D. (2002) *Angles on atypical psychology*. Cheltenham, Nelson Thornes.

MURRAY, R., HILL, P. AND MCGUFFIN, P. (1997) *The essentials of postgraduate psychiatry*. Cambridge, Cambridge University Press.

# Erikson's theory of lifespan development

## The Idea

$E$RIK ERIKSON WAS A PSYCHOANALYST AND A FOLLOWER OF Sigmund Freud (see p.64). Like Freud, he was interested in personality development, but unlike Freud (who considered the adult personality to be largely formed in the first few years of life), he thought in terms of development as a lifelong process. He used the term *psychosocial development* to distinguish his approach from Freudian psychosexual development. Erikson believed that development could be thought of as a series of stages each of which was characterised by a psychosocial problem to overcome.

- ❋ Developmental tasks
- ❋ Stages of psychosocial development

Erik Erikson

### Developmental tasks

ERIKSON proposed that the *ego,* or 'self', matures through the individual's handling of a number of developmental crises. Each crisis is social in nature, involving the relationship between the individual and others – hence the term 'psychosocial.' For each crisis there is a developmental task, which is to overcome the crisis and progress to the next level of development. Everyone goes through the same crises in their development in the same sequence, although there is some variation in the age at which each individual encounters and negotiates their crisis. Development of a mature ego and hence mental health depends on successfully negotiating each developmental crisis.

## Stages of psychosocial development

BASIC TRUST VS MISTRUST (0–1 YEAR)  The child's focus in its first year is its relationship with its primary carer. It is this first relationship that gives a child a sense of security or *basic trust* in the world and in other people. If the primary carer manages to create a secure, reliable and comfortable environment the child will trust them and transfer this trust to its dealings with the rest of the world. Inconsistent, neglectful or abusive care on the other hand will leave the child with a sense of mistrust that will affect its later development.

AUTONOMY VS SHAME AND DOUBT (1–3 YEARS)  The child is now aware of its identity as a separate person. This brings with it the challenge to assert its own wishes and to 'do its own thing' (i.e. to have *autonomy*) whilst maintaining a close relationship with its parents. The child is developing its own identity at this point, but this could be crushed by heavy-handed or overly critical parenting. Accidents, for example in toilet training, can be a source of shame to the child and it is essential that this shame does not overwhelm the child's developing sense of self. Firm but gentle parenting is needed to get the child past this period.

INITIATIVE VS GUILT (4–6 YEARS)  At this point the child is developing physically and intellectually very rapidly, and the child is generally keen to explore the world and its own abilities. Having established that it is a person the child now needs to find out what *sort* of person it is. The child is thus very inquisitive and starts to show curiosity about sex. The child also indulges in considerable fantasy play at this stage as a way of exploring its place in the world. This fantasy typically includes imagining taking the place of the same-sex parent in the relationship with the opposite-sex parent. If parents respond to the child's curiosity and fantasy with embarrassment or treat the child as a nuisance it can develop a sense of guilt. If, however, it is encouraged in these activities it will develop a sense of initiative that will continue into adulthood.

INDUSTRY VS INFERIORITY (7–12 YEARS)  The child is beginning to focus on what it can learn about the world. Erikson believed that all cultures have the equivalent of school where the child can learn the practical and technological skills emphasised by the particular culture. The word 'technological' in this context means anything from weapons through manual tools to computers, depending on the culture. Relationships with others outside the family start to assume particular importance at this stage as the child compares its developing skills with those of its peers and begins to form significant relationships with its teachers. If the child succeeds in forming new relationships outside the family and in its mastery of technology it develops a sense of industry – the capacity to be busy. If it fails to achieve these goals the child could be left with a sense of inferiority.

IDENTITY VS IDENTITY-DIFFUSION (12–18 YEARS)  This is adolescence, a time of rapid change on physical, psychological and social levels. Erikson believed that the developmental task of adolescence is to maintain a stable identity in the face of these changes. At the physical level the young person experiences rapid and dramatic changes in their body, which requires a period of adjustment. On a social level adolescence is a *moratorium*, a period where we delay responsibilities such as work and marriage in order to give the adolescent time to adjust. However, this moratorium can cause as much difficulty as it prevents; adolescents are often expected to act in an adult manner and to make adult career decisions, yet they are excluded from the benefits of adulthood. The adolescent who overcomes all these difficulties develops a stable adult identity; however, there is a risk of *identity diffusion* in which during the struggle for identity they identify with labels such as 'delinquent' or extreme youth cultures such as violent gangs. The role of parents is particularly important here; Erikson believed that parents who are tolerant of adolescent crises and refuse to apply labels like 'delinquent' are enormously helpful in avoiding identity diffusion.

INTIMACY VS SELF-ABSORPTION (19–25 YEARS) The developmental task at this age is to develop successful platonic, romantic and sexual relationships. Erikson believed that this could only be achieved if the individual had successfully achieved an identity during adolescence. While Erikson emphasised the importance of sexual relationships, he applied the same principles to the establishment of adult friendships and adult relationships to other family members. The developmental conflict of early adulthood is to achieve intimacy in relationships while retaining autonomy. Unsuccessful outcomes of this conflict include isolation and loneliness (or superficial, meaningless relationships) at one extreme and submerging one's individuality in a relationship and becoming 'under the thumb' at the other. Erikson considered the capacity for *distantation* very important. Distantation is the ability to distance oneself from others and to oppose them and what they represent, when necessary even going to war.

GENERATIVITY VS STAGNATION (26–40 YEARS) *Generativity* is the capacity to maintain interest in the next generation. This is manifested in an interest in work, family and the world as a whole, but particularly in one's children and in that which will affect future generations of humanity. A failure in generativity (*stagnation*) may lead to loss of the will to work or in impoverished interpersonal relationships. Erikson (1959) observed that many parents he saw in his child-guidance work had been unable to maintain an appropriate interest in their children because of their own parenting. Erikson believed that those who did not have children but who channelled their energies into creative or altruistic work were still displaying generativity and could successfully negotiate this stage of development.

EGO INTEGRITY VS DESPAIR AND DISGUST (41 YEARS+) As you enter the second half of your life and have achieved most of what you are going to achieve, and as your physical and cognitive abilities begin to decline, there is psychosocial conflict to overcome between *ego integrity*, as you look back at your achievements with contentment, and *despair and disgust* as the unsatisfied individual looks back with regret. Despair results from the awareness that life is too short to start again. The despairing individual may also feel disgust at his or her own lack of achievement. This feeling of disgust is commonly projected onto others; thus the individual may appear to be angry, critical and contemptuous of others. Erikson believed that the main determinant of whether a state of integrity or despair and disgust develops in an individual is whether generativity has been achieved in the previous stage. If you have thrown yourself wholeheartedly into the development of the next generation you are more likely to sit back and watch contentedly as they take their turn in achievement.

# The Idea Today

BECAUSE ERIKSON PLACED MORE EMPHASIS ON INDIVIDUAL EXPERIENCE THAN ON observable behaviour his ideas can be quite difficult to test. However, there is research to support a number of Erikson's ideas. Much of this research has focused on adolescence. The importance of parenting in avoiding delinquency has been well supported. Carlo et al. (1998) assessed 80 young people for levels of parental support, aggression, antisocial behaviour, sympathy and prosocial behaviour. A strong relationship was found between parental support and all the other variables, suggesting that Erikson was correct in his emphasis on supportive parenting in adolescence. In another study Vitaro et al. (2000) tested the idea that parental support can directly influence delinquency. They found that the chances of an individual becoming a delinquent were greatly increased if their best friend was delinquent. However, the effect was much smaller when the individual had supportive parents.

Research has also supported Erikson's ideas about the shift from adolescence to young adulthood. In a longitudinal study Whitbourne et al. (1992) measured intimacy and sense of identity in 20, 31 and 42-year-old subjects. They found that, as predicted, both measures increased substantially between 20 and 31 years. An interesting twist to the Whitbourne study was that during the course of the study two new groups of 20 year olds were assessed at the same time as the first group were being reassessed at 31 and 42, and the second group was reassessed at age 31 at the same time as the first group were having their 42-year assessment. No difference was found between the levels of intimacy or identity at 20 or 31 in the different groups despite massive social changes between 1966 (when the study began) and 1988. This suggests that, as Erikson believed, development is dependent on age rather than societal factors. It may be, however, that Erikson's theory does not take sufficient account of gender differences in development. A study by Patterson et al. (1992) showed for example that, whereas men tend to base their identity on work, women have a wider variety of influences, including work, relationships and parenthood.

Generativity has also been the subject of some recent work. McAdams and St Aubin (1992) developed a psychometric test to measure generativity called the Loyola Generativity Scale. McAdams et al. (1997) compared the life stories of adults classified as high and low in generativity by means of this scale. Generative adults were more likely to take a positive view of adversity and to use analogies such as myth, folklore and biblical stories to make sense of their life events. They also scored higher on commitment to others. This is in keeping with Erikson's theory.

## Current status of the idea

ERIKSON'S main influence has been in clinical work. In mainstream academic psychology his ideas have proved more palatable to many than those of Freud. However, in the psychology of adulthood developmental theories in general have been out of fashion for some time, and there is a current emphasis on the stability of the adult personality and responses to particular life events. It is widely felt that developmental theories like Erikson's generalise too much about the challenges people face at different ages, and underestimate the aspects of the personality that do not change with age. Also, as we have seen, Erikson's theory is more applicable to men than women.

## The Idea in Action

THE MAJOR APPLICATION OF ERIKSON'S THEORY HAS BEEN IN THERAPEUTIC WORK, WHERE therapists trying to make sense of their patients' lives have benefited from an understanding of the developmental tasks that typically affect people at particular ages. For example, adolescents in crisis are likely (though a good therapist would not make too many assumptions about this) to be struggling with issues of identity. A 40-year-old might be struggling to maintain generativity and an older person might be battling with despair and disgust. Clearly, therapists can take different approaches depending on the developmental task their patient is dealing with. There are also cases where advice can be given based on an understanding of Erikson's theory. For example, parents of an adolescent can be educated on the importance of non-judgmental support.

Erikson's theory has recently been applied to understanding the appeal of particular entertainment genres. Schlozman (2000) has thus explained the appeal of *Buffy the Vampire Slayer* to adolescents in terms of Erikson's views on adolescent identity crisis. According to Schlozman each character (including the monsters) represents an adolescent anxiety. For example Oz the teenage werewolf symbolises the difficulty of coping with rapid identity change in adolescence. We might interpret the facial hair and raging hormones of the werewolf as symbolic of puberty.

## Further Reading

BEE, H. (1998) *Lifespan development*. New York, Harper Collins.

ENGLER, B. (1999) *Personality theories*. Boston, Houghton Mifflin.

JARVIS, M., RUSSELL, J., FLANAGAN, C. AND DOLAN, L. (2000) *Angles on psychology*. Cheltenham, Nelson Thornes.

# Evolutionary psychology

❖

## The Idea

THE IDEAS USED IN EVOLUTIONARY PSYCHOLOGY ARE NOT NEW. THE UNDERPINNING explanation, that of evolution, dates back to the nineteenth century and is of central importance to many academic fields such as biology, palaeontology and molecular genetics as well as psychology. The origins of what has become today's evolutionary psychology lay in the theoretical analyses of animal behaviour of the 1960s and 1970s. There was a theoretical shift in that period from the immediate 'triggers' of behaviour towards the 'ultimate causes' or adaptive benefits of the behaviour.

A clear problem for evolutionary psychologists lies in the absence of direct evidence for the selection pressures existing during early human evolution. Evolutionary psychologists must therefore rely on indirect evidence from general evolutionary principles, comparisons between species, cross-cultural studies and human behaviour today. Speculations about how these modern behaviours have arisen are difficult (although not impossible) to test empirically. The hypotheses generated are, however, useful because they take a different view of present-day human behaviour than those arising from typical social science models.

* Natural selection
* Sexual selection
* Genes
* Kin selection
* Parental investment

## Natural selection

THE theory of evolution by natural selection, proposed by Charles Darwin (1859), is an explanation of change. It offers a way of understanding how organisms adapt to their environments and how the results of random mutations affect their survival and reproduction. The theory of evolution, and hence evolutionary psychology, would predict that individuals evolve behaviours that enhance their survival and reproductive success. For our early ancestors, these behaviours might have included seeking out foods high in energy, responding with alarm to potentially harmful situations, aggression in competition for scarce resources such as good mates and caring for offspring.

Charles Darwin

According to the theory of evolution behaviours, like physical structures, change by degree. Three key factors are responsible for this adaptation, making animals better suited to survival and reproduction in their environment.

- Firstly, individuals vary; they differ from one another.

- Secondly, such differences may be passed on from parent to offspring; they are heritable characteristics.

- Thirdly, these differences in characteristics lead to differential reproduction; some individuals will reproduce more successfully than others.

This capacity to survive and reproduce is called fitness, hence 'survival of the fittest'. So, if some early humans were, say, better at fighting than others, their ability to protect themselves and their offspring from attack would increase the likelihood of their survival and reproduction. Thus, in an environment where attack was likely this would act as a source of selection pressure and so aggression would be adaptive.

## Sexual selection

DARWIN was also responsible for identifying *sexual selection*, differences between individuals of the same sex and species that confer specific advantages in terms of reproduction. Two processes result in sexual selection. Competition arises between members of one sex (usually the males) for the scarce resource of the other sex (usually the females). This effect, called *intersexual selection*, tends to result in favouring a capacity to win fights with competitors (through size, strength or tactical advantage). In addition, a competing individual's reproductive success will also be affected by their attractiveness to the opposite sex. Thus when males compete for females, those with attributes preferred by the females will be more likely to mate, a process called *intrasexual selection*. This results in the selection of ornamentation (as in the peacock) and courtship behaviour that increase the probability of being chosen as a mate.

## Genes

ALTHOUGH the study of genetics had already begun when Darwin described natural selection, the two levels of explanation were not united for many years. Now, because we understand so much more about the structure and function of deoxyribonucleic acid (DNA), the molecule from which genetic material is made, Darwin's theory can be thought of in genetic terms. The heritability of differences relies on the control of those characteristics by genes, individually inherited factors. Variation can arise because individuals carry two alleles (gene forms) for each gene. These are united in different combinations for each individual through the process of sexual reproduction as genetic material from the mother and father are combined. Further variation can arise as different combinations of genes from the parental ones can be generated during egg or sperm production. Finally mutations, the random errors that occur in DNA replication, can introduce changes into an individual's genetic make-up that could be inherited by its offspring. There are few, if any, behaviours that are controlled by single genes. Many genes act in combination to influence any particular behaviour. Additionally, in most cases genes only play a part in the development of any particular behaviour in the repertoire of an individual. Experience is also important (see p.20).

## Kin selection

ALTHOUGH natural selection is able to explain the evolution of behaviours that act to the advantage of the performer, it cannot readily explain instances where individuals appear to behave in a way that carries costs for themselves but benefits others. In fact, natural selection would be expected to eradicate such behaviours. The existence of helping or *altruistic* behaviours is a well-documented phenomenon and so requires explanation. The theory of kin selection provides one account of the way in which such behaviours may evolve. An individual that sees a predator should, in terms of survival of the fittest, hide or retreat to maximise its chances of escaping unharmed. In fact, members of many species give alarm calls in the face of danger, putting themselves at risk by being easy targets but assisting the safety of others. In terms of fitness this seems counterintuitive until we look closely at those individuals who benefit. Many animals remain in loose family groups and relatives receive the benefits from such helping behaviour. As a consequence, the helpful behaviour will promote the survival of related individuals and since they share some genes with the altruist, the altruist benefits indirectly through an enhanced contribution to the gene pool. Those individuals that have been helped will have an increased chance of surviving and reproducing, thus contributing more of the genes shared with the altruist to the next generation. This indirect measure of genetic success is called *inclusive fitness*, accounting for the genes that are represented in the next generation by one's own offspring and those in the offspring of related individuals.

## Parental investment

MOST species are *anisogametic*, that is they produce gametes (sex cells) of different sizes; sperm are much smaller than eggs. This leads to a situation in which, for any given offspring, the mother is likely to have expended more energy than the father at the point of conception. In many species this 'traps' the mothers into continued parental care – having invested so much already a strategy of continued care is, for females, more successful. This may not be the case for males, for them the strategy of embarking on new opportunities to impregnate other females may be a better way to enhance fitness. The underlying difference in investment in gametes thus has several consequences. In general, females are more likely than males to offer parental care to their offspring, and males are likely to depart and seek new opportunities to mate if the female can rear the offspring alone. Females, being the scarce resource, are in a position to choose and will prefer males that are able to provide benefits for them or their offspring.

This mate choice may be based on indicators of 'good genes' such as strength, size or performance in a courtship ritual or it may be influenced by the contribution the potential mate can make to survival of offspring. Mates that have an ability to build nests or provide food, or are 'trapped' into staying by a prolonged courtship would be preferred. There are also situations in which males provide extended parental investment as two parents may be vital to the offspring's survival (such as in many bird species). Finally, for either parent, there comes a point where their reproductive success will be maximised by ceasing to invest in any current offspring and embarking on another breeding opportunity. This leads to the parent-offspring conflict; it is in the offspring's interest to continue to receive care but in the parents' interests to begin anew.

The Idea Today

THE FRAMEWORK OF EVOLUTIONARY PSYCHOLOGY IS BEING USED TO PROVIDE alternative explanations both for behaviours that appear to be adaptive and for ones that appear now, but may not previously have been, maladaptive. Buss (1999) describes the link between levels of evolutionary explanations as a hierarchy. Natural selection, at the top of the hierarchy, is the guiding principle for evolutionary thinking, beneath which there are broad principles such as kin selection and parental investment. The theory of natural selection itself is supported by two centuries of diverse geological and biological evidence. The second-level principles derived from this are based on wide-ranging studies of comparative psychology; evidence from similarities and differences between the behaviour of animals with similar evolutionary histories. From these broad principles, evolutionary psychology can make specific predictions about individual species, such as humans. A further level predicts in even more specific circumstances, such as differences in behaviour of males and females of individuals of different ages.

Finding a partner with high Darwinian fitness would enhance the reproductive success of an individual, hence sexual selection would predict that people might choose partners using some indicator of fitness. Cartwright (2000) found that adults prefer photographs of members of the opposite sex who have more symmetrical faces. Facial symmetry, a trait which is in part hereditary, may thus be used as an indicator of fitness. Not only is it likely that offspring of such mates will inherit this attractive characteristic but also facial symmetry may provide direct evidence of good health. Individuals who have been well fed and who have resisted disease are more likely to avoid facial asymmetry. Furthermore, facial symmetry is a good indicator of body symmetry (another attractive characteristic) – asymmetric males and females report having fewer sexual partners than those with greater symmetry. Cartwright (2000) also found that women with breasts of equal size were more fertile than women with uneven breasts and that women were likely to have more orgasms if their partners were more symmetrical. Although these effects could be the direct result of symmetry indicating health or other aspects of physical fitness they could also be explained indirectly. More symmetric people may be more confident or dominant, making them more appealing.

Evolutionary theory would also predict a difference in the frequency with which males and females seek sexual partners. Men would be expected to desire more partners than women in accordance with sexual selection and parental investment ideas. Buss and Schmitt (1993) found evidence to support this by asking undergraduates the number of different sexual partners they would like to have over different periods of time. The males consistently wanted to have more sexual partners than females. In addition, Buss and Schmitt also investigated how soon after meeting a potential partner men and women would be willing to have sex with them. Again, the male participants were far more inclined to consider sex with a comparative stranger than were women.

In terms of parental investment, males' reproductive success should depend on finding fertile, and therefore younger, mates whilst females would benefit from older mates with more resources to help to raise the offspring. This pattern, of men preferring younger women but women preferring older men, has been confirmed (e.g. by Isaacson, 2001). Men may use hair length as an indicator of potential fertility. Hinsz et al. (2001) found a negative correlation between hair length and age; younger women had longer hair and this, in turn, was positively correlated with health.

Aggression has an effect on fitness. Fighting would have been adaptive to attain and protect resources so would have been preserved by natural selection and, in young men in particular, sexual selection would have operated to enhance this behaviour. However, although successful as a strategy to compete for and protect females in our evolutionary history, aggressiveness has obvious costs. As a consequence, threat displays evolve to limit the risk of engagement in an unwise dispute with a potentially stronger opponent. In the modern world, two features – alcohol and guns – have altered the value of such assessments before escalation. Studies of bar-room fights suggest that men do appraise their rivals before embarking on a fight (Graham and Wells, 2000) but under the influence of alcohol they are likely to over-estimate their own prowess and enter into fights with people who are likely to beat them. The use of guns creates a situation in which assessments are worthless and escalation is immediate – in the absence of a measure of the relative chances of losing aggression is unrestrained.

Altruistic behaviour, such as blood donation, where there are clear costs to the donor and gains to the recipient can also be investigated from an evolutionary perspective. This is an interesting example as the particular behaviour cannot have been exposed to evolutionary pressures because the medical technique is too recent. However, evolution can have shaped a tendency to help others so hypotheses can be generated to explain the tendency of people to give blood. If donated blood was always reserved for relatives the behaviour could be explained by kin selection but we know that this is not the case. What possible gains could there be for the altruist? Perhaps a kind of reciprocal altruism is at work. People may give blood in order to affect other people's impression of them; if survival and reproduction were dependent on co-operation and 'being liked' then it would be adaptive to perform acts to gain a good reputation. Low and Heinen (1993) tested this prediction by finding out whether blood donors tended to hide their participation or to let people know that they had given blood. They found that students were more likely to donate at fundraising events where they received a pin or tag they could wear to advertise their status as a blood donor. Perhaps a kind of *reciprocal altruism* is at work here – an altruistic behaviour is maintained because short-term benefits are accrued by both an original helper and another individual, who returns the favour.

## Current status of the idea

THE scope of behaviours to which evolutionary principles are being applied is rapidly expanding. The challenge to explain from a new perspective behaviours that cannot have been directly shaped by evolution is offering new opportunities for psychology. However, there is a risk of appearing to accept some behaviours, especially antisocial ones such as cheating, rape or aggression, whereas evolutionary psychology neither suggests that such behaviours are inevitable nor attempts to justify them, only to explain how they may have arisen.

W HAT USE IS EVOLUTIONARY PSYCHOLOGY? SADLY, KNOWING WHY A BEHAVIOUR HAS arisen and that it is (or may once have been) adaptive does not necessarily help us to control it. Evolutionary explanations of rape and aggression can be criticised for merely telling us why these behaviours may have been adaptive strategies rather than providing solutions to criminal behaviour. There are, however, some useful observations that may help to guide the ways that we can support victims.

Evolutionary theory provides two hypotheses to explain why men rape women despite the severe penalties they incur if caught.

- Rape may have evolved as an adaptive strategy for men who are unable to reproduce because they cannot attract a sexual partner.

- Alternatively, rape may be a maladaptive consequence of males' high sexual arousability and motivation to seek many sexual partners.

In practice, these two hypotheses lead to similar predictions (such as rape victims will tend to be women in their peak reproductive years) and this prediction is supported by evidence (Thornhill and Thornhill 1983). Women who are raped may suffer further as their male partners may feel jealous (as, in terms of evolutionary theory, the partner's fitness may have been jeopardised). Women who have been hurt during the rape, suggesting to their partner that they were not complicit in the act, are less likely to be subject to such additional trauma. Such findings could be used to guide the way we help rape victims; consideration of whether they are single or part of a couple and the response of their partner could ensure that appropriate support is provided.

Throughout our evolution, humans have been faced with diseases of many kinds. Natural selection has adapted our immune systems to fight many of these effectively.

However, the on-going battle between our evolving immunity and the co-evolution of the bacteria and viruses we are attempting to resist resembles the evolutionary arms race described by Dawkins and Krebs (1979) between predators and prey. As one species evolves a new strategy to overcome the opposition, so the other adapts to compete more effectively. Darwinian medicine uses this type of evolutionary explanation to understand the relationship between humans (the host or 'prey') and disease-causing agents (the pathogen or 'predator). Understanding the relationship between the evolution of pathogens and the immune system has helped us predict the effects of behaviour change on disease symptoms. The human immunodeficiency virus (HIV) is responsible for destroying the immune system of individuals it infects, making them vulnerable to other infections that cause the symptoms of acquired immune deficiency syndrome (AIDS) responsible for killing the sufferer. Diseases spread by direct contact (contagious diseases) tend to be less virulent (cause less damage to the host) than airborne or insect-carried diseases – by ensuring the host's survival, the pathogen is able to spread more widely as the infected individual interacts with other people. HIV, however, is both highly virulent and contagious. Reducing sexually and intravenously transmitted infection would not only lower the number of new cases of HIV infection but would also precipitate the evolution of a less virulent form of the virus – in order to survive it would become adaptive to cause *less* harm to the host.

 Further Reading

ALCOCK, J. (1998) *Animal behavior, An evolutionary approach*. Sunderland, MA, Sinauer.

CLAMP, A. (2001) *Evolutionary psychology*. London, Hodder and Stoughton.

DARWIN, C. (1859) *The origin of species by means of natural selection*. London, John Murray.

DAVIES, R. (1995) Selfish altruism. *Psychology Review* 1, 2–9.

# Freudian psychoanalysis

❖

## The Idea

SIGMUND FREUD IS WITHOUT DOUBT THE MOST famous psychologist of all time. He developed a collection of ideas, which have together formed what is perhaps still the most complex and complete theory of the human personality. Freud was a therapist and his ideas are based largely on what his patients told him during therapy: indeed, one of Freud's achievements was the development of effective psychological therapy. Freud wrote on a wide variety of topics and developed his ideas throughout the period of his writing. It is not possible to look at all (or even most) of Freud's ideas in this short section, but we can briefly overview some of the more important areas.

Sigmund Freud

- ❀ The unconscious mind
- ❀ Dreams
- ❀ Psychological defences
- ❀ The structural model of personality
- ❀ Psychosexuality

## The unconscious mind

THE most fundamental idea in Freudian theory, and in the whole psychodynamic approach to psychology, is that of the unconscious mind. Freud described his approach as 'depth psychology,' comparing himself to an archaeologist digging away layers of the human mind. Freud distinguished between the conscious mind, which consists of all the mental processes of which we are aware, the preconscious mind, which contains memories that can be recalled to consciousness under certain circumstances and the true unconscious mind, which contains our biologically based instincts, most importantly the primitive urges for sex and aggression. These instincts are not accessible to consciousness. While we are fully aware of what is going on in the conscious mind, our feelings, motives and decisions are powerfully influenced by our past experiences, stored in the preconscious, and instincts from the unconscious.

Freud believed that the influences of the preconscious and unconscious reveal themselves in a variety of ways, including dreams, apparent accidents, myths and stories and in action slips or *parapraxis*, most commonly of the tongue, now popularly known as 'Freudian slips.' Freud (1914) gave a number of examples of parapraxes: a woman talking about her unsuccessful life commented that 'men just need *five* straight limbs'; another asked her friend to wait 'for a few *movements*' while she went into a chemist for a laxative. Not all parapraxes are verbal: one of Freud's medical colleagues once went to shake the hand of an attractive female patient and instead undid her dressing gown.

## Dreams

FREUD called dreams 'the royal road to a knowledge of the activities of the unconscious mind' (Freud, 1900). He went on to propose that the major function of dreams was the fulfilment of wishes. Freud distinguished between the *manifest* content of a dream – what the dreamer remembers – and the *latent* content – the underlying wish represented by the manifest content. The process whereby the underlying wish is translated into the manifest content is called *dream-work*. The purpose of dream-work is to transform the forbidden wish into a non-threatening form, so reducing anxiety and allowing us to continue to sleep.

Dream-work involves four processes:

- *Displacement* takes place when we alter whatever we are *really* bothered about into someone or something else. An example of displacement comes from one of Freud's patients, who hated his sister-in-law. He used to refer to her as a dog, and once dreamed of strangling a small white dog. Freud interpreted this as displacement of his feelings towards his sister-in-law onto the dog.

- *Condensation* takes place when we combine different factors into one aspect of the manifest content. For example, if we are angry at two people they might be represented by one person.

- *Symbolisation* occurs when one object represents another. For example, a patient in hospital for a penis operation dreamed of having a smaller, bleeding sword than his friends.

- *Secondary elaboration* is the final part of dream-work, and occurs when the unconscious mind strings together wish-fulfilling images into a logical story. Freud suggested that this is why the manifest content of dreams can be in the form of plausible chains of events.

## Psychological defences

FREUD suggested that there are psychological mechanisms by which we protect ourselves from painful, frightening or guilty feelings (Freud, 1894). The mind has a number of such defences at its disposal: *denial* occurs when we refuse to admit an unpleasant fact, *repression* involves the inability to remember painful events, *displacement* involves redirecting a strong emotion such as anger from one person to another, *reaction formation* takes place when we adopt an attitude opposite to what we really feel. Other defences include *sublimation*, in which we channel a strong emotion into creative activity and *regression*, in which we use childlike behaviours to comfort ourselves.

The idea of psychological defences was further developed by Anna Freud (Sigmund's daughter) (Freud, 1936). She proposed that the tendency for defensiveness was acquired in childhood as a result of trauma, especially that which related to parents, and that different defences were associated with relationship difficulties at specific ages. Anna Freud also suggested that defences can be triggered by conflicts between instinctive impulses and societal disapproval (the *id-ego/superego conflict*).

## The structural model of personality

FREUD (1933) tried to show how instinct and past experience affects personality by dissecting the personality into three parts – 'I' 'it' and 'above-I'. Each of these parts represents a different aspect of the person and plays a different role in deciding on a course of action.

- *It* represents the instinctive aspect of the personality, present from birth. *It* wants to be satisfied, and *it* does not willingly tolerate delay or denial of its wishes.

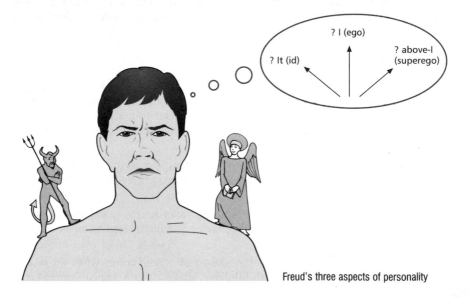

Freud's three aspects of personality

- *I* is the aspect of the person that is aware of both the demands of *it* and the outside world, and which makes decisions. *I* develops through experience of dealing with the world, and has the capacity to think logically.

- *Above-I* is the aspect of the personality formed from the experience with authority figures such as the parent, which poses restrictions on what actions are allowed. Your *above-I* can reward you with pride and punish you with guilt according to whether you go along with its restrictions.

These three aspects of the personality are sometimes called the *id* (it), the *ego* (I) and the *superego* (above-I).

## Psychosexuality

THIS is perhaps the most controversial aspect of Freud's theory. In 1905 Freud proposed that psychological development in childhood takes place in a series of fixed stages. These are called *psychosexual stages* because each stage represents the fixation of libido (roughly translated as sexual drives or instincts) on a different area of the body. If this sounds slightly odd, it is important to realise that Freud's use of the word 'sexual' was quite broad in meaning, and he did not mean that the child experiences these instincts as 'sexual' in the adult sense. Libido is manifested in childhood as *organ-pleasure*, centred on a different organ in each of the first three stages of development.

In the *oral stage* (the first year of life), while the child is breast-feeding and being weaned, the focus of organ-pleasure is the mouth. As well as taking nourishment through the mouth, children in the oral stage are taking comfort and their knowledge of the world via their mouth. Freud proposed that if the person experiences a trauma in the first year they can become fixated in the oral stage and continue to display oral characteristics into adulthood. Oral habits can include thumb-sucking, smoking, tastes such as oral sex and attitudes such as *gullibility*, which represents the unquestioning taking in of information as children do in their first year.

In the *anal stage* (years 2–3), the focus of organ-pleasure now shifts to the anus. The child is now fully aware that they are a person in their own right and that their wishes can bring them into conflict with the demands of the outside world. Freud believed that this type of conflict tends to come to a head in potty training, in which adults impose restrictions – for the first time in the child's experience – on when and where the child can defecate. The nature of this first encounter with authority can determine the child's future relationship with all forms of authority. Early or harsh potty training can lead to the child becoming an *anal-retentive personality* who hates mess, is obsessively tidy, punctual and respectful of authority. Alternatively the child may turn out an *anal-expulsive personality*, who is messy, disorganised and rebellious.

In the *phallic stage* (years 3–6), the focus of organ-pleasure has shifted to the genitals, as the child becomes fully aware of its gender. This coincides with a growing awareness of the child's exclusion from some aspects of its parents' lives, such as sleeping in the same room. The resulting three-way relationship is known as the *Oedipus complex*, named after Oedipus, who in Greek legend killed his father and married his mother (not realising who they were). In the Oedipus complex a rivalry relationship develops between the child and the same-sex parent for the affection of the opposite-sex parent. Freud believed that on an *unconscious level* the child is expressing instinctive wishes to have sex with his mother and kill his father. This is not to suggest that children possess a conscious awareness of sexual intercourse or death in the adult sense.

Freud believed that the phallic stage was the most important of the developmental stages. When boys realise that they have a penis and girls do not, their unconscious response is *castration anxiety*, the belief that girls have already been castrated and the fear that they might share the same fate! Their response is to repress their desire for the mother and identify with the father (in much the same way as we might identify with a bully and become like them in order to overcome our fear of them). Freud was somewhat perplexed by how girls dealt with the Oedipus complex on an unconscious level. He speculated (Freud, 1924) that when girls discover they lack a penis they feel that they have somehow come off worse, and are left with a sense of *penis envy*, the wish to have a penis. Penis envy is later sublimated into the wish to have a baby, and eventually relieved by actually having a baby.

M ANY OF FREUD'S IDEAS HAVE PROVED VERY DIFFICULT TO RESEARCH, AND HENCE VERY frustrating to psychologists. We cannot directly access the unconscious mind, so studying its influence calls for some clever methodology. A study by Harris and Campbell (1999) looked at the role of unconscious motivation in unplanned pregnancy. Pregnant women whose pregnancies were either planned or unplanned were interviewed about the *secondary gains* that they would expect from becoming pregnant. These included gaining higher status in their family and strengthening relationships with partners. It was found that 81% of the unplanned group expected secondary gains as opposed to 16% of women whose pregnancy was planned. This suggests that the beliefs about the secondary gains of pregnancy were unconscious motivating factors in the women with unplanned pregnancies.

The role of wish fulfilment in dreams remains a much-argued idea. This is difficult to research because, although we can look at the manifest content of dreams there is no objective way to measure what latent content it might represent. Roussy et al. (1996) collected pre-sleep thoughts and accounts of current wishes and anxieties of eight participants and made records of their dreams. There was no apparent association between dream content and what was on the minds of the participants (however, we would not expect much association if the manifest content contains only disguised elements of wishes). Some recent neurological evidence does support the link between dreams and wishes. Solms (2000) has reviewed cases of brain-damaged patients and isolated an area of the brain that, when damaged, abolishes both dreaming and wish-fulfilling behaviour.

There have been many attempts to research psychological defences. There is evidence that reaction formation plays a role in homophobia. In a study by Adams et al. (1996) homophobic men and non-homophobic men watched pornographic films showing heterosexual, lesbian and gay scenes. Both groups became aroused during the lesbian and heterosexual scenes but 80% of the homophobic men (as opposed to 30% of the control group) had erections during scenes of sex between men. This shows a link between homophobia and homosexual arousal, and suggests that homophobia may be reaction against this arousal. Repression is a highly controversial subject and many psychologists do not believe in its existence. However, there is some supporting evidence. Walker et al. (1997) had participants keep a diary of pleasant and unpleasant events. When tested later they showed good recall of pleasant events but poor recall of unpleasant events, suggesting that these may have been repressed.

Psychosexuality is controversial, and may even appear bizarre, yet there is surprisingly strong support for some aspects of Freud's theory, particularly with regard to anality. We can assess anality by measuring people on three scales: obstinacy (stubbornness), orderliness (need for order) and parsimony (stinginess). O'Neill et al. (1992) measured these three traits in 40 women and assessed their responses to toilet humour. Not only did the three traits cluster together (i.e. they were most apparent in the same participants), but those highest in anality found the toilet humour the funniest. There is also evidence linking anality to parenting style. Flett et al. (1995) found that children whose parents were particularly authoritarian (harshly disciplinarian) tended to have a greater tendency for orderliness than others. One area in which psychologists have firmly decided against Freud's view is in the Oedipus complex. Freud believed that this was extremely important in moral and gender role development. However, a number of modern researchers (e.g. Tasker and Golombok, 1997) have compared moral and gender development in single-parent and gay parent families with that of two-parent heterosexual families and concluded that not having two parents of opposite sex has no influence on children's development.

## Current status of the idea

MANY of Freud's ideas, including psychological defences and the importance of parenting style, remain important in modern psychology. His work has a clear application in treating psychological problems, although most psychologists now tend to favour therapies derived from other psychological theories. Other ideas on which Freud placed great emphasis, most notably the Oedipus complex, have been firmly discredited. Because of Freud's emphasis on the unconscious mind, his ideas have proved very frustrating to researchers in psychology. Moreover, Freud's emphasis on sexuality has proved something of an embarrassment to psychologists, and feminists have objected to ideas like penis envy. For these reasons, Freud is generally not well liked in contemporary psychology.

THE MAJOR APPLICATION OF FREUD'S WORK IS IN THE USE OF PSYCHOLOGICAL THERAPY to treat mental disorder and psychological distress. Freud discovered in his early work that one of his patients, Anna O (Breuer and Freud, 1895), gained relief from her symptoms as she talked of traumatic events. This reliving of painful memories is called *abreaction* and the accompanying discharge of painful emotions is called *catharsis*. In a later case, that of Dora (Freud, 1905), Freud discovered the phenomenon of *transference*, whereby feelings about a significant person in the life of a patient are transferred on to the therapist, so that the patient displays tremendous anger or affection towards them. The interpretation of transference, so that the patient realises the way feelings from past relationships are brought to bear on new ones is, like catharsis and abreaction, important in psychoanalytic therapies.

There are now many psychological therapies: some remain true to Freud's techniques and others have diverged considerably, abandoning interpretation and placing much less emphasis on catharsis. A critical question in psychology concerns the relative effectiveness of different psychological therapies. For many years it seemed that there was relatively little evidence that psychoanalytic therapies (as opposed to more modern styles of therapy) were effective in treating psychological problems. However, this has changed in the last 5–10 years as the National Health Service has become committed to *evidence-based practice*, providing only therapies that have been demonstrated by research to be effective. Recent studies have supported the effectiveness of psychoanalytic therapies. Bateman and Fonagy (1999) compared the outcomes for a group of patients suffering from borderline personality disorder in conventional hospital treatment with those given both individual and group psychoanalytic therapy. The patients receiving the therapy showed significantly less depression, self-harming, anxiety and drug abuse than the control group, showing that they were helped by the therapy. Other studies have investigated the effectiveness of psychodynamic therapies for depression and anxiety disorders. Holm-Hadulla et al. (1997) allocated 117 patients suffering from depression and anxiety disorders to a condition of brief psychodynamic therapy whilst a control group of 116 patients received no therapy. Six months after the course of therapy the control group showed little or no improvement whilst the therapy group displayed very substantial improvements.

A major research issue is the extent of differences between classical psychoanalysis and the slightly less intensive and long-term psychoanalytic psychotherapy. This, as well as the general effectiveness of psychoanalytic treatments, has been addressed in a recent series of Swedish studies. Sandell (1999) studied outcomes for 756 patients receiving state-funded psychoanalysis or psychoanalytic psychotherapy and found strong support for the effectiveness of long-term psychodynamic therapies and for the difference between the two therapies. Psychoanalysis was defined by having 4–5 sessions per week, in contrast to psychotherapy, which took place once or twice a week. Therapy continued for up to 3 years. At the end of treatment both groups showed substantial gains, but there was no difference between the two groups. However, at 3-year follow-up the psychoanalysis group were rated as having significantly fewer symptoms. It seems that, unlike the patients receiving psychotherapy, the psychoanalysis group continued to improve after the end of the treatment. This is a highly significant study, being the first to demonstrate that classical psychoanalysis really is different from psychoanalytic psychotherapy.

ANDREWS, B. AND BREWIN, C. (2000) What did Freud get right? *The Psychologist* 13, 605–623.

BATEMAN, A. AND HOLMES, J. (1995) *Introduction to psychoanalysis*. London, Routledge.

JARVIS, M. (in press) *Psychodynamic psychology: Classic theory and contemporary research*. London, ITP.

# Gay and lesbian psychology

UNTIL VERY RECENTLY, PSYCHOLOGY AND ITS RELATED DISCIPLINES HAVE ADOPTED A negative attitude towards homosexuality and have been generally unhelpful to gay people. Psychological literature was dominated by attempts to explain how homosexuality might come about, and in the main these efforts were characterised by an assumption that homosexuality needed explaining because it was in some way abnormal. Indeed, until the publication in 1980 of the third edition of the *Diagnostic and Statistical Manual of Mental Disorder*, homosexuality was classified as a mental disorder. This classification has now been dropped however, and in recent years a shift has occurred in the ways psychologists talk of gay issues. The new field of gay and lesbian psychology is more concerned with issues that are of interest to gay people themselves, and aims to be of use in improving their quality of life.

The term 'gay' can be used to refer generically to all people who have a sexual preference for their own sex or specifically to homosexual men. The terms 'gay people' or 'lesbians and gay men' are thus synonymous. Many psychologists prefer not to use the term 'homosexual' as this is associated historically with the DSM classification of a mental disorder. The terms 'gay psychology' and 'gay and lesbian psychology' also mean the same thing and are both acceptable. The term 'gay psychologist' is used to describe someone who studies psychological issues of particular importance to gay people (it does not describe the psychologist as gay themselves any more than 'sport psychologist' describes one as an athlete or 'clinical psychologist' suggests that one has a clinical condition).

- ✻ Essentialism versus the social construction of homosexuality
- ✻ Gay and lesbian identities
- ✻ Lesbian and gay relationships
- ✻ Homophobia

## Essentialism versus the social construction of homosexuality

ONE of the most fundamental issues in gay and lesbian psychology is whether it is most helpful to think of homosexuality as an internal state, created through genetic and/or environmental influences, which the individual discovers and either acknowledges or denies. This view is called the *essentialist* position because it sees people as essentially either gay or not. This is in fact the 'common sense' position adopted by most non-psychologists. There is now, however, a radical alternative in the form of the social constructionist view (see p.135 for a general discussion of social constructionism). Social constructionists reject the idea that sexual orientation is a fixed internal state, and instead explore the social influences that lead people to describe themselves as having a particular sexual orientation. Whereas essentialists see being gay as something within the person, social constructionists see it as outside them, taking place on a social rather than individual level.

To social constructionists, terms like 'gay' originate in particular historical and political contexts and are misleading in that they pigeonhole people and lead us to underestimate the range of individual differences between people with the same sexual orientation. To get around this pigeonholing effect, some psychologists now refer to 'men that have sex with men' or 'women that have sex with women' in their publications. From a social constructionist viewpoint these phrases have the advantage that they refer to one aspect of the lives of the people being discussed rather than applying the overarching label of 'gay.'

## Gay and lesbian identities

IDENTITY is the subjective experience of knowing who we are and what we are like. Everyone has an identity based on their understanding of their age, gender, ethnicity and socio-economic and occupational group. Identities change throughout life (see Erikson's theory, p.52, for a discussion), and certain ages are associated with shifts and potential difficulties in identity. It has been suggested that gay people are likely to have particular difficulties with identity, especially at certain life stages. 'Coming out,' which takes place most frequently in adolescence, can be a particular issue for young people who are already struggling to find their feet in the adult world and who face the additional problem of disapproval or rejection from family and friends. Where gay people have encountered serious prejudice they may take this on board and accept that the problem they are facing lies within them rather than others. This is known as *internalised homophobia*. Internalised homophobia has a serious impact on self-esteem, and may prevent the individual developing a healthy gay identity.

## Lesbian and gay relationships

AN ongoing issue in gay psychology has been the extent to which the nature of gay romantic relationships mirrors that of heterosexual couples. Some researchers (e.g. Peplau, 1991) have placed their emphasis on the similarities between gay and heterosexual relationships. Both gay and heterosexual people tend to see their ideal relationship status as being with one person. Both groups fall in love, and the same factors appear to be involved in determining the success of relationships in gay and heterosexual couples. However, as Kitzinger et al. (1998) point out, gay couples have additional pressures to deal with in relationships. For example, there may be disputes within couples over the timing and extent of coming out to acquaintances and colleagues (often brought to a head when couples begin to cohabit). There is also the question of to what extent partners should adopt gender-stereotypical roles in relationships – should one partner play a more 'feminine' role and one a 'masculine' role? Gay couples may face particular issues as parents. Currently, under the 1989 Children's Act, gay and lesbian couples cannot adopt children, although there are a fairly large number of families in which a mother or father goes into a gay relationship having had children, meaning that the children effectively have an adoptive gay parent. Research has been quite clear that children of same-sex parents are indistinguishable from those of heterosexual couples but in some circles there is still something of a social stigma attached to gay parenting.

## Homophobia

HOMOPHOBIA refers to the negative reaction of some heterosexuals towards lesbians and gay men. Like all prejudices homophobia can manifest itself in a number of behaviours, ranging from avoidance and verbal abuse to murder. It can be institutionalised as well as individual, and gay people have much less protection in law than most other minority groups. Traditionally, homophobia has been seen as a factor within the individual. We have already looked at research into the role of the authoritarian personality (p.12) and reaction formation (p.68) in homophobia. However, whilst these variables are important in explaining individual differences in homophobia, contemporary gay psychology places more emphasis on homophobia as a social rather than an individual phenomenon. Herek and Berrill (1992) have suggested that homophobia should be seen as the systematic oppression of a minority group by society at large rather than by a few individuals.

## The Idea Today

SOMETHING OF A GULF REMAINS BETWEEN ESSENTIALIST AND SOCIAL CONSTRUCTIONIST perspectives on homosexuality (Kitzinger et al, 1998); however, there is evidence to suggest that gay people find both positions useful. Morrow (1999) analysed the family narratives (stories told by individuals about their family life) of lesbians and gay men, and found that they found it helpful to think of being gay as an essential quality (something one is) when asserting gay rights, but as a social construct when emphasising the similarities between gay people and heterosexuals.

There has been a wealth of research examining gay identities, relationships and parenting, and the phenomenon of homophobia. The emergence of a healthy gay sexual identity in adolescence appears to hinge largely on the attitudes of others, in particular family. Waldner and Magruder (1999) surveyed 172 gay and lesbian adolescents and found that the confidence to come out depended on good family relationships. Floyd et al. (1999) interviewed 72 gay and lesbian adolescents, and found that parental acceptance was the only factor that predicted their development of a healthy sexual identity.

Recent studies have supported the principle that relationships between same-sex couples have strong similarities to but also some differences from heterosexual relationships. Rose and Zand (2000) interviewed 38 lesbian women aged 21–63. As is the case for heterosexuals, the women reported that the distinguishing features of sexual relationships as opposed to friendships were greater emotional intensity and sexual contact. Respondents used the same verbal and non-verbal cues to initiate sexual contact as is typical of heterosexual couples. However, some distinctive features of lesbian relationships emerged from the interviews. Women reported that they had the positive experiences in lesbian relationships of being freed from their gender roles, and of being able to combine close friendship and romance with the same person (which many heterosexual women find difficult). Lesbian relationships also developed much faster than is typical in heterosexual couples.

Research into gay and lesbian parenting is particularly important as it has policy implications. Research comparing children from same-sex and opposite-sex parent families has made it quite clear that in virtually every way children are indistinguishable. Patterson (1997) assessed the social development – including gender identity – of American children both born to and adopted by lesbian mothers and found no difference from children born to or adopted by heterosexual families. Tasker and Golombok (1997) found similar results in Britain. Although Tasker and Golombok found that the children of lesbian families were more likely to have considered or tried a same-sex relationship they were no more likely to settle on a homosexual orientation than children of heterosexual families. It seems that same-sex couples parent children in the same ways as do opposite-sex couples, although they may experience extra pressures. Kurdek (2001) surveyed gay, lesbian and heterosexual parents and found few differences in parenting strategies. Interestingly the lesbian parents reported the best quality of relationships, although gay and lesbian parents received less support from the rest of their families than did heterosexual parents.

Homophobia has also attracted much research. A crucial research question concerns just how homophobic heterosexuals are. Ellis and Fox (2001) conducted an experiment to see if people are less helpful to a gay person in difficulty. They telephoned people, apologised as they 'realised' they had reached a wrong number and asked the person answering to relay a message to their partner (in the experimental condition the partner was of the same sex and in the control condition of the opposite sex). Overall people were less helpful in the experimental condition, but a gender difference also emerged, men being less helpful, in particular to gay men. Women were no less helpful to lesbians than to heterosexual women. A recent survey of heterosexual students in university halls of residence (Bowen and Bourgeouis, 2001) found that most students believed themselves to be less homophobic than their peers, but that they believed homophobia to be widespread. Attitudes tended to cluster in particular halls or corridors, suggesting that students largely took on the attitudes of their neighbours (this is called pluralistic ignorance). Homophobic attitudes were least in evidence where students had a gay or lesbian neighbour, suggesting that homophobia is associated with lack of experience of gay people.

## Current status of the idea

GAY and lesbian psychology as we currently think of it is a relatively new field, and at the time of writing it is a growth area. A minority of psychologists have challenged the belief that lesbians and gay men require their own branch of psychology; however, there is widespread support for the idea that gay people are in a sufficiently unique position to warrant study in their own right. Moreover, there are a number of ways in which gay and lesbian psychology has been applied to improve quality of life.

The Idea in Action

RESEARCH INTO GAY AND LESBIAN PSYCHOLOGY HAS A NUMBER OF PRACTICAL applications. One of these has been in reducing homophobia. The study by Bowen and Bourgeois (2001) showed that regular contact with gay people is associated with lower levels of homophobia, so it may be possible to base strategies for reducing homophobia on increasing contact between gay people and heterosexuals. Another strategy for tackling homophobia involves helping heterosexuals understand what it feels like to be a member of an oppressed minority. Rabow et al. (1999) asked 76 students to wear a pink triangle and to record the reactions of others and their own responses to these reactions. Having experienced the responses of those who assumed them to be gay, the majority of participants reported an increase in their understanding of and empathy towards the experiences of gay people.

From a social constructionist perspective, homophobia is embedded in our use of language, so it follows that we may be able to tackle homophobia by changing language. Burn (2000) surveyed American students on their attitudes towards gay people and their use of insults like 'fag' and 'queer' in their everyday conversation. It emerged that around half the male participants who used terms like these had homophobic attitudes, but that the other half did not, and appeared to be using homophobic language to win approval from their peers. Burn suggests that campaigns to reduce the use of these terms may be effective in reducing their use by non-homophobic individuals and hence to reduce the frequency of homophobic sentiment in everyday language.

Further Reading

KITZINGER, C., COYLE, A., WILKINSON, S. AND MILTON, M. (1998) Towards lesbian and gay psychology. *The Psychologist* 11, 529–533.

TASKER, S.L. AND GOLOMBOK, F. (1998) *Growing up in a lesbian family*. London, Guildford Press.

# Humanistic psychology

## The Idea

HUMANISTIC PSYCHOLOGY IS SOMETIMES CALLED THE 'THIRD FORCE' IN PSYCHOLOGY because it emerged in rebellion against learning and psychodynamic approaches to psychology (the first and second forces respectively). By the 1940s and 1950s a number of psychologists were disillusioned at the complex and rather speculative theories of personality development being put forward by psychoanalysts, and even more so by the laboratory experiments of learning theorists. The humanistic movement aimed to restore some balance in psychology by looking at human needs and ordinary human experience with a minimum of theory. The humanistic movement owes most to two early theorists, Carl Rogers and Abraham Maslow.

* Intrinsic and extrinsic values
* The actualising tendency
* The self-concept
* The fully functioning person
* The hierarchy of needs
* Peak experiences

## Intrinsic and extrinsic values

IN some ways humanistic psychology is not so much a theoretical perspective on psychology as a value system. Humanistic psychologists place enormous value on human individuality and dignity, and they see people as inherently good and creative. They see the pursuit of *intrinsic values* such as intimacy, personal development and membership of a community as both morally superior and more mentally healthy than pursuit of *extrinsic values*, which include wealth and social status. This is not to say that people should not pursue career success or material possessions, rather that they will appreciate them in a healthier way if they see them in terms of personal development rather than satisfying externally imposed standards of status or wealth.

## The actualising tendency

ROGERS (1959) proposed that human behaviour is guided by an underlying motive, the tendency to *self-actualise*. Self-actualisation means the attainment of the highest level of 'human-beingness' we can reach; in other words fulfilling our potential. Many humanistic psychologists have used the metaphor of plant growth: people can be seen as flowers that grow to their potential if the conditions are right, but which are constrained by their environment. An unconscious influence called the *valuing process* leads us towards behaviours that will help us achieve our potential. Two important factors interfere with the operation of the valuing process: overly strict social rules and a poor self-concept. Rogers believed that people are inherently good and creative. Destructive behaviour results when a poor self-concept or external constraints derail the valuing process.

## The self-concept

ROGERS and Maslow placed great emphasis on the ways people perceived and felt about themselves (their *self-concept*). Rogers, who was a therapist, noticed that his clients would often refer to themselves, saying things like 'I wonder who I really am'. He began to place great importance on this use of the word 'I' and suggested that the most important part of people's self-concept is their *self-esteem* (Rogers, 1961). Self-esteem is the emotional-evaluative aspect of the self-concept, in other words how much we like ourselves. Rogers believed that we hold in our mind images of ourselves as we are currently and as we would like to be. If these images are the same (Rogers called this *congruence*), we will develop good self-esteem.

To develop congruence and hence a high level of self-esteem depends on receiving *unconditional positive regard* from other people. This comes in the form of acceptance, love and affection. Without sufficient unconditional positive regard people are incapable of self-actualisation. Some children lack unconditional positive regard in childhood due to harsh or inattentive parenting or a parenting style characterised by *conditional love* (love that is available only when the child conforms to certain conditions).

## The fully functioning person

ROGERS' *fully-functioning person* has developed good self-esteem following their experiences of unconditional positive regard, either in their upbringing or in humanistic therapy. Rogers (1959) identified five characteristics of what he called mature behaviour.

- The first is *openness to experience*. The fully functioning person can accept every-thing that happens to them, both good and bad, without using psychological defence mechanisms.

- A second characteristic, closely related to openness to experience, is *existential living*. This essentially means being able to live in and enjoy the present, without looking back to the past or forward to the future.

- The third characteristic is *trust in oneself*. We need to believe that our own life-decisions are the correct ones and we should trust ourselves to make the right choices.

- The fourth characteristic of the fully functioning person is *experiential freedom*. By this Rogers meant that we should be free of influences from our past.

- Finally, and most importantly, the fully functioning person is distinguished by their *creativity*. In Rogers' terms, creativity means the ability to adapt happily to changes in circumstances.

## The hierarchy of needs

MASLOW was, like Rogers, interested in human needs. In 1954 he proposed a theory of human needs that aimed to rank them in the order in which people prioritise them. A critical distinction is between *deficiency needs* (D-needs), requirements for food, rest, safety etc., and *being-needs* (B-needs), which represent our actualising tendency and so lead us to fulfil our potential. We cannot strive towards our B-needs until our D-needs have been met. Therefore we prioritise D-needs until these are met but once they are met we focus instead on out B-needs. Maslow broke down D and B-needs further and constructed a triangular hierarchy, intended to encompass all human needs. This is shown in the figure below.

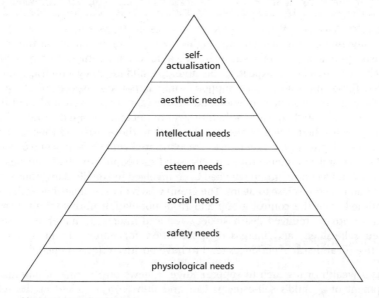

Maslow's hierarchy of needs

Maslow's idea is that we ascend this hierarchy, satisfying each need in turn. The first priority is to satisfy our physiological needs (including food and warmth), as we cannot survive without them. When they have been satisfied we seek out safety. Once we are safe, we worry about our social needs to belong to a group and have relationships with other people. When our social needs have been satisfied our esteem needs become paramount. To satisfy our esteem needs we need to achieve things, to become competent and for our competence to be recognised by others. Once this has been achieved the focus shifts to satisfying our intellectual needs. These include gaining understanding and knowledge. Above intellectual needs in the hierarchy come aesthetic needs (the need for beauty, order and balance). The ultimate human need is for self-actualisation.

## Peak experiences

TOWARDS the end of his life Maslow's interest shifted towards *peak experiences*. He saw such experiences as moments when the world appears complete and we feel at one with it. Such experiences stay with us and permanently alter our view of the world for the better. Peak experiences are associated with self-actualisation. The fortunate few people that self-actualise are much more likely than others to have peak experiences. Peak experiences are associated with the area in which we achieve our potential – they can be triggered by art, music or sporting moments for example. For some people peak experiences are spiritual in nature and associated with religious experience.

SOME ASPECTS OF HUMANISTIC PSYCHOLOGY, SUCH AS THE ACTUALISING TENDENCY AND the fully functioning person, are highly resistant to research. Furthermore, as humanistic psychology is in some ways a value system rather than a theoretical approach, we would not expect to be able to validate it by empirical methods. However, there are studies that support some important aspects of Rogers' and Maslow's ideas. For instance, Sheldon and Kasser (2001) reviewed studies of lifestyle and mental health and concluded that, in general, people oriented towards intrinsic values experience better health and well-being than those oriented towards external values. Interestingly, certain experiences are associated with shifts in value orientation. Groth-Marnat and Summers (1998) interviewed 52 people who had had near-death experiences and a control group who had been involved in equally dangerous incidents but who had not come close to death. The group who had experienced near death were distinguished from the control group and from population norms by an increase in concern for others, reduced death anxiety, reduced interest in material possessions, increased self-esteem and increased appreciation for nature. From a humanistic perspective, near-death experiences tend to have positive effects on people.

There is a wealth of research to support Rogers' views on the role of parents in the development of a child's self-esteem. Lau and Pun (1999) looked at the relationship between parents' evaluations of children in 974 families and the self-esteem of the children, who were aged 8–13 years. Where parents had positive views of their children, the children tended to have higher self-esteem. This was especially the case where the positive parental attitude was shared by both parents. In another study Burnett (1999) collected information from 269 Australian primary school children regarding their self-concept and the frequency of positive and negative comments from teachers. It was found that positive comments from teachers were associated with improved self-concept, which was in turn associated with greater achievement. This supports the view that achievement (actualisation) is dependent on self-esteem, which is in turn dependent on positive regard from others.

A problem with humanistic psychology is that it is highly culture bound. The view held by both Rogers and Maslow of individuals as striving for personal achievement is firmly located in the highly individualistic culture of the USA. Cross-cultural research by Kitayama and Markus (1992) has shown that, whilst positive feelings in American students were associated with personal achievements, Japanese students by contrast tended to associate positive feelings with good relations with others. The idea of actualisation as individual achievement thus has limited application in cultures other than North America.

## Current status of the idea

DESPITE the grandiose label of the 'third force' in psychology, actually humanistic psychology now has little influence on academic psychology or on most branches of applied psychology, the exception being in counselling. In 2002 over half the members of the British Association for Counselling adopted a humanistic approach. However, most of these counsellors are not psychologists and the proportion of psychologists adopting a humanistic approach is rather smaller. In academic psychology humanistic psychologists once played a useful role as the dissenting voice against practices such as psychiatric classification and undervaluing groups such as women. One reason for the decline in the influence of humanistic psychology is that this function now tends to be carried out more effectively by psychologists of another orientation, the *social constructionists* (see p.135 for a detailed discussion).

THE MAJOR PRACTICAL APPLICATION OF HUMANISTIC PSYCHOLOGY IS IN COUNSELLING. Rogers developed the technique of *person-centred therapy* or counselling. In line with the philosophy of humanistic psychology, Rogerian counselling aims not just to treat mental disorder but to allow the client to move towards self-actualisation. This is sometimes called the fulfilment model of counselling. Rogers (1961) suggested three core conditions that facilitate clients in their personal growth.

- *Empathy* is the ability to follow what the client is feeling, and an important task of the person-centred counsellor is to follow precisely what the client is feeling and to communicate to them that they understand.

- *Congruence*, also called genuineness, refers to the fact that the Rogerian therapist allows the client to experience him- or herself as they really are.

- The final core condition is *unconditional positive regard*. Rogers believed that for people to grow and fulfil their potential it is important that they are valued as themselves. The person-centred counsellor thus always maintains a positive attitude to the client, even if horrified by the client's actions.

Person-centred counselling is unquestionably helpful for clients when applied appropriately. Greenberg et al. (1994) reviewed the results of 37 outcome studies looking at the effectiveness of person-centred therapy in a variety of situations and conditions. They concluded that overall person-centred counselling is as effective as other approaches to therapy, and more successful than no treatment. Some case studies appear to show that, for some people, adopting a humanistic approach to therapy is the most effective intervention. Siebert (2000) describes the case of an 18-year-old girl diagnosed with severe paranoid schizophrenia and expected to remain institutionalised for life; all her symptoms disappeared following person-centred counselling. Of course, this is a one-off case and very few psychologists would recommend a humanistic approach to schizophrenia.

JARVIS, M. (2000) *Theoretical approaches in psychology*. London, Routledge.

MERRY, T. (1995) *Invitation to person-centred psychology*. London, Whurr.

THORNE, B. (1992) *Carl Rogers*. London, Sage.

# Hypnosis

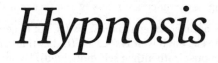

## The Idea

THE FIRST DOCUMENTED PRACTITIONER OF WHAT IS NOW CALLED HYPNOSIS WAS FRANZ Anton Mesmer (hence the term *mesmerised*). He aimed to use his skills therapeutically and believed that the effects he induced in people were a result of his own 'magnetism.' His activities aroused the fears of the authorities, who conducted a series of rather well controlled experiments. From these it was concluded that neither Mesmer nor the effects he had on his clients demonstrated any signs of magnetism and that imagination, rather than magnetism, was responsible for the effects. As a consequence Mesmer was discredited. Mesmer is unlikely to have been magnetic; his clinical practice, however, was demonstrably effective. Present-day hypnotists use such induction techniques as relaxation, eye fixation – focusing on an object – and verbal cues such as feeling heaviness in the eyelids or a sensation of moving downwards. Effectively administered to a susceptible person these procedures lead to the condition of relaxed suggestibility called hypnosis, which can indeed have useful clinical effects.

Hypnosis can be used to treat phobias

- ❀ The nature of hypnosis
- ❀ Susceptibility
- ❀ Tests of susceptibility
- ❀ Age regression
- ❀ Hypnotic analgesia
- ❀ Posthypnotic suggestions
- ❀ The hidden observer

## The nature of hypnosis

DESCRIPTIONS of the sensation of being hypnotised vary, but in general hypnotic subjects report feeling relaxed, awake but inwardly focused (rather than unaware) and receptive or responsive to the hypnotist (rather than self-motivated). Hypnotised subjects demonstrate limited reality testing (i.e. they tolerate logical inconsistencies). This is described as *trance logic*. Trance logic resembles our lack of concern in a dream when we step out of a first floor window straight into a car on the ground. In addition to the introspective reports given by subjects after hypnosis, observers can describe changes in behaviour and cognition. Hypnotised subjects are more *suggestible*, that is they have an increased imaginative capacity, but neither compliance nor obedience is enhanced. They are also better able to enact a role; a suggested situation will be simulated more effectively under hypnosis than would otherwise be achievable. Subsequent behaviour may also be affected by suggestions made during hypnosis (posthypnotic suggestions).

## Susceptibility

ONLY about 15% of the population is capable of experiencing deep hypnosis. Most of the population, about 85%, can be hypnotised but differ in the depth they can achieve. This is described as *susceptibility*. Subjects tend to be consistent in their response to hypnotic induction from one occasion to the next, suggesting that susceptibility is a stable trait. What kinds of observable characteristics are associated with high susceptibility? The following factors have been identified as indicators, but are neither essential nor exhaustive: age affects hypnotisability; young people hypnotise better than adults, peaking at about 12 years of age; children become very absorbed in imagery and are less concerned with reality testing and separating fact from fantasy than are adults; one's willingness and attitude towards hypnosis is important.

There is no evidence that even highly susceptible subjects can be hypnotised against their will and subjects with negative attitudes rarely hypnotise well, but among those with increasingly positive attitudes there is a spread of susceptibility. This suggests that a positive attitude towards hypnosis allows, but does not ensure, high susceptibility. Being able to become absorbed in an activity is a key indicator of hypnotisability. People who can become highly engrossed in a pursuit, such as reading, music or mountain climbing and become oblivious to irrelevant stimuli are likely to be highly susceptible. People who can tolerate trance-like experiences that might be bizarre or disturbing are more susceptible. Finally, individuals who can readily conjure up vivid imagined scenarios tend to be more highly hypnotisable. This capacity, described as *creative imagination,* has become a basis for testing susceptibility.

## Tests of susceptibility

SOME tests of susceptibility, such as the *Creative Imagination Scale* (CIS), measure characteristics believed to relate to hypnotisability. The CIS consists of a series of statements read to non-hypnotised participants who imagine the scenes described and report the intensity of their imagined experience. Other tests are more direct, measuring the effects of graded hypnotic procedures to assess the depth of a subject's hypnosis. The *Stanford Hypnotic Susceptibility Scale* is a sequence of hypnotic suggestions that are put to the subject after a standardised hypnotic induction. The hypnotist observes the subject's responses to each suggestion, the more items to which an appropriate response is exhibited, the deeper the subject's hypnosis.

## Age regression

THE hypnotist uses direct suggestions to guide the subject to recall past events very clearly (this is called *hypermnesia*) or to re-live events as if they were happening (called *revivification*). The experience of going back in time differs between hypnotic subjects. It may be directed by the hypnotist, perhaps with reference to a time travelling vehicle, or by the subject, focusing on images of themselves, on past events or on a representation of each phase of their life. The regression might be experienced as feeling smaller and smaller, as a journey on a 'time vehicle' or as passing through doorways representing past years as the subject moves backwards in time. This serves to illustrate that, whilst the hypnotist makes a general suggestion, it is the subject who provides the hallucinatory experiences.

## Hypnotic analgesia

BOTH *analgesia*; the numbing of pain, and *anaesthesia*; the loss of sensation, are possible through hypnosis. A measure of analgesia may arise spontaneously during hypnosis; as the subject becomes absorbed in the imagery, their awareness of other sensations diminishes. This is comparable to not realising we have gone numb from sitting still for hours reading a good book. A greater analgesic effect can be achieved by direct suggestion. This can result from suggested loss of sensation, e.g. as a 'glove' protecting the hand from pain, or by guiding the subject to feel separate from that part of the body. Other techniques use age progression or regression to take the client forwards or backwards in time to a pain-free age, and suggestions to 'forget' the pain (Yapko, 1995).

## Posthypnotic suggestions

A *posthypnotic suggestion* is one given to the subject during hypnosis to affect their behaviour, cognition or emotions after the session. A commonly used suggestion is that the subject will 'find becoming deeply hypnotised easier next time', making the process of induction quicker and more successful. Such suggestions can also be used to affect the individual outside the context of hypnosis, and these are arguably the most useful therapeutically (Yapko, 1995) as they can provide a lasting effect on the client. Amnesia for events during hypnosis is not, as many people assume, automatic. In fact, even direct suggestions of amnesia are often ineffective (Yapko 1995). However, indirect suggestions, such as being 'allowed to forget' may be useful in the therapeutic context to repress hurtful memories.

## The hidden observer

THE phenomenon of the hidden observer was discovered accidentally when Ernest Hilgard was demonstrating hypnosis to a group of students using a subject who was blind. During the session Hilgard suggested that the subject would be unable to hear and that the deafness would cease when his shoulder was touched. The unresponsive subject failed to acknowledge noises or voices as expected. Then, questioning whether he was really as deaf as he seemed, Hilgard quietly asked if, even though he was hypnotically deaf, there was any part of his brain which could hear, and if so to raise a finger. To the surprise of Hilgard, his class and the unsuspecting subject, the subject raised a finger. Hilgard reinstated the student's hearing by touching the subject's shoulder and asked him what he could recall. The subject reported that everything had become still and boring, so he'd resorted to thinking about statistics until he became aware that his finger had moved and he wanted to know why. When asked for an account from 'the part of his brain which had listened before and made your finger rise' the subject reported accurately all that had happened (Hilgard 1977). Hilgard referred to this monitor of all the events during hypnosis, even those of which the subject is not consciously aware, as the *hidden observer*.

Other situations can also be used to illustrate the hidden observer, for instance in experiments where hypnotic analgesia is used to mask the experience of pain. In the *cold pressor* test, the hypnotic subject immerses their hand in (usually) unbearably cold water but reports no pain. If the hidden observer is asked, however, pain is reported. During age regression a hidden observer (who may be an adult) can be introduced to report the activities of the 'child'.

# The Idea Today

*STATE THEORISTS* SUCH AS HILGARD FOLLOW THE WIDELY HELD AND TRADITIONAL VIEW that hypnotic induction takes the subject from a waking state into a trance-like state, which is responsible for the behavioural changes seen in hypnosis. Hilgard's view of hypnosis is now referred to as the *neodissociationist theory*. He proposes that the state of hypnosis arises as a result of the dissociation of cognitive systems, the operation of which is normally integrated. The influence of the hypnotist is to separate (dissociate) levels of cognitive processing such that we are aware of some aspects of our thinking but not others. The aspects of which we are aware result in the primary experience of hypnosis (hallucinations for instance) and the suppressed levels of awareness account for amnesia, analgesia, etc. In the neodissociationist theory, Hilgard (1977) suggests that the hidden observer provides access to the otherwise unavailable level of consciousness – the level that has become dissociated from conscious experience.

If state theories like Hilgard's are correct we would expect to be able to see a distinctive physiological state in the brain during hypnosis. It was believed until very recently that there was no evidence for a physiologically distinctive state of hypnosis, or that it is no different from relaxation. However, Williams and Gruzelier (2001) have succeeded in differentiating between the physiological state of hypnosis and relaxation, using electroencephalography (EEG) to demonstrate that the brain activity seen during hypnosis (alpha waves) differs from the theta wave activity typical of relaxation. Similarly, de Pascalis et al. (2001) report brain correlates of hypnotic analgesia. Interestingly, the location of brain activity in response to hypnotically induced analgesia differed between subjects with high and low hypnotisability. Furthermore, Jensen et al. (2001) have shown that EEGs of *event-related potentials* (brain waves occurring in response to a particular stimulus) are different in high and low hypnotisables and waking subjects.

Non-state theorists, such as Wagstaff, deny that hypnotic induction generates a trance state. Wagstaff, one of the first and most critical of the non-state theorists, identifies absorption in imagery as the central factor causing the phenomena experienced during hypnosis. Wagstaff (1986) proposed a relationship between the actions of the hypnotist, the observed characteristics of hypnosis and the subjects' imaginative activities. In this view, hypnosis can be explained in terms of familiar socio-cognitive processes, without the need to invoke the idea of a 'trance' to explain the phenomena observed. Instead, the experiences of the hypnotic subject are explained as the result of a desire to comply with the suggestions of the hypnotist. This is not the same as 'shamming'; the experience of a hypnotic subject is neither pretence nor, as Wagstaff comments, motivated by an urge to 'put one over on the hypnotist for a laugh.' Patients using hypnosis in place of general anaesthesia during medical procedures would be unlikely to pretend that they feel no pain. Of course, this does not mean that no other phenomena are faked.

## Current status of the idea

HEAP (1996) concludes that the fundamental dispute, whether or not there is a special state of consciousness called 'hypnosis,' is irreconcilable and is the result of a failure to agree exactly what we are talking about when we use the term *hypnosis*. State and non-state theorists are essentially talking at cross-purposes and discussing differing aspects of the hypnosis phenomenon. Despite these reservations, new directions for research are emerging, such as investigating the relationship between hypnotisability and biorhythms. Lippincott (2001) has established that '*larks*' (people who are more alert in the morning) are more hypnotisable at night and those of us who are '*owls*' (evening people) are more readily hypnotised in the morning. At a theoretical level, Oakley (1999) has proposed a new model for understanding hypnosis, based on neurophysiological evidence. His model suggests that hypnotic effects are possible because the brain operates in parallel processing; the executive control system that determines awareness is central to the subjective experiences associated with hypnosis.

## The Idea in Action

THE MAJOR CURRENT APPLICATIONS OF HYPNOSIS ARE CLINICAL: HYPNOSIS HAS BEEN used within the framework of therapy and for pain relief since the days of Mesmer. In these applications, hypnosis is generally being used to assist a pre-existing system, rather than as a solution in its own right. Oakley et al. (1996) observe that, in itself, hypnosis is *not* a form of therapy. Rather, it can be used as an adjunct, providing a situation in which psychological therapies can be delivered more effectively. They reject the use of labels such as 'hypnotherapy'; being an effective therapist must be the starting point from which the additional deployment of hypnosis may help clients. A useful analogy is to anaesthesia; surgery is highly effective with or without an anaesthetic, but patients are more likely to benefit from the experience overall if they are anaesthetised. In therapy, clients can gain from therapeutic procedures more readily via hypnosis.

The effectiveness of hypnosis as an adjunct to therapy can only be assessed by comparing similar procedures with and without the addition of hypnosis. Kirsch et al. (1995) conducted a meta-analysis of studies comparing cognitive-behavioural therapy delivered with hypnosis and alone. They found a substantial advantage to clients receiving therapy with hypnosis both immediately after treatment and after a follow-up period. This may have been because many clients are taught self-hypnosis so can continue to benefit after therapy has ceased.

Treatment of phobias using hypnosis in conjunction with systematic desensitisation is particularly effective. The benefits here are twofold.

- The phenomenon of trance logic (the capacity of hypnotised subjects to suspend reality) allows the client to react 'as if' they were experiencing the situation. The event appears to be real, but is less threatening and more easily controlled (Yapko, 1995). A hallucinated spider, for example, is much less likely to accidentally escape from its box and disappear into a corner of the room!

- Secondly, relaxation can be readily achieved and more easily maintained if a person is hypnotised. Morgan (2001) successfully used hypnosis to desensitise a client with a phobia of driving and being a passenger in a car. Similarly, Oakley (1998) success-fully used hypnosis combined with other therapeutic approaches to help a woman suffering from trichotillomania (compulsive hair pulling).

In addition to the treatment of fear of pain, hypnosis can also be used to reduce experi-ence of actual pain. Langenfeld (2000) tested the use of hypnosis in pain management for patients with AIDS. By the end of the 12-week period of study, all patients reported experiencing less pain. Anbar (2001) found that four out of five children taught self-hypnosis to help with recurrent, unexplained, abdominal pain had ceased to experi-ence pain within 3 weeks. Pain relief during surgery is, for most patients, achieved by chemical anaesthesia but this is only strictly necessary for incisions into some tissues: many areas, such as subcutaneous tissue, bone, brain, lungs, stomach, liver and kidney are insensitive to incision. In hypnotically induced anaesthesia, local anaesthetic is generally applied only to the skin, which does respond with pain to incision.

Posthypnotic suggestions may be used with clients who want to give up smoking – for example, the suggestion could be made that cigarettes will cause an unpleasant sensa-tion of nausea. In a meta-analysis of more than 600 studies of 72, 000 people from a range of nations, Viswesvaran and Schmidt (1992) found that of techniques employed to help people to quit smoking (including smoke aversion, acupuncture or nicotine gum) hypnosis had a success rate of 30%. Only people warned of serious cardiac condi-tions were more likely to stop. Given that on average only 19% of people who try to give up actually succeed, hypnosis appears to be effective. Barber (2001) has shown that a hypnotic procedure combined with rapid smoking treatment (an aversive process) was successful with over 90% of participants.

Another clinical application of hypnosis is in relief from speech impediments. For example, Moss and Oakley (1997) used a series of hypnosis sessions to teach a client with a severe stutter anxiety management and self-hypnosis as well as using standard reading materials. Following post-hypnotic suggestion and directed practice, the client's speech markedly improved, both in the laboratory and in everyday situations. In addition, the client reported improvements in general physical and mental well-being.

# Further Reading

GIBSON, H.B. AND HEAP, M. (1991) *Hypnosis in therapy*. London, Lawrence Erlbaum Associates.

HEAP, M. (1996) The nature of hypnosis. *The Psychologist* 9, 498–501.

HILGARD, E.R. AND HILGARD, J.R. (1994) *Hypnosis and the relief of pain*. New York, Brunner/Mazel.

NAISH, P.L.N. (Ed.) (1986) *What is hypnosis?* Milton Keynes, Open University Press.

OAKLEY, D., ALDEN, P. AND DEGUN MATHER, M. (1996) The use of hypnosis in therapy with adults. *The Psychologist* 9, 502–505.

YAPKO, MD. (1995) *Essentials of hypnosis*. New York, Brunner/Mazel.

# Individual
# psychology

✿

## The Idea

ALFRED ADLER WAS A CONTEMPORARY OF SIGMUND FREUD
(see p.64), and for some years he was a Freudian
psychoanalyst. However, in 1911 Adler split with Freud and
formed his own approach to psychology. He called this
new school 'individual psychology' because he felt that
existing psychological approaches such as that of Freud
did not take enough account of the great diversity among
individuals. Like Freud, Adler was interested in the role of
families in development, but Adler placed more emphasis
on the effects of early social interactions on individual
development and less on the workings of the unconscious
mind than did Freud. He also took more account of the
importance of the whole family on child development, in
contrast to Freud's emphasis on parents.

Alfred Adler

- ✿ The inferiority complex
- ✿ Family climate
- ✿ Family constellations
- ✿ Style of life and personality
- ✿ Social interest

## The inferiority complex

ADLER believed that the fundamental motivating force in all humans is to escape the feelings of inferiority we all have as young children surrounded by older, more competent adults. He called this motivation the *drive towards superiority*. Adler saw all human achievement as the result of *compensation* for feelings of inferiority. He cited numerous cases of people who responded to particular weaknesses by excelling in the area of that weakness. For example, the concert pianist Klara Schumann had suffered hearing problems as a child, and Demosthenes (the great orator) had stuttered as a child.

Achievement results when people tackle their feelings of inferiority by taking on the problem. Some people adopt maladaptive strategies to cope with inferiority, by tackling the emotions associated with inferiority – they do things to make themselves feel better rather than to solve their problems. People adopting this approach to life are said to suffer from an *inferiority complex*. Instead of striving for superiority they have a *lust for power*. This can manifest itself in bullying behaviour, including domestic violence, as the individual who feels weak tries to gain a feeling of strength by bullying someone vulnerable. The temporary sense of strength resulting from this strategy is called *autointoxication* and only partially relieves feelings of inferiority. The inferiority complex may also reveal itself in helplessness and can manifest in various ways, for example in being particularly timid and dependent on others, or in psychopathology such as agoraphobia. Adler believed that agoraphobia represented giving up all contact with the outside world in the face of insurmountable inferiority.

## Family climate

ADLER placed considerable emphasis on the role of family relationships in shaping children's development. He used *family climate* to refer to the quality of relationships in the family and to the type of interactions children have with other family members. Generally, if relationships within the family are poor a child will have poor experiences of interacting with other people, which leads to an inferiority complex. However, good relationships in families can pamper children. Adler believed that pampered children were no better off than neglected children because they would not learn to adapt to the needs of others and to take up a socially useful position.

## Family constellations

THE term *family constellation* refers to a person's position in their family. The most important aspect of family constellation is birth-order. First-born children begin life with a sense of royalty as only child, but experience what Adler called *dethronement* when siblings are born. They remain motivated throughout their lives to regain this lost sense of importance. First-borns are thus typically more intelligent, and power seeking. They are also the most likely to be the most conforming and least rebellious children. However, subsequent children, although usually less power seeking, are highly motivated to catch up with their older sibling and frequently achieve more than the first-born. Last-born children are typically the most dependent on others, and this dependency can continue into adulthood. If the first-born is a girl and siblings are male particular problems can occur, because girls mature faster than boys and the later-born boys can see their older sister pulling further ahead of them as they get older.

## Style of life and personality

ADLER (1927) proposed that personality could be explained in terms of the different strategies used to overcome inferiority. He proposed four major strategies or *styles of life,* which can be seen by the time a child reaches 5 years of age and remain fairly stable throughout life. The term 'style of life' is the origin of the modern term 'lifestyle.'

- People of Adler's *ruling type* are aggressive and dominating, with little interest in social affairs.

- Those of the *getting type* are dependent individuals who require considerable support from others whilst contributing little in return.

- *Avoiding type* people avoid life problems and tend not to involve themselves in intimate relationships or take on challenges.

- *Socially useful* people are characterised by social interest – the tendency to involve oneself with others and take an interest in social affairs.

Ruling, getting and avoiding styles of life are all maladaptive, and only people of the socially useful type are, in Adler's view, mentally healthy.

Although most people fall broadly into one of these four types, style of life is also highly individual, and in this sense Adler saw everyone as unique. We acquire a style of life as we organise our behaviour around particular goals. The major goal of the ruling type is to acquire power over others (to avoid feeling powerless); that of the dependent type is to acquire support from others, and that of the avoiding type is to avoid situations requiring meaningful interaction with others (so as to avoid being hurt).

## Social interest

ADLER (1939) suggested that all humans have a tendency towards *social interest* and that it is this that predisposes us to make social contact with other individuals. Social interest is not simply an interest in particular individuals but an overarching interest in people, individually and collectively. Interests in social issues and politics are thus expressions of social interest, as is the capacity to have relationships with other individuals. Adler saw social interest as an evolutionary mechanism designed to lead groups of humans to live together cooperatively. Although there is a tendency in all of us to develop social interest, the extent of its development is affected by childhood experiences. Pampered and neglected children do not develop much social interest, and both these groups tend to experience difficulty in adult relationships and are likely to be socially irresponsible. This is seen in three of the four styles of life.

SOME OF ADLER'S IDEAS ARE QUITE DIFFICULT TO RESEARCH – IT IS, FOR EXAMPLE, PRETTY much impossible to assess directly the extent to which people are actually motivated to escape infantile feelings of inferiority. However, research has supported the idea that childhood events that would be expected to lead to feelings of inferiority are associated with particular patterns of adult behaviour. Kiracofe (1992) assessed style of life in 417 adults using a test called the *Lifestyle Inventory* and looked for relationships with early experiences. In line with Adler's theory, people who believed that they were not their parents' favourite child tended to be more rebellious as adults. Other research has focused on the links between early family experiences and adult domestic violence. Dutton and Holtzworth-Munroe (1997) researched the backgrounds of a group of male wife-batterers and found that childhood experiences of abuse, neglect and shaming were more common than in a control group. In a review of the adult characteristics of batterers Holtzworth-Munroe et al. (1997) reported that a sense of powerlessness was one of five characteristics consistently found. This supports Adler's concept of the *ruling type*, people that attempt to escape feelings of inferiority by dominating others.

Perhaps the most extensively researched aspect of Adlerian theory is birth order. Research has generally supported Adler's observation that first-borns have higher IQ than later-born children, but there are other explanations for this apart from Adler's motivation to regain a lost sense of importance. Downey (1995) examined data from 25, 000 children and found a strong negative relationship between number of children in a family and the resources available to each child (toys, time spent with parents, etc.). First-borns could be brighter simply because they have more stimulation in their early lives. Some research has also supported Adler's view of first-borns as more conformist, although the picture is rather mixed. Freese et al. (1999) found no difference in social attitudes of first-born and later-born children, as measured by a questionnaire called the *General Social Survey*. However, Zweigenhaft and Von Ammon (2000) looked at arrests and found that later-born children were significantly more likely to have been arrested for civil disobedience than first-borns – supporting Adler's view of later-borns as more rebellious.

## Current status of the idea

ADLER'S position in psychology is slightly unusual in that, although many of his ideas remain of considerable importance, he himself is rarely referred to nowadays, except in the one current journal devoted to individual psychology. Terms like 'lifestyle' and 'inferiority complex' have become so commonly used that it is easy to forget where they came from. Ideas like emotion and problem-focused coping, despite originating in Adler's work, have since been better explained and more effectively put to use in other branches of psychology. However, Adler is remarkable for having developed so many ideas of contemporary importance, and he was vastly ahead of his time.

## The Idea in Action

A DLER WAS A THERAPIST, AND THE MAJOR APPLICATION OF HIS IDEAS CONTINUES TO BE in psychological therapy. Adlerian therapy is a psychodynamic therapy, with a focus on the quality of the therapist–patient relationship and on the patient gaining insight into their behaviour. It is a relatively informal approach to therapy, with thera-pist and patient co-operating as equals. Adlerians see insight in terms of identifying inferiority complexes and poor styles of life to their patient so that he or she can realis-tically assess their behaviour and choose healthier ways of functioning. *Transference*, emphasised by other psychodynamic schools of therapy, is not of primary importance in Adlerian therapy: the therapist–patient relationship is used to give the patient a positive experience of a relationship with another person and to foster social interest. Some research supports the effectiveness of Adlerian psychotherapy. Rogner (1994) compared 45 patients completing 160 hours of therapy with a control group just commencing therapy, and found them to have fewer physical symptoms, more frequent positive emotions and better emotional regulation.

Adler's ideas have other applications in modern psychology. His contrast between tackling problems and tackling emotions has been taken up by Lazarus and Folkman (1984) in their influential distinction between problem-focused and emotion-focused coping styles. Research in a variety of situations has shown that, as Adler believed, problem-focused coping is associated with more positive emotion in stressful situa-tions, such as sporting competition. For instance, Ntoumanis and Biddle (1998) asked athletes to recall a particularly stressful competition, to describe how they coped with the stress and how they then felt. Athletes whose coping responses were classified as problem-focused generally showed more positive emotion than those whose responses were emotion-focused. Sport psychologists can improve athletes' responses to stressful competition by training them in problem-focused coping strategies.

 **Further Reading**

ENGLER, B. (1999) *Personality theories*. Boston, Houghton Mifflin.

JARVIS, M. (in press) *Psychodynamic psychology: classic theory and contemporary research*. London, ITP.

LUNDIN, R.W. (1996) *Theories and systems in psychology*. Lexington, Heath.

# Milgram and the study of obedience

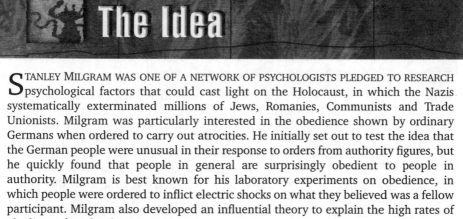

## The Idea

STANLEY MILGRAM WAS ONE OF A NETWORK OF PSYCHOLOGISTS PLEDGED TO RESEARCH psychological factors that could cast light on the Holocaust, in which the Nazis systematically exterminated millions of Jews, Romanies, Communists and Trade Unionists. Milgram was particularly interested in the obedience shown by ordinary Germans when ordered to carry out atrocities. He initially set out to test the idea that the German people were unusual in their response to orders from authority figures, but he quickly found that people in general are surprisingly obedient to people in authority. Milgram is best known for his laboratory experiments on obedience, in which people were ordered to inflict electric shocks on what they believed was a fellow participant. Milgram also developed an influential theory to explain the high rates of obedience found in his experiments.

* Milgram's laboratory procedure
* Variations on the procedure
* Agentic and autonomous states
* Moral strain

### Milgram's laboratory procedure

MILGRAM advertised for male volunteers to take part in a 'memory' experiment for a fee of $4.50. When they arrived at the university, the participants were told they would be either a teacher or a learner. They were then introduced to a fellow participant named 'Mr Wallace,' a mild-mannered and pleasant middle-aged man who was in fact an actor working for Milgram. By fiddling an apparently random selection procedure, Milgram ensured that the real participant was always the teacher and 'Mr Wallace' was always the learner. 'Mr Wallace' was then strapped into a chair and given a memory task involving remembering pairs of words. Every time 'Mr Wallace' made a mistake a confederate ordered the participant to give him an

© Stanley Milgram 1965. From the film 'Obedience', distributed by Penn State Media Sales

electric shock. Of course there were no real shocks, but there was no way for the participant to realise this. Following each mistake the level of the 'shock' appeared to increase. The shock levels on the machine were labelled from 0 to 450 volts and also carried signs saying 'danger – severe shock' and, at 450 volts, 'XXX'. Milgram's confederate ordered participants to continue increasing the shocks whilst the learner shouted and screamed in pain then appeared to collapse. When participants protested they were told: 'the experiment requires that you continue.'

To Milgram's great surprise, all the participants gave 'Mr Wallace' electric shocks of at least 300 volts, and 65% continued to the end of the scale, giving the full 450 volts to an apparently dead man. Most participants protested and some wept and begged in their distress, obviously believing that they had killed him, but most people did not feel that they could stop when ordered to continue by Milgram. This dramatic study demonstrates the power of authority over our behaviour. What is particularly remarkable about the results is that participants were clearly very upset by what they had to do, but saw no alternative except to obey. The results were also notable in the disparity between the observed rates of obedience and estimates obtained by Milgram from other psychologists and psychiatrists, who thought that only a tiny percentage of participants would give the full 450-volt shock.

## Variations on the procedure

IN a series of variations on the original experiment, Milgram found that the circumstances in which the procedure was carried out affected the percentage of people who would follow orders to the point of killing. When the setting was moved from a prestigious university to a run-down office block the number of people willing to give 450-volt shocks declined to 47.5%. When Milgram gave orders by telephone from another room the percentage dropped to 20.5%. When the teacher was required to force Mr Wallace's hand down on to an electrode, the percentage willing to go to 450 volts was 30%. We can see then that the situation is important in determining how obedient we are to authority.

## Agentic and autonomous states

MILGRAM (1974) proposed that our general tendency to obey people we perceive to be in authority has evolved in order to maintain a stable society. For humans to exist in complex societies we need social rules, and sticking to these rules requires that at least some of the time we give up a degree of our free will. Milgram suggested that in order to accomplish this we have evolved two social states.

- In the *autonomous state* we are free to act as we wish, including how our conscience dictates.

- However, in our *agentic state* we surrender our free will and conscience in order to serve the interests of the wider group. When we are in an agentic state we see ourselves as primarily the agents of those in authority and only secondarily as individuals.

We are socialised into developing the capacity for the agentic state during childhood. In school, we learn to put aside our individual wishes in favour of maintaining order, putting the good of the class as a whole first. Milgram believed that, like children in the classroom, we are all constantly subordinating our own needs and wishes to those of society. We can see this tendency in our job-related behaviour: in theory, most people would say that they work for their own benefit and would not go out of their way for their employers but in reality, once people are in a job and they identify themselves as part of an organisation, they have a tendency to put the needs of their employer above their own.

## Moral strain

AN important aspect of the agentic state is the strategies we use to deal with *moral strain*. Moral strain results when we have to do something we believe to be immoral in order to function as an agent of authority, and so benefit society. Milgram suggested that we use Freudian defence mechanisms (see p.66) to avoid the distress of having to perform acts we would normally find abhorrent. *Denial* was found to be particularly common in participants in the Milgram studies, and in the Holocaust, as perpetrators refused to confront what they were doing.

The Idea Today

A LARGE NUMBER OF LABORATORY STUDIES HAVE BEEN CONDUCTED ON OBEDIENCE, USING a range of procedures and set in a variety of societies. It is tempting to make judgements about cultural differences in obedience based on these studies, but this is difficult because studies in different countries have involved different procedures, and even in studies resembling the Milgram procedure the stooge has not always resembled 'Mr Wallace' (Smith and Bond, 1998), which may affect results. Blass (1996a) later concluded that people have not become any less obedient to authority since the time of the original study and that there are no gender differences in obedience. However, in more recent studies, when people have been asked to estimate the rate of obedience the estimates were much more accurate than those obtained by Milgram. This is interesting as it suggests that Milgram's research has altered public perceptions of obedience.

There are many ways of investigating obedience outside the laboratory. Lichtenberg (2000) investigated the tendency for obedience using a real-life situation: the responses of American motorists to police searches of their cars. Police records from two American States, Maryland and Ohio, revealed that between 90 and 95% of people obeyed instructions to allow police officers to search their cars – despite their consti-tutional right to refuse. Age, race and sex had no effect on obedience. Interviews with some of those who had obeyed the instructions revealed that they thought that disobe-dience would be futile, and that to disobey would result in punishment. Interestingly, when police advised motorists of their constitutional right to leave it made no differ-ence to the obedience rates. This provides strong support for Milgram's concept of agency, because people responded to authority figures irrespective of the actual power of the authority figures.

Replication of Milgram's original procedure would now be widely regarded as ethically dubious. However, in a related approach Blass (1996b) showed undergraduate students an edited film of Milgram's study and questioned them about the relative responsibility of Milgram and his participants in administering shocks. Respondents identified Milgram as in the role of authority figure and attributed responsibility for the treatment of 'Mr Wallace' to him rather than the participant. In another study, Hamilton and Sanders (1995) presented participants from the USA, Japan and Russia with stories of crimes set in the workplace, some of which were at the orders of superiors and some of which were the actor's own idea. Respondents attributed little responsibility for the crime to the perpetrators when they were acting under orders, but a lot of responsibility when they acted independently. This supports agency theory because the criminals were seen as responsible for their actions when they were autonomous but *not* when they were seen as the agent of an authority figure. Some cultural differences emerged, with the American respondents attributing more respon-sibility to criminals following orders than those from Russia and Japan.

## Current status of the idea

ALTHOUGH Milgram's research is nearly 30 years old, and although relatively few laboratory studies of obedience are now conducted, Milgram's findings remain highly relevant. More recent studies of obedience conducted in natural settings have confirmed the remarkable tendency of people to obey authority figures and, in the main, have also supported agency theory as a general explanation for obedience. This is not to say, however, that Milgram's work has answered every question about obedi-ence. There are large individual differences in both the tendency of individuals to obey orders and to be obeyed. Little is known about the motives of those who consistently oppose authority, but they are certainly not neatly explained by agency theory.

## The Idea in Action

ONE IMPORTANT APPLICATION OF OBEDIENCE RESEARCH IS THE UNDERSTANDING OF THE state of mind of people who commit atrocities. The diaries of Adolph Eichmann, the Nazi administrator who had organised the Holocaust, revealed his surprise that anyone could hold him responsible for any deaths as he had merely followed his orders. He clearly saw himself as an agent of society and therefore individually blameless. There is no shortage of more recent atrocities, and psychologists have investigated the motives of people who obeyed orders to kill. Peters and Richards (1998) interviewed child soldiers in Sierra Leone. One such interview was with a young woman who had been in the army from the age of 16. She had killed numerous rebels, both in battle and as prisoners (to save bullets she had killed captives by hand). She believed that she had been defending her country and therefore had done nothing wrong by killing so many people. This belief was frequently voiced by the soldiers interviewed – like Eichmann, they saw themselves as agents of their society and therefore on the moral high ground in spite of their actions.

Obedience research has other applications, for example in accident prevention. Krackow and Blass (1995) asked 68 nurses about the last time they had carried out a doctor's order with which they disagreed or which they had refused to carry out. The nurses reported that, by and large, they considered doctors to be legitimate authority figures, and rarely refused orders. There were no apparent differences between the individuals who had refused doctors' orders and those who had obeyed. This is all in line with agency theory, although nurses took into account the effects of following the inappropriate orders on patients as well as the authority of the person giving the order. Where there were few consequences to patients nurses attributed most responsibility to the doctor but when there were serious consequences they saw the nurse as responsible by following the doctor's orders. Tarnow (2000) examined the role of obedience to inappropriate orders in plane crashes, analysing the findings of official reviews of 37 crashes. In 25% of cases following inappropriate orders might have contributed to the crash. Tarnow has proposed procedures for reducing the obedience of pilots and hence to avoid crashes.

## Further Reading

BARON, R.A. AND BYRNE, D. (1998) *Social psychology*. Boston, Allyn and Bacon.

HAYES, N. (2000) *Foundations of psychology*. London, ITP.

# *Moral reasoning*

❦

## The Idea

MUCH OF OUR CURRENT UNDERSTANDING OF THE DEVELOPMENT OF MORAL REASONING comes from the work of Lawrence Kohlberg. Like Piaget (see p.122), Kohlberg was a cognitive-developmental psychologist, interested in the changes in children's thinking that come with age. Kohlberg wrote on several issues in child development, but he is perhaps best known nowadays for his views on the development of moral reasoning. Piaget did considerable work on moral development, but he believed that by adolescence young people had achieved formal operational reasoning and were essentially morally mature. Kohlberg questioned this, and his theory is concerned with changes in moral reasoning through adolescence. In the 1970s Carol Gilligan proposed that, whilst Kohlberg's theory might explain moral development in men, women's development took a different course. She supplemented Kohlberg's theory with a complementary view of women's moral development.

❀ Moral dilemmas

❀ Stages of moral development

❀ Moral development across cultures

❀ Gilligan's studies of moral reasoning in women

❀ Moral orientations

## Moral dilemmas

ONE of Kohlberg's major contributions was to develop a series of moral dilemmas as a way of researching moral reasoning. This technique involves presenting children and adolescents with made-up scenarios in which people have to make difficult decisions with a strong moral component. They are then interviewed about what decision they think the character in the scenario should have made and their reasons for believing this. Kohlberg (1963) investigated morality in 10–16-year-old boys, using a set of these scenarios. The best known of these is that of Heinz and the pharmacist.

---

### Case example: Kohlberg's 'Heinz dilemma'

Heinz's wife was very ill with a rare form of cancer, and was close to death. A local pharmacist had developed a drug that might save her but he was charging $2000 for a small dose, ten times what it cost to make. Heinz managed to raise $1000 and begged the pharmacist to sell the drug cheaply or allow him to pay in instalments. However, the pharmacist refused and in desperation Heinz broke into the pharmacy and stole the drug.

---

## Stages of moral development

ON the basis of young people's answers to a series of dilemmas like that of Heinz Kohlberg classified their moral reasoning into three broad levels of development.

- *Preconventional morality* develops at the age of about 5–12 years. Morality is based entirely on external influences. During this period there is a shift from deference to authority based on the avoidance of punishment – the earliest conception of morality – to a realisation that conformity brings rewards (a more advanced reasoning).

- *Conventional morality* develops at 13–15 years. Moral judgements can now be applied to others. Although the reactions of adults are still important these are seen not in terms of reward and punishment but in terms of approval – being seen as 'good' is an important motivator. By the end of the conventional period morality is internalised (the child makes moral decisions based on their own judgement rather than the anticipated responses of others). By this point the child has developed a respect for society and sees the law as very important.

- *Postconventional morality* develops at around 16–20 years. This level is characterised by the awareness that people have a variety of values and opinions and that rules are to some extent arbitrary. There is a shift during this period from a stage of general acceptance of rules for reasons of impartiality and because they constitute a social contract towards the highest moral state, that of *universal ethical principles* (equality and respect for individual dignity). This involves the realisation that, although laws and conventions usually reflect moral principles, when they come into conflict the ethical principles rather than the rules must be upheld.

Kohlberg believed that only around 10–15% of people achieved the highest moral state and acquired universal ethical principles. He named Jesus Christ, Martin Luther King, Mahatma Gandhi and himself as amongst the few. In his later writing Kohlberg stopped referring to universal principles as the end-point of normal development and instead wrote of them as an ideal.

## Moral development across cultures

ONE of the important criteria against which theories like Kohlberg's need to be assessed is their *cross-cultural validity* – the extent to which the theory can be applied to a range of societies. Many psychologists do not take account of this, and it is to Kohlberg's credit that he did conduct cross-cultural research. Kohlberg (1969) researched moral development in a number of countries and reported the same pattern of development in societies as diverse as those of America, Taiwan, Mexico and Turkey. A number of studies have supported Kohlberg's belief that his pattern of moral development is universal. However, as we will see, there is some contemporary debate about whether Kohlberg's stages can truly be generalised to all cultures.

## Gilligan's studies of moral reasoning in women

GILLIGAN (1977, 1982) challenged Kohlberg's then widely supported theory of moral development by pointing out that he had not addressed differences in the development of moral reasoning in boys and girls. In his original studies Kohlberg only used male participants and some early studies using male and female participants found that girls appeared to be at a lower level of moral development than boys of the same age. Gilligan investigated moral reasoning in women, and developed a theory of how their reasoning differed from that of men. In her original study, Gilligan (1977) interviewed 29 women aged 15–33 recruited from pregnancy or abortion advice services. She aimed to discover the factors underlying their decision for continuing or terminating their pregnancy. Responses were classified into three levels of moral reasoning: self-interest, self-sacrifice and *universal care* (balancing the needs of self and others).

## Moral orientations

BASED on this study Gilligan (1982) proposed that men and women use different criteria when making moral judgements. They can thus be said to have different *moral orientations*. Although Gilligan's three levels of female moral reasoning are roughly equivalent to Kohlberg's preconventional, conventional and postconventional levels, they are based on different principles. Gilligan suggested that whereas men's moral reasoning is based on their understanding of justice, women's reasoning is based on their understanding of caring. She referred to these two ways of thinking as the *justice orientation* and the *caring orientation*.

Comparison of levels of moral reasoning in males and females (after Gilligan, 1982)

|  | Male | Female |
| --- | --- | --- |
| Level of reasoning 1 | Preconventional | Self-interest |
| Level of reasoning 2 | Conventional | Self-sacrifice |
| Level of reasoning 3 | Postconventional | Universal Care |
| general moral orientation | Justice | Caring |

Gilligan explained the difference between male and female moral orientations in terms of their development in early childhood. Some psychologists believe that boys and girls have a different relationship with their mother, because girls can remain close to their mother and acquire their female identity from her whereas boys have to break away to form a separate male identity. Gilligan suggested that this difference means that girls retain a sense of *connectedness*, which characterises their reasoning. Boys, having had to detach themselves from their mother in order to develop a male gender identity, develop a sense of *separateness*, which characterises their later social development. It is this sense of separateness that leads boys to rely on logical decisions about justice.

In her early work Gilligan believed that male and female moral reasoning were completely different, that men based their judgements purely on justice and women based theirs purely on care. However, researchers soon revealed this to be an oversimplification and Gilligan altered her original idea. Instead, she proposed that the justice orientation is dominant in men whereas the caring orientation is dominant in women (Gilligan and Attanucci, 1988).

KOHLBERG'S APPROACH TO MORAL DEVELOPMENT STILL UNDERLIES A LARGE PROPORTION of contemporary research into moral development. This not to say that research universally supports his ideas; there is disagreement, for example, over cross-cultural validity. Snarey (1985), in his review of 44 studies covering 26 countries, concluded that generally Kohlberg's theory could be applied to a wide variety of cultures. However, not all cultures place the same value on the freedom to make individual moral choices, so postconventional morality may not be the universal endpoint of development. When Okwonko (1997) gave Kohlberg-type moral dilemmas to Igbo children in Nigeria she found that they often produced highly sophisticated answers that demonstrated advanced reasoning. However, because of Nigerian cultural values of obedience to parents, belief in a divine being and the close interdependence of all members of a community their answers did not fit neatly into Kohlberg's classification and could not be classified as postconventional.

There are further problems with Kohlberg's research and theory. One important limitation lies with his choice of research method. His interviews centred on hypothetical situations, quite different from the types of moral dilemmas that his participants had ever faced. Millis (1999) demonstrated the importance of the context in which moral dilemmas are presented. She presented children with four moral dilemmas set in school and four set out of school. The children were much more conventional when dilemmas were set in school, and were more likely to give responses classifiable as postconventional in out-of-school situations.

Although Gilligan's early idea that men and women have entirely different moral orientations is considered extreme and not supported by research, contemporary research does tend to support Gilligan's more moderate view that women place more emphasis on care and men on justice when making moral decisions. In one study Garmon et al. (1996) tested the moral reasoning of 543 participants aged 9–18 using a standard interview called the Sociomoral Reflection Measure and found that girls were more likely to refer to issues of care and idealism than boys.

## Current status of the idea

THE cognitive-developmental approach remains the dominant way of looking at moral development, and Kohlberg-type dilemmas are still frequently used in research. The broad principles of Gilligan's moral orientation remain widely believed, although there is some criticism of her research methods, and there is still disagreement about the extent to which males and females differ in moral orientations. There are, however, some exciting new directions in moral development research, addressing important aspects of moral development not easily addressed by traditional theory. For example, the development of children's theory of mind (see p.157) and the quality of family relationships have been implicated by recent studies in individual differences in moral reasoning.

ALTHOUGH MORAL DEVELOPMENT IS PRIMARILY OF ACADEMIC INTEREST, THERE HAVE been some practical applications. In criminal psychology, for example, it has been proposed that one aspect of criminality is a lack of moral reasoning ability. Support for this idea comes from a study by Aleixo and Norris (2000) in which 101 male offenders aged 16–21 were assessed using Kohlberg-type dilemmas, IQ and personality tests. The participants came out on average as less morally mature than the population at large, and of significantly lower IQ, suggesting that poor reasoning was indeed a factor in criminality. However, the criminals also differed significantly in personality from the population norm, so moral reasoning is not the only factor in criminal behaviour.

An understanding of moral reasoning has also proved useful in education, where a major task is to influence children's citizenship. The general idea that children's understanding of morality becomes more sophisticated with age is generally supported by psychologists, and has helped teachers to teach morality in a form suitable to the age of the children. Goodman (2000) has suggested that the approach to teaching morality at school must be tailored to the cognitive development of the children, and that younger children (who lack the subtleties of postconventional morality) will benefit from knowing and sticking to firm rules. Once they achieve postconventional morality, negotiation and an appreciation of *moral relativism* (i.e. the idea that morality is not fixed but changes according to situation) can be introduced.

DURKIN, K. (1995) *Developmental social psychology*. Oxford, Blackwell.

JARVIS, M. (2001) *Angles on child psychology*. Cheltenham, Nelson Thornes.

THOMAS, R.M. (2000) *Comparing theories of child development*. Belmont, Wadsworth.

# Observational learning

❁

OBSERVATIONAL OR *SOCIAL LEARNING* OCCURS WHEN ONE INDIVIDUAL, THE LEARNER, acquires a new behaviour by imitating another individual, known as the *model*. The mere presence of other individuals may enhance learning by increasing competition or reducing fear but this is not true social learning. The model need not be aware of their status as a role model. A child who learns a swear word because it hears the word uttered by its parents is learning by observation, although the model is likely to be surprised by their child's new-found skill. Observational learning can provide a short-cut to the acquisition of new and complex behaviours by imitating conspecifics (members of the same species). This offers animals in their natural habitats a relatively safe, error-free way to learn about social behaviours, foraging and responses to predators.

❁ Conditions for observational learning

❁ Mimicry

❁ Competence versus performance

❁ Characteristics of an effective model

❁ Vicarious reinforcement

❁ Observational learning in humans

## Conditions for observational learning

BANDURA (1977) proposed four prerequisites for observational learning:

Albert Bandura

- *attention* to the model
- *retention* of the observed behaviour
- *reproduction* of the observed action and
- *motivation* to generate the learned behaviour in return for a reward.

Attention is clearly vital, as without it the necessary information about the behaviour cannot be taken in. However, it is also necessary to be able to recall the sequence of actions observed and to be able to reproduce the behaviour. Finally, the learner needs to be motivated to demonstrate their newly acquired skill. To return to our example of a child learning to swear, it must first notice a parent or other model swearing (attention). It must then remember the incident (retention), and repeat the swear word or words on a later occasion (reproduction). The response it receives for swearing determines the child's motivation to repeat the swearing.

## Mimicry

TRUE imitation leads to indirect or delayed reward; mimicry, however, appears to be a special case of imitation in which there is no obvious reward. Captive primates such as orang-utans show mimicry when they copy human behaviours such as pouring drinks, touching glasses and using paint brushes (Pearce, 1997). Although no obvious rewards are evident in these situations, it is possible that the orang-utans may be reinforced by the attention their behaviour attracts from humans. However, it appears that mimicry occurs in some cases even when this type of reward is not present. Moore (1992) reported an experimental procedure in which an African grey parrot mimicked behaviour it had seen performed by a human. The parrot was videotaped performing the behaviour in the absence of an audience.

## Competence versus performance

AN animal or human that has learned through observation may *acquire*, but not necessarily *display*, the new behaviour. Just because you have seen someone roll a cigarette, for example, doesn't mean that you will necessarily follow suit. This is an important difference between conditioning and observational learning. When we learn a behaviour by operant conditioning we need to have it rewarded or *reinforced*. Observational learning has no requirement for reinforcement in acquiring a behaviour although reinforcement can play a part in expression of the behaviour – we may know the words to a trashy pop song but we are unlikely to demonstrate our ability to sing them unless a karaoke opportunity offers rewards!

## Characteristics of an effective model

NO species imitates all the behaviour of their conspecifics. One important variable in determining whether behaviour is imitated is the nature of the individual doing the modelling. Duck (1990) suggests that the extent to which the model resembles the observer may determine their effectiveness as a model: for instance, same-sex models are more effective than opposite-sex models. Other important attributes of effective models include power, social status and likeability – in humans parents and soap opera stars are powerful models; social animals (including humans) are more likely to imitate the behaviour of individuals with high social status in their community.

## Vicarious reinforcement

WE can learn *how* to behave in a certain way without reinforcement but reward does play a role in the likelihood of our actually repeating the behaviour. However, we do not have to experience such rewards ourselves. The behaviour can also be reinforced when we observe the model receiving a reward for expressing it. This process of learning from 'second-hand' rewards is called *vicarious reinforcement*.

## Observational learning in humans

IN a classic series of experiments in the 1960s Albert Bandura demonstrated that children would imitate a role model engaged in aggressive behaviour towards an inflatable doll (see Jarvis et al., 2000 for a full description of the original procedure). In variations on their procedure Bandura and colleagues demonstrated that children's imitation of adult aggression increased when the model was of the same sex and when they witnessed the model receiving a reward for their behaviour. Thus it seems that the factors that influence observational learning in animals are also important in humans.

CONTEMPORARY RESEARCH HAS CONTINUED TO SUPPORT THE PRINCIPLES OF observational learning. In a recent naturalistic observation by Ottoni and Mannu (2001) it was noted that 10% of instances of adult capuchin monkeys using tools to crack nuts were closely observed by their young. Competence in nut cracking increased with age, suggesting that the juveniles were learning their technique by watching the adults. Altshuler and Nunn (2001) demonstrated the importance of modelling in migratory humming birds, which in the wild have to learn to feed from a variety of plant species. Captive birds that watched a model learned more quickly to use an artificial feeder than those learning by trial and error. The importance of sex and social status in the likelihood of imitation of a model was tested in a study of chickens by Nicol and Pope (1999). They found that chickens exposed to different demonstrators in a feeding task imitated the feeding locations of dominant hens in preference to those of submissive ones or cockerels.

One criticism of observational learning theory is that the learning demonstrated may not be the result of imitation but of *stimulus enhancement*. This means that models, rather than offering behaviour to imitate, simply attract the observer to a particular characteristic of the environment. Fritz and Kotrschal (1999) looked at learning of feeding techniques in ravens in an attempt to test this, but found that either observational learning or stimulus enhancement could have responsible for the acquisition of the feeding skill. The ravens had been fed meat in boxes without lids but were then offered food in closed boxes, which could be opened either by jumping on the lid or by pulling a small tab. When naïve ravens were exposed to models competent in the latter technique, the observers acquired both techniques, whilst control birds with no models used only the former approach. The presence of a model did affect the observers' behaviour but Fritz and Kotrschal concluded that either stimulus enhancement or imitation could be responsible for these findings. The naïve ravens may have observed the model's interaction with the tabs and thus been attracted to them; they became enhanced stimuli. Alternatively, they might have observed and imitated the model's technique. However, evidence for imitation as an explanation for observational learning (as opposed to stimulus enhancement) comes from Hirata and Morimura (2000), who found that naïve chimpanzees learning to use tools for 'honey fishing' by observing others tended to watch before their first attempt or after a failure but not following successful attempts. This suggests that they were focusing on the details of how to fish for honey rather than just where to look for the source of the food.

## Current status of the idea

THE essence of observational learning remains unchanged and classic experimental research and recent naturalistic evidence demonstrate essentially the same findings. Humans and animals seem to learn through observation very much according to the same rules, and children will acquire a range of behaviours from adults through observational learning. Some ideas have changed, however. For example, in contrast to previous beliefs about competence versus performance, recent research suggests that the opportunity to perform socially learned behaviours between observations does improve performance (Deakin and Proteau 2000).

THE THEORY OF OBSERVATIONAL LEARNING IS IMPORTANT IN UNDERSTANDING AND influencing the development of children's behavioural repertoire. Although there is evidence that observational learning plays a part in the acquisition of problem behaviour in children from aggressive families (e.g. Onyskiw 2000, Onyskiw and Hayduk 2001) it can also be used to provide examples of prosocial behaviour. Huston and Wright (1998) investigated the educational impact of television programmes that contained prosocial models that children could imitate, such as *Mister Rogers' Neighbourhood*, *Sesame Street* and *Lassie*. They found that children who viewed programmes that emphasised behaviours such as kindness, sharing, and helpfulness demonstrated more kind and helpful behaviours than children who did not.

We may also learn our fears through observation of our families. Although both common sense and traditional psychological explanations would suggest that direct experiences of trauma would be necessary to develop fears and phobias, this may not be the case. Zinbarg and Mineka (2001) explain how observational learning is an important developmental pathway in the acquisition of anxiety during childhood and offer ways to prevent and treat fears learned through observation.

Observational learning techniques have been used to assist language learning in children in both mainstream education and those with learning disabilities. Horner (2000) tested the effect on preschool children of a model's attention to the print when reading. She found that if a child model asked questions about the print in an alphabet book the children who viewed this behaviour were significantly more likely to pay attention to the print themselves and that this leads to an improvement in letter-naming ability. Similar improvements in children's references to the print were found by Ezell's and Justice's (2000) study of children observing adult models in a shared book-reading situation. Keel et al. (2001) investigated the effects of observational learning on the language use of groups of children with learning disabilities. Students who were able to observe other students writing on the board significantly improved in reading ability.

Another important application of observational learning is in sport psychology, where it is used to enhance the acquisition of motor skills. Instructors use a combination of demonstration, verbal instruction and practice to help learners acquire new skills. Al-Abood et al. (2001) tested the usefulness of observational learning in acquiring an aiming skill by comparing modelling with verbal instruction and learning by practice alone. Verbal instruction and modelling proved equally effective and more so than simple practice. This suggests that demonstration is an effective coaching technique.

# Further Reading

FLANAGAN, C. (1996) *Applying psychology to early childhood development*. London, Hodder and Stoughton.

PEARCE, J.M. (1997) *Animal learning and cognition: An introduction*. Hove, UK, Psychology Press.

# Operant conditioning

❋

## The Idea

WHEREAS CLASSICAL CONDITIONING (SEE P.30) INVOLVES LEARNING TO ASSOCIATE TWO events with one another so that we respond to them in the same way, operant conditioning involves learning to repeat or not repeat behaviours according to their consequences. Edward Lee Thorndike carried out the first work in this area at the end of the nineteenth century; however, the study of operant conditioning came to dominate psychology for a time in the 1930s and 1940s, largely due to the influence of Burhus Frederic Skinner.

- ❋ Thorndike's law of habit formation
- ❋ The operant
- ❋ Positive and negative reinforcement
- ❋ Primary and secondary reinforcers
- ❋ Uncontrollable reinforcers
- ❋ Punishment
- ❋ Schedules of reinforcement
- ❋ Equipotentiality and preparedness

## Thorndike's law of habit formation

THORNDIKE demonstrated that many apparently logical decisions made by animals could be explained by a simple learning process in which actions with positive consequences increase in frequency and those with negative consequences decrease. Thorndike found that 6-day-old chicks could learn to find their way through a twisting pen to find other chicks, taking 3 or 4 minutes initially but only 5 or 6 seconds after several attempts (Thorndike, 1905). Using a puzzle box from which a kitten must escape to obtain food, he also showed that following a period of trial and error the time taken for the kitten to operate the button that opened the door decreased with the repeated experience of obtaining food on release.

Based on these observations, Thorndike (1905) proposed his *Law of Habit Formation,* saying that any act that in a given situation produces satisfaction becomes associated with that situation, so that when the situation recurs the act is more likely than before to recur. Conversely, any act that in a given situation produces discomfort becomes dissociated from that situation, so that when the situation recurs the act is less likely than before to recur.

## The operant

THORNDIKE'S procedure required observing the kitten and returning it to the box after each escape. A simpler, more controlled procedure for recording behaviour was developed by B.F. Skinner, using apparatus now called the 'Skinner box'. The behaviours exhibited by animals in such situations are called *operants* because the animal is operating on (i.e. changing) its environment. In a Skinner box that contains a bar, a rat can alter its environment by pressing the bar (the operant). The consequences of such behaviours form the basis of the theory of operant conditioning.

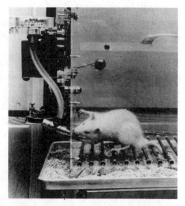

The Skinner box, courtesy Pfizer Inc.

## Positive and negative reinforcement

SKINNER extended Thorndike's notions of satisfaction and discomfort, focussing on the way in which the consequences of a behaviour affect the probability of it being repeated. His *law of conditioning* states that 'If the occurrence of an operant is followed by presentation of a reinforcing stimulus, the strength is increased' (Skinner, 1938).

The rewards used by Skinner and Thorndike are referred to as *reinforcers*. Reinforcement may be achieved in two ways:

- A *positive reinforcer* is a pleasant experience, such as receiving food or being taken out for a treat.

- *Negative reinforcement* is the pleasant experience that occurs when an unpleasant stimulus is removed, for example cessation of an electric shock or not being shouted at any more.

Both of these reinforcement techniques increase the frequency of the behaviour they follow (Skinner, 1953).

## Primary and secondary reinforcers

REINFORCERS can also be classified as primary or secondary:

- *Primary reinforcers* fulfil some basic need: food, water, sex and social contact may be used as primary reinforcers.
- *Secondary reinforcers* acquire their reinforcing properties by association with a primary reinforcer.

A rat in a Skinner box may learn to press the bar in order to hear the 'click' of the mechanism because it associates this action with the dispensing of food. An example of a secondary reinforcer used to motivate humans is money. People work for money which, of itself, has no survival value but is directly associated with food and other essentials.

## Uncontrollable reinforcers

WHEN a positive consequence follows a behaviour we will tend to repeat that behaviour, even if it was not the cause of the reward. Positive consequences that occur regardless of our behaviour are called *uncontrollable reinforcers* – 'uncontrollable' because they occur regardless of our behaviour and 'reinforcers' because they increase the probability of the behaviour being repeated.

The power of uncontrollable reinforcers was demonstrated by Skinner (1948). Eight pigeons were placed in Skinner boxes and given a food pellet every 15 seconds, regardless of their behaviour. Six of the birds acquired repetitive and bizarre behaviours. It seemed that they linked whatever they were doing when the food arrived to the food and therefore when they wanted more food they repeated the behaviour: one bird turned anticlockwise, another hopped and another swung its head in a pendulum motion. As the frequency of the food delivery decreased the pace of the learned behaviours increased. Skinner claimed to have produced in the pigeons a superstitious belief of the power of their behaviour to influence food delivery.

## Punishment

SKINNER believed that behaviour was shaped and maintained its consequences, and that those consequences could be good or bad. Whereas pleasant consequences (reinforcers) increase the frequency of the behaviours that precede them, unpleasant consequences (*punishers*) reduce the likelihood that the behaviour will be repeated. Like reinforcement, punishment can take two forms:

- *Positive punishers* are unpleasant, such as getting an electric shock or being caned.
- The unpleasantness of *negative punishers* arises because something good is withdrawn, such as deprivation of social contact or being grounded.

Both of these processes reduce the frequency of the behaviour they follow.

## Schedules of reinforcement

A reinforcer might not be applied in every instance that an individual exhibits the required behaviour. Where every performance is rewarded, the reinforcement schedule is described as *continuous reinforcement*. In real life this rarely occurs; a child is unlikely to hear 'well done' each time it says 'thank you', nevertheless, children generally acquire this courtesy. It would seem that rewarding every instance of a behaviour is the least effective way of ensuring the rapid and lasting acquisition of a behaviour. The regulation of reinforcement can be achieved by varying either the minimum number of responses required before reinforcement is obtained or the minimum time for reinforcement to occur.

Reinforcement schedules governing the number of responses are *ratio schedules*, those controlling the time between reinforcements are *interval schedules*. Either of these partial or intermittent reinforcement systems may operate as a *fixed schedule*, in which the number or time interval remains the same on every occasion or as a *variable schedule*, in which the number or interval is varied around an average. Consider a rat in a Skinner box. In a 'fixed ratio (FR) 5' schedule the rat would receive reinforcement on every fifth response. In a 'variable ratio (VR) 10' schedule the rat would receive reinforcement for every tenth response *on average* – it might receive reinforcement twice in succession but then not for several responses. A 'fixed interval (FI) 20' schedule would reinforce the rat every 20 seconds if it had pressed the bar at all during the preceding 20 seconds. Finally, a 'variable interval (VI) 60' schedule would reinforce the rat on average every minute if, in the period since the previous reinforcement, it had pressed the bar. Different reinforcement schedules produce differing response patterns and extinction rates. Continuous reinforcement results in the slowest response rate and fastest extinction whereas variable schedules produce the fastest response rates and behaviour that is most resistant to extinction.

## Equipotentiality and preparedness

FOLLOWING early research into the parameters governing operant conditioning, when it was believed that a reinforcer could be used to shape the acquisition of any response by any animal (this is called *equipotentiality*), it has become apparent that this is not the case. As early as the 1970s, Skinner's views were changing; he observed that 'the fact that operant conditioning, like all physiological processes, is the product of natural selection throws light on the question of what kind of consequences are reinforcing and why' (Skinner, 1975). It has now been shown that not only are different consequences effective for different species in different ways but that some responses can be acquired by some species but not others. For example, rats or pigeons will readily learn to avoid a shock by jumping away from it or to obtain food by pressing a lever but cannot easily be conditioned to press a lever to avoid a shock. Thus there appears to be a 'preparedness' to learn about some relationships but not others.

# The Idea Today

RESEARCH HAS CONTINUED TO REFINE OUR UNDERSTANDING OF THE PROCESSES OF operant conditioning. Although first identified many years ago (e.g. Grice 1948), the importance of the effect of *delayed reinforcement* on learning has been the subject of recent research. Lattal and Gleeson (1990) tested rats in a Skinner box with a delay of up to 30 seconds between bar pressing and reinforcement. Although the rats could acquire the correct response under these conditions, their learning was very slow and they performed at a low rate. Research has also focused on the role of uncontrollable reinforcement in the development of superstitious behaviour. Matute (1996) demonstrated that students whose computers periodically emitted a loud noise would press buttons to try to stop it, and that they would learn to use a particular response to stop the noise. In fact the noise stopped anyway after a few seconds, but the participants did not realise this and continued to use the keyboard to try to stop it. Interestingly, participants instructed to wait before trying to stop the noise learnt that it stopped anyway and did not acquire the button-pressing response.

*Incentive* (the attractiveness of the reinforcer) also affects reinforcement. Two factors influence incentive: the value of the reinforcer and the delay before receiving it. Kirby and Herrnstein (1995) offered university students a range of different financial rewards after different length delays: most students chose to receive $12 after 6 days rather than waiting 12 days to receive $16. The act of waiting seems to devalue reinforcement. This phenomenon is exploited by the financial services industry. It is very tempting to opt for 'buy now pay later' deals and hire purchase even when they result in greater cost in the long run.

The neurological basis of operant conditioning has also been investigated in recent research focusing on the role of the amygdala. Parkinson et al. (2001) lesioned the amygdalas of 12 marmosets, and tested them on their responses to primary and secondary reinforcers. They responded normally to primary reinforcement but did not respond to secondary reinforcement. A similar finding was obtained by Blundell et al. (2001), using rats. These studies suggest that the amygdala plays a role in identifying or assessing the value of particular reinforcers.

## Current status of the idea

THE existence of operant conditioning is uncontroversial. The fact that we acquire behaviours that have positive consequences is self-evident, and the work of Skinner and later researchers has undoubtedly helped us understand this process. However, Skinner's belief that most or all human behaviour can be explained by operant conditioning is no longer popular with psychologists. Operant conditioning can not account for our instinctive tendencies to behave in certain ways. It also fails to account for learning by observation of others and by having behaviour strengthened by *almost* receiving a reward (this is called the *near miss*). Both of these types of learning require much more complex mental processes than those proposed by Skinner.

OPERANT CONDITIONING HAS APPLICATIONS IN CLINICAL PSYCHOLOGY. HENRIQUES AND Davidson (2000) tested depressed and non-depressed participants on a verbal memory task under three monetary pay-off conditions: reward, punishment and neutral. The non-depressed participants maximised their earnings by altering their responses (relative to the neutral condition) in both reward and punishment conditions. The depressed participants, however, did not alter their responses in response to reward. This finding supported earlier physiological evidence of decreased responsiveness to rewards in depressed individuals. This has implications for understanding depression. Addiction can also be explained in terms of operant conditioning. If we are rewarded for a behaviour, then the likelihood of it being repeated increases. Activities such as gambling involve variable reinforcement schedules – because winning occurs irregularly – as does reinforcement when searching for Internet pornography (Putnam, 2000). Hence these behaviours are particularly easy to become conditioned to repeat compulsively and difficult to extinguish.

Operant conditioning is also used in treating mental disorder. Clinical techniques using operant conditioning are thus described as *behaviour modification*; the patient's behaviour is being modified by its consequences. Ghosh and Chattopadhyay (1993) employed behaviour-modification techniques including positive reinforcement, the *Premack Principle* and *programmed learning*. The Premack Principle involves using the opportunity to perform a more frequent event to reinforce the occurrence of another, less probable, one. Programmed learning sequences learning opportunities such that tasks are short and feedback is rapid, so performance is reinforced by success on the tasks. In the treatment of a 7-year-old boy with Attention Deficit Hyperactivity Disorder, Ghosh and Chattopadhyay found that the programme was effective in improving both his behaviour (for instance staying on-task, co-operation and social interaction) and his academic achievement.

Operant conditioning is currently being used as a means to measure the responses of captive animals to their environment. This has allowed us to improve their quality of life. Cooper and Mason (2000) looked at how powerful a range of benefits were as reinforcers for behaviour in farmed mink. Tunnels, water bowls, toys and spaces emerged as the most powerful reinforcers, and as a result of this farmers have a better idea of how to improve their animals' quality of life. Phillips and Morris (2001) investigated factors affecting cows' passageway preferences. When tested on an operant conditioning task in which they had to choose a passageway in a Y-shaped maze, cows demonstrated the strongest preference for a lit passageway over a dark one (regardless of the size of the reward the cows avoided the dark aisle). The cows did not, however, avoid passageways containing slurry. The knowledge that cattle have a strong preference for well-lit environments can be used to improve their conditions.

 **Further Reading**

CLAMP, A.G. AND RUSSELL, J. (1998) *Comparative psychology*, London, Hodder and Stoughton.

LEIBERMAN, D.A. (2000) *Learning: behaviour and cognition*. London, Wadsworth.

# Parapsychology

❈

## The Idea

P ARAPSYCHOLOGY FORMS PART OF THE WIDER FIELD OF ANOMALISTIC PSYCHOLOGY, THE study of out-of-the-ordinary human experiences, sometimes called the paranormal. Anomalistic psychology includes the study of ghost phenomena, UFOs and monsters. The narrower field of parapsychology focuses on those anomalistic experiences that lend themselves to study under controlled conditions, principally extrasensory perception (ESP) and psychokinesis (PK). ESP refers to the perception of information without the use of the known senses, and PK to the mental influence of matter, living or non-living. Collectively ESP and PK are known as psi phenomena. The scientific study of psi phenomena dates back to the formation of the psychical research society in 1888 (Beloff, 1993). The study of psi formally became part of psychology in the 1920s with the establishment of a parapsychology laboratory at Duke University by J.B. Rhine. Much of the current research in parapsychology is based on refinements of Rhine's methods.

* ❈ Zener cards and general ESP
* ❈ Telepathy and the ganzfield
* ❈ Clairvoyance and remote viewing
* ❈ Precognition
* ❈ Psychokinesis
* ❈ The sheep–goat effect

## Zener cards and general ESP

J.B. RHINE and a colleague Karl Zener developed the distinctive Zener cards tradition-ally used in ESP research. These came in packs of 25, five with each symbol. Initially Rhine used Zener cards to investigate general ESP (GESP). A participant's task was to perceive the order in which the symbols would appear in a shuffled pack. Chance would predict that participants were correct 20% of the time. Rhine (1934) published the results of 800 trials using Zener cards, showing that results were consistently higher than would be expected by chance alone.

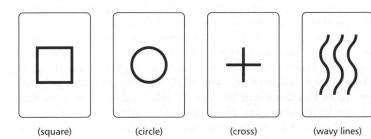

| (square) | (circle) | (cross) | (wavy lines) | (5-pointed star) |

The five symbols of Zener cards

A difficulty in using Zener cards was in telling whether participants were using telepathy (picking up the information from the experimenter) or clairvoyance (visual-ising the cards in the pack). Rhine managed to eliminate the possibility of telepathy when he wanted to study clairvoyance by making sure no-one saw the cards after they were shuffled. Cards could not be used to test telepathy without the possibility of clair-voyance, however, because there would always be a chance that participants were picking up information from the cards rather than another person. A further limitation of Zener cards is that they lack ecological validity – they simply do not contain the sort of information we might pick up using telepathy or clairvoyance in everyday life. Because of these limitations Zener cards are not generally used in current research.

## Telepathy and the ganzfield

RHINE studied telepathy by asking 'receivers' what Zener symbol a 'sender' was thinking of (in the absence of an actual card, which would have allowed clairvoyance). However, as we have seen, Zener cards have their limitations, and the modern study of telepathy involves a procedure called the *ganzfield,* developed by Honorton (1974). The ganzfield is a form of sensory deprivation believed to maximise the likelihood of ESP. The ganzfield does not involve complete sensory deprivation because this leads to hallucinations; instead participants are subjected to featureless vision and sound by viewing a red light shone into the face as if through ping-pong balls whilst listening to white noise (static). In typical ganzfield studies the receiver sits in a ganzfield while a sender is shown randomly selected pictures. The receiver then tries to select the images the sender was thinking about from a choice of four, thus having a 25% probability of being right due to chance. A limitation with early ganzfield studies was that the exper-imenter administered them, and participants may have picked up subtle cues about the nature of the pictures selected. To get around this Bem and Honorton (1994) intro-duced the autoganzfield, essentially the same procedure except that it is administered by computer rather than by people. Most contemporary studies of telepathy use the autoganzfield procedure, and there is substantial evidence to suggest that, at least for some people, some degree of telepathy takes place.

## Clairvoyance and remote viewing

CLAIRVOYANCE is the visual experience of information not actually available through the eyes. There are corresponding terms for the other senses, for example clairaudience is an auditory experience of perceiving information not in earshot. In his early Zener card studies Rhine managed to isolate clairvoyance from telepathy by making sure that no one knew the order of the cards until after the participants had suggested one. Variations of the ganzfield procedure have been used to test clairvoyance – if the receiver successfully identifies pictures before anyone else knows what they are then clairvoyance rather than telepathy must have been employed. However, the most popular way of investigating clairvoyance is by *remote viewing*. Targ and Puthoff (1974) reported the case of a retired police officer who could describe locations (chosen randomly) that were visited by members of the research team, although he did not go with them and did not know where the researchers were going. Modern remote viewing studies follow Targ and Puthoff's procedure closely but employ a double blind procedure. The experimenter who remains with the participant does not know what sites are being visited, and independent judges are used to match descriptions with sites.

## Precognition

PRECOGNITION is the perception of events before they happen. Rhine (1940) investigated precognition using a simple variation on the procedure for assessing clairvoyance and telepathy. The participant's task was to list before the pack was shuffled the order in which Zener cards would appear after shuffling. Rhine obtained comparable results in precognition to those of his clairvoyance and telepathy studies, suggesting that precognition was as powerful as other forms of ESP. A newer laboratory procedure has been developed (Radin, 1997 cited in Hayes, 2000) to investigate another form of precognition. It involves testing whether physiological arousal occurs in response to threatening events before participants have access to sensory information about the threat. The arousal of participants is monitored as they randomly select unseen photographs to appear on a computer screen. Interestingly, threatening photographs (e.g. of autopsies) produced a strong physiological reaction before they were seen, although non-threatening pictures did not. A further line of research into precognition has involved the study of pets that appear to know when their owner is returning home, regardless of whether it is the usual time (Sheldrake, 1994). Controlled studies have in fact failed to show that pets can reliably predict the return of their owners once times are randomised and other clues removed.

## Psychokinesis

PSYCHOKINESIS (literally translated as 'movement by the mind') involves the ability to influence physical matter. There are three categories of psychokinesis: micro-PK, macro-PK and bio-PK.

- Micro-PK involves influencing systems where there is a degree of randomness, for example in throwing a die. Rhine found that in trials of dice-throwing PK could produce very modest but consistent improvements in score, and this has been supported by later studies (e.g. Radin and Ferrari, 1991).

- Macro-PK involves the influence on stable systems, the classic example involving bending of spoons and other metal objects in stage shows. Macro-PK has proved much harder to demonstrate under controlled conditions and numerous performers of macro-PK have been exposed as frauds.

- An interesting recent variation on macro-PK studies is bio-PK or DMILS (direct mental interaction with living systems). The classic real-life situation in which this occurs is when we become aware that someone is looking at us even though we have no visual information to suggest this. Some controlled studies have supported the existence of this 'eyes-in-the-back-of-the-head' phenomenon.

## The sheep–goat effect

AN interesting and consistent finding from decades of parapsychology research has been the relationship between apparent psi ability and belief in psi phenomena. Sceptics (goats) tend to score below the levels we would expect according to chance on a variety of tests including telepathy and psychokinesis. By contrast believers in psi (sheep) often score moderately but consistently above chance levels. The existence of sheep and goats is in itself evidence for psi phenomena, as it seems that people can affect their psi according to their wishes.

The Idea Today

RECENT STUDIES HAVE PROVIDED SOME SUPPORT FOR THE EXISTENCE OF PSI phenomena. Most, though not all, telepathy studies in recent years have involved the ganzfield. Honorton et al. (1990) performed a meta-analysis of 42 ganzfield studies and concluded that the ganzfield led to strong telepathy effects. However, not all such meta-analyses have found the same results, and the existence of telepathy remains controversial. In an interesting variation on the usual procedure Willin (1996) tested whether music can be communicated telepathically. Four pairs of participants took part in four trials each, in which they attempted to communicate music telepathically. The results were in line with the 25% success that would be expected according to chance – one pair scored 50% correct, two pairs 25% and one pair 0% – and thus there is no evidence that music can be communicated by telepathy. Rather more encouraging results were achieved by Dalkvist and Westerlund (1998) in a study of transfer of emotion by telepathy. A series of slides containing positive and negative images were shown to 337 participants, who were given the task of transmitting these emotions. Receivers correctly identified the evoked emotion significantly more often than would be expected according to chance.

However mixed the evidence for the existence of telepathy, there is little doubt that a substantial proportion of the population believe in telepathy in everyday life. Sheldrake (2000) surveyed people by phone in Bury and London, asking them about the experience of knowing when people were about to phone them. Around half the respondents reported occasions when they had known someone was going to phone just before they did so. The effect was significantly more common in London.

Some recent studies have cast doubt on the assumption that telepathy, clairvoyance and precognition are actually separate phenomena. Morris et al. (1995) conducted a ganzfield study in which there was no sender. Lacking a sender had little effect, and some participants were still able to identify the target picture in the absence of the possibility of telepathy. A meta-analysis by Steinkamp et al. (1998) of clairvoyance and precognition studies revealed no difference in success rates, suggesting that the distinction between clairvoyance and precognition may be false. It is unclear whether this means that there is only one psi ability, or whether we simply substitute one form of psi for another according to the situation.

There is some evidence that we can influence systems with a random element (micro-PK). An experiment by Stevens (1999) is typical of research into micro-PK: participants accessing a web page were invited to try to influence the path of a laser beam. The path of the beam in this condition was altered significantly more often than in a control condition where there was no attempt to change its course, suggesting that participants had successfully altered the path of the beam through micro-PK.

Much recent interest has focused on bio-PK or DMILS. Delanoy and Morris (1999) tested whether participants could alter the electrodermal activity (electrical activity in the skin) of targets when shielded from them so that no electromagnetic, verbal or visual influence was possible. Times were randomised so that targets did not know when the sender was trying to influence their electrodermal activity. Their electrodermal activity was reliably different when the sender was trying to influence them, supporting the DMILS phenomenon. DMILS has also been tested outside the laboratory, for example in the eyes-in-the-back-of-the-head phenomenon (properly called the *staring detection effect*) in which people believe they can detect an unseen person staring at them. Controlled studies have found mixed results. Braud et al. (1995) found that galvanic skin response (a measure of arousal) was consistently associated with unseen staring. However, other studies in which people are forced to guess when someone is staring have tended to produce negative results, perhaps because of the pressure of forced guessing.

## Current status of the idea

PARAPSYCHOLOGY remains a small, specialist area in psychology, and most psychologists remain unconvinced of the existence of psi phenomena. However, the evidence for psi is sufficiently strong to warrant further study, not least to investigate why psychologists, who generally claim to be unbiased researchers, are so negative about the possibility of ESP and PK in the face of the available evidence.

## The Idea in Action

BY AND LARGE, THE STUDY OF PARAPSYCHOLOGY HAS BEEN OF ACADEMIC INTEREST rather than having widespread applications. One important use of parapsychology within psychology has been to develop our understanding of the more subtle influences on research findings in general. The history of fraud, bias and cynicism surrounding the study of psi phenomena has led to the development of a sophisticated critical thinking in relation to research. Morris (2000) has proposed a role for parapsychology in the general teaching of psychology in order to develop skills of critical thinking in psychology students.

Other applications of parapsychology are largely military and research findings are not easily available to the public. Utts (1996) reported the results of a CIA review of remote-viewing studies, which concluded that around 1% of the public can reliably remote view. It is not difficult to see why the CIA was so interested – if it works remote viewing has a clear application in espionage.

 Further Reading

BELOFF, J. (1993) *Parapsychology, a concise history*. London, Athlone Press.

BROUGHTON, R. (1991) *Parapsychology, the controversial science*. London, Rider.

HAYES, N. (2000) *Foundations of psychology*. London, ITP.

# Piaget and cognitive development

P IAGET WROTE ABOUT CHILDREN'S INTELLECTUAL OR *cognitive* development from the 1930s until the 1970s, and has been without question the most influential writer in this area. Piaget was the first psychologist to suggest that children don't just know less than adults but actually think in quite different ways. Piaget was a philosopher and sociologist as well as a psychologist, but in psychology we are interested primarily in his work on how children think and acquire knowledge.

Jean Piaget

- Operations, schemas and equilibration
- Object permanence
- Conservation
- Egocentrism
- Formal reasoning
- Stages of cognitive development

## Operations, schemas and equilibration

PIAGET proposed two mental structures: operations and schemas. *Operations* are rules about how the world operates. The operations of which a child is capable increase as the brain matures. *Schemas* are mental structures, each of which contains all the information the individual has relating to one aspect of the world. We have schemas for people, objects, actions and more abstract concepts. Piaget believed that we are born with a few innate schemas that enable us to interact with others and that throughout childhood we acquire more. Unlike operations, which develop with brain maturity, most schemas are acquired by experience.

When we can comprehend everything around us we are said to be in a state of *equilibrium*. Whenever we meet a new situation that cannot be explained by our existing schemas we experience the unpleasant sensation of *disequilibrium*. According to Piaget we are instinctively driven to gain an understanding of the world and so escape disequilibrium. Because we are motivated to equilibrate, humans are not passive learners but active *agents* in their learning. Piaget identified two processes by which this process of *equilibration* takes place: assimilation and accommodation.

- *Assimilation* takes place when a new experience can be understood by altering an existing schema. For example, when an infant who has a 'bird' schema based on the family canary first encounters sparrows in the garden it will assimilate sparrows into the 'bird' schema.

- *Accommodation* takes place when a new experience is so radically different that it cannot be assimilated into existing schemas and a new schema is formed. An example of accommodation occurs when the infant in the above example first encounters an aeroplane; this new object is just too different to incorporate into the 'bird' schema, and so an 'aeroplane' schema is formed.

## Object permanence

OBJECT permanence refers to the understanding that objects exist permanently even when they are no longer visible. Piaget observed the behaviour of infants who were looking at an attractive object when it was removed from their sight. Until about 8 months, children would immediately switch their attention away from the object once it was out of sight. From about 8 months, however, they would actively look for the object. If, for example, it were pushed behind a screen within their reach they would simply push the screen aside. Piaget concluded from this that, before about 8 months of age children do not understand that objects continue to exist once they are out of sight. Support for Piaget's idea comes from a variation in his procedure in which a sheet is used to cover the hidden object and the object's shape is still clearly visible. Children still did not respond to the object, suggesting they really did not understand that it continued to exist.

## Conservation

CONSERVATION refers to the understanding that a quantity of objects can remain the same even if their appearance changes. Piaget (1952) reported that young children had difficulty with tasks of conservation. He demonstrated this in a number of situations, two of which are particularly well known.

NUMBER CONSERVATION  Piaget found that if two rows of counters are laid out side by side, with the same number of counters spaced apart at the same distance, children correctly spotted that there were the same number of counters in each row. If, however, the counters in one of the rows were pushed closer together, young children typically thought that there were now fewer counters in that row.

LIQUID CONSERVATION  Piaget found that if children see two glasses together with liquid coming up to the same height in each they can correctly spot the fact that they contain the same amount of liquid. If, however, liquid was poured from a short, wide glass to a taller, thinner container, young children typically believe there is now more liquid in the taller container.

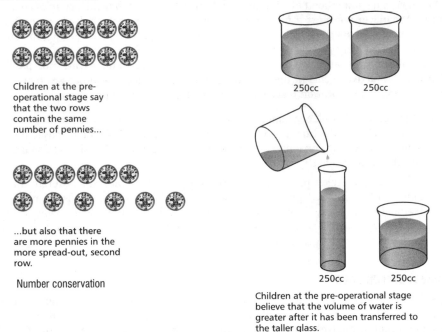

Children at the pre-operational stage say that the two rows contain the same number of pennies...

...but also that there are more pennies in the more spread-out, second row.

Number conservation

250cc    250cc

250cc    250cc

Children at the pre-operational stage believe that the volume of water is greater after it has been transferred to the taller glass.

Liquid conservation

## Egocentrism

*EGOCENTRISM* is the tendency to see the world entirely from our own perspective, and to have great difficulty in seeing the world from the viewpoint of others. Unlike difficulty with object impermanence, which is associated with specific ages, egocentrism declines gradually throughout childhood. Piaget saw egocentrism as applying to both abstract and concrete concepts. A classic study by Piaget and Inhelder (1956) (the *three mountains experiment*) illustrated egocentrism in the physical environment. Each model mountain had a different marker on the top: a cross, a house or a covering of snow. A doll was positioned to the side of the three mountains. A child seated in front of the scene was shown pictures of the scene from different viewpoints and asked to select the picture that best matched what the doll could 'see.' Children under 7 years old had difficulty with this task, and tended to choose the picture of the scene representing their own point of view. You can demonstrate egocentrism for yourself by watching the news on television with a young child, and asking them what the newsreader can see. Young children will often find this difficult, believing that the newsreader can see *them*.

Piaget and Inhelder's three mountains experiment

## Formal reasoning

PIAGET believed that from about 11 years of age children became capable of abstract or formal reasoning. The term *formal* indicates that children capable of this type of reasoning can focus on the *form* of an argument and not be distracted by its content. For example, if a child capable of formal reasoning is presented with the syllogism 'All green birds have two heads. I have a green bird called Charlie. How many heads does Charlie have?' he or she should be able to answer 'two' (Smith et al., 1998). Before a child becomes capable of this type of reasoning they would be more likely to become distracted by the content and state that birds do not really have two heads.

## Stages of cognitive development

BASED on the types of logical error Piaget identified as typical of children of different ages, he proposed a stage theory of development containing four stages:

- *sensorimotor stage* (0–2 years)
- *preoperational stage* (2–7 years)
- *concrete operational stage* (7–11 years)
- *formal operational stage* (11 years+).

THE SENSORIMOTOR STAGE This lasts approximately the first 2 years of life. Piaget believed that our main focus at this point is on physical sensation and on learning to coordinate our bodies. We learn by trial and error that certain actions have certain effects. By the second year of life infants are quite mobile, and so are well equipped to actively explore their environment. They are extremely curious and often experiment with actions to discover their effects. By the end of the sensorimotor stage infants are fully aware of themselves as separate from the rest of the world and have begun to develop language.

THE PREOPERATIONAL STAGE By the end of their second year, a child has sufficient grasp of language for its thinking to be based around symbolic thought rather than physical sensation. However, the child has not developed sufficiently to grasp logical rules or operations (hence the term *preoperational*) and it deals with the world very much as it appears rather than as it is. Preoperational children are thus highly egocentric and have difficulty in conservation.

THE CONCRETE OPERATIONAL STAGE The child's mind is now mature enough to use logical thought, but children can apply logic only to objects and situations that are present and physical (hence *concrete* operational). They become less egocentric and better at conservation tasks. However, children in this stage have great difficulty in carrying out logical tasks without the objects physically in front of them. They find syllogisms very difficult.

FORMAL OPERATIONAL STAGE In the formal operational stage children become capable of formal reasoning. Formal operational thinkers can respond to the form of arguments and syllogisms, and they can devise and test hypotheses. Piaget took this to mean that a child had entered a new stage of adult logic, where abstract reasoning was possible. As well as systematic abstract reasoning, use of formal operations permits the development of a system of values and ideals, and an appreciation of philosophical issues.

The Idea Today

IT IS WIDELY AGREED THAT SOME OF PIAGET'S IDEAS ARE CORRECT, FOR EXAMPLE THAT there are fundamental differences in the ways children and adults think. There is also some support for Piaget's idea of agency, that we are active in seeking out knowledge and constructing our mental representation of the world (see Niaz and Caraucan, 1998 for a review). Interestingly, whilst Piaget saw motivation as leading to learning, Bandura (1989) has suggested the opposite relationship – self-efficacy theory, in which successful learning increases motivation. In a review of the relationship between motivation and learning, Andreani (1995) has concluded that both views are partially correct and that learning and motivation each influence the other.

Modern variations on Piaget's tests of children's thinking have produced mixed results. Baillargeon and DeVos (1991) developed an alternative method for assessing object permanence. When 3-month-old infants were shown an 'impossible scene', in which carrots were passed behind a screen with a window through which they should have been visible but were not, the infants spent significantly longer looking at the carrots than in a 'possible' control condition. This suggests that very young children have an understanding of object permanence. Li et al. (1999) tested 486 primary school children in China on the classic liquid conservation task. In line with Piaget's theory, the percentage of children getting the answer correct increased with age. However, the researchers also found significant variations from one school to another, schools with a good academic reputation achieving better results. This suggests that individual differences in cognitive development are related to education as well as brain maturation. Modern tests of formal thinking have suggested that Piaget was over-optimistic in suggesting that all or most people acquire the ability to think formally in their teens. In one recent study Bradmetz (1999) followed 62 French children up to 15 years, testing them on a number of formal reasoning tasks. At 15 only one of the 62 was reliably capable of formal reasoning tasks.

An important limitation of Piaget's theory is his lack of attention to the role of instruction by adults and other children in learning. A contemporary of Piaget, L.S. Vygotsky, addressed this by proposing that children acquire from adults and older children a 'mental toolkit' with which they understand the world. Contemporary research seems to favour Vygotsky's position. For example, in the study by Li et al. discussed above children from better schools did better in conservation tasks, suggesting that the quality of instruction has an impact on cognitive development.

## Current status of the idea

A small volume of research is still generated based on Piaget's ideas, and his theory can therefore be said to be of current as well as historical interest. Certainly his work has important practical applications in education but Piaget no longer dominates the field of cognitive-developmental psychology. Rival approaches include that of Vygotsky, who emphasises the role of instruction from others in development, and the *innatist modular* approach, which emphasises the activation of particular neural systems at different ages (as opposed to the individual) as an agent of learning. As well as this range of *domain-general* theories (i.e. theories that aim to explain all cognitive development) there are now *domain-specific* approaches to cognitive development, which just aim to explain particular mental functions. For example, much research is currently being undertaken into the development of *theory of mind* (children's understanding of the emotions and motives of others; discussed on p.157). This provides an alternative explanation for the development of a child's ability to see other perspectives in contrast to Piaget's idea of egocentrism.

THE MAJOR APPLICATION OF PIAGET'S IDEAS HAS BEEN IN EDUCATION. PIAGET'S approach suggests that children learn best when allowed to construct their own schemas, and that the teacher's task is not to lecture but to set up situations where students can discover ideas for themselves (as happens when they are given Internet search tasks). This approach, sometimes called *child-centred learning*, has been extensively introduced in the last 30 years, but research comparing traditional and child-centred methods shows no consistent advantage for either approach, and cooperative learning (as proposed by Vygotsky) has been shown to be more effective than either, at least in some situations. For example, Mevarech et al. (1991) compared the rates of learning of students who worked alone or shared a computer. Those sharing the computer did significantly better, supporting Vygotsky's view over that of Piaget. Piagetian theory also has implications on what students are taught at school.

The development of the National Curriculum was influenced by Piaget's theory: the Primary Curriculum begins with ideas appropriate to preoperational thinking and progresses to tasks requiring concrete operational thought. The secondary curriculum includes ideas and tasks that require formal reasoning.

 **Further Reading**

JARVIS, M. (2001) *Angles on child psychology*. Cheltenham, Nelson-Thornes.

PHILLIPS, J.L. (1975) *The origins of intellect: Piaget's theory*. San Francisco, Freeman.

SMITH, P.K., COWIE, H. AND BLADES, M. (1998) *Understanding children's development*. Oxford, Blackwell.

# Reconstructive
# memory

❦

## The Idea

**M**OST LAY-PEOPLE BELIEVE THAT OUR MEMORY OPERATES IN THE SAME WAY AS A VIDEO recorder; that we keep in some form a complete, sequential record of everything that has happened to us. However, psychologists tend to believe instead that memory involves an active process of *reconstruction*: when we try to recall an event, we actively piece it together using a range of information. Although Freud (1899) had previously identified the distorting effect of emotional factors on memories of childhood events, the study of the cognitive processes in recon-structive memory really began with the work of Frederick Bartlett. Bartlett (1932) described memory as 'an imaginative recon-struction' of past events, influenced by our attitudes and our responses to those events at the time they occurred. Many of Bartlett's ideas are borne out by modern research and have important practical applications in the legal system.

- ❀ Serial reproduction and repeated reproduction studies
- ❀ Schemas and the search for meaning
- ❀ Stereotyping and confirmation bias
- ❀ Eyewitness testimony and the reconstruction of crimes

## Serial reproduction and repeated reproduction studies

BARTLETT developed the *serial reproduction* method of studying reconstructive memory. Serial reproduction is rather like the children's game of 'Chinese whispers': one person tells another a story and they tell it to a third person, who in turn tells it to a fourth and so on. The idea of serial reproduction is that it can be used to replicate under controlled conditions the process in which information is passed from one person to another in real life. Bartlett famously used the Native American story, 'The War of the Ghosts' in serial reproduction studies because it was unfamiliar and different in cultural origins to the participants.

> One night two men from Edulac went down the river to hunt seals, and while they were there it became foggy and calm. Then they heard war-cries, and they thought; 'maybe this is a war-party.' They escaped to the shore, and hid behind a log. Now canoes came up, and they heard the noise of paddles and saw one canoe coming up to them. There were five men in the canoe and they said: 'What do you think? We wish to take you along. We are going up the river to make war on the people.'... So one of the young men went and the other returned home... the young man went ashore to his house and made a fire. And he told everybody and said: 'behold I accompanied the ghosts and went to fight. Many of our fellows were killed and many of those who attacked us were killed.'... When the sun rose he fell down. Something black came out of his mouth. His face became contorted. The people jumped up and cried. He was dead.

An edited version of 'The War of the Ghosts'

Bartlett found that once it had been reproduced through a sequence of half a dozen people the story became distorted in distinctive ways. It became shorter, on average to 55% of its original length. The details that were left out tended to be those specific to Native American culture. Thus the story came to resemble an English story. Bartlett also used stories like The War of the Ghosts in his *repeated reproduction* procedure. In repeated reproduction the same participant retells the story on a number of occasions. Bartlett found that, as in the serial reproduction method, the story became shorter and more anglicised.

## Schemas and the search for meaning

BARTLETT (1932) proposed that the reason for the distortions of stories like The War of the Ghosts in serial and repeated reproduction was the fact that remembering involves a *search for meaning* – an effort to make events coherent and logical. Because of its different cultural origins, English participants tended not to see the story as logical in its original form. They therefore distorted it during the process of remembering to make it make more sense to them. We can only reconstruct memories in this way if we have a fixed understanding of the world. Bartlett proposed that our world knowledge is stored in units of memory called *schemas*. We each have a schema for every aspect of our world. When we reconstruct memories we activate the relevant schemas and make use of the information in them. For example, when trying to recall The War of the Ghosts we might make use of our ghost-schema, war-schema and death-schema. The reason that Bartlett's participants distorted the story in reproduction is that, having searched their relevant schemas when remembering the story, they eliminated information that did not fit into their understanding of ghosts, war, etc.

## Stereotyping and confirmation bias

ONE way of describing the effect of reproduction on stories like The War of the Ghosts is to say that versions of the story became increasingly *stereotyped*. By this we mean that they increasingly fitted in with the participants' preconceived ideas about what a story involving ghosts and war should be like. This stereotyping process also operates when we remember information about people. This was demonstrated in a serial reproduction study by Allport and Postman (1947). They showed White participants a picture in which a scruffy White man armed with a cutthroat razor was arguing with a Black man in a suit. Descriptions of the scene were passed on to other participants through serial reproduction. After a few reproductions the descriptions changed so that, for example the Black man was typically described as holding the razor. Presumably the participants held positive stereotypes of White people and negative stereotypes of Black people, so that when they accessed their 'Black-schema' and 'White-schema' the information they found there required that they distort the scene to make it logical to them. This distortion of memories to fit in with existing schemas is called *confirmation bias*, because it involves *bias* towards accepting an interpretation of remembered material that *confirms* our existing stereotypes.

## Eyewitness testimony and the reconstruction of crimes

IN a classic series of experiments in the 1970s Elizabeth Loftus applied the principle of reconstructive memory to understanding evidence given by eyewitnesses to crimes. She pointed out that one of the sources of information we use to reconstruct memories of events is how the questions we are asked are worded. This is called post-event information. Loftus noted that lawyers were expert in using misleading questions to distort witnesses' memories. In one study (Loftus and Palmer, 1974) participants watched a 30-second film in which two cars collided. They were asked to estimate the speed of the cars when the crash occurred, but in different conditions the question was phrased slightly differently – when the cars 'smashed,' 'collided,' 'bumped,' 'hit' or 'contacted.' The estimates of speed ranged from averages of 41 mph for 'smashed' to 32 mph for 'contacted.' In another study by Loftus (1975) participants watched a film of a car travelling through the countryside. In one condition they were asked how fast the car was going when it passed the white barn. There was in fact no barn, yet a week later 17% of the participants said there was. This demonstrates the ease with which new information can be added to people's memories after the event.

IN THE MAIN CONTEMPORARY RESEARCH HAS SUPPORTED THE PRINCIPLE OF RECONSTRUCtive memory. Sherman and Bessenoff (1999) have found new support for the stereotyping effect: they gave 93 college students biographical accounts of fictitious characters presented them with a set of behaviours and asked which had been included in the biographies. In keeping with the reconstructive memory hypothesis participants made a significant number of errors, attributing behaviours to the characters with which the target behaviours were most stereotypically associated. In the absence of an obvious stereotype for memory accounts to conform to there is much less distortion in serial and repeated reproduction. When Wynn and Logie (1998) asked first-year undergraduates to describe their first week at university on several occasions throughout their first year there was no decline in the accuracy of their reports.

Wright et al. (2000) provided new support for Loftus' principle that post-event information can distort memories. They set up an experiment where pairs of participants saw slightly different information (they were unaware of this), and were then asked together to recognise the information. The aim was to see whether the recognition of each participant was distorted by the influence of the other, who would of course not recognise the same information. Participants were individually shown 50 pictures of cars from *Auto Trader* (they were paired so that each pair saw 40 identical pictures but 10 different pairs). After doing a 20–minute filler task (i.e. a task not directly related to the experiment but designed to occupy the participants) each pair was shown 100 cars, including the 40 they had each seen and the 20 of which each participant had seen only 10. They were asked together to identify the pictures they had already seen. Recognition was accurate for the 40 cars that they had both seen, but much less so for the 10 remaining cars. This is an example of the *memory conformity effect*, in which people rely on each other's accounts of events as a source of information with which to reconstruct events. Carli (1999) demonstrated the related phenomenon of *hindsight bias*. In this study 135 undergraduates were given a story to read and asked to reproduce it. In one condition the story ended abruptly without a conclusion and in the other it ended with a rape scene. In the second condition participants of both sexes tended to distort the story more than in the first. These distortions tended to be consistent with the theme of rape – retellers tended to describe the rapist in more threatening terms than had been used in the original story. In a second part to the study 69 students reproduced a story ending in either rape or a proposal of marriage. In both cases participants distorted the story in line with the ending.

## Current status of the idea

THE idea that memory is a reconstructive process is widely accepted in psychology. Schemas are also widely accepted and there is a wealth of evidence to show that we both interpret new information and reconstruct past information in the light of our schemas. Perhaps most importantly the idea of reconstructive memory has proved invaluable in understanding inaccuracies in eyewitness testimony, particularly in understanding the effects of post-event information. Although there is little doubt about the reconstructive nature of memory or the practical applications of emphasising its reconstructive nature, this is not to say that reconstruction can answer all questions about remembering. One problem is that the whole idea of reconstruction is highly cognitive; it neglects the importance of other factors in remembering, for example the emotional. Understanding memory as a purely reconstructive process does not help us understand the impact of trauma, fantasy or the emotional significance of events on our ability to accurately remember them. Despite this limitation, reconstructive memory remains an important idea in psychology.

# The Idea in Action

THE MAJOR APPLICATION OF OUR UNDERSTANDING OF RECONSTRUCTIVE MEMORY remains in eyewitness testimony. Wright et al. (2000) have gathered some frightening statistics concerning the impact of inaccurate eyewitness testimony on the justice system: it remains the most common cause of wrongful conviction, and the vast majority of prisoners recently released following newly available DNA evidence were convicted on the evidence of eyewitnesses. From the available data Levi (1998) has estimated that up to 25% of eyewitness identifications of suspects are incorrect.

A phenomenon that has been the focus of much recent research has been the memory conformity effect. Reports of other witnesses are now recognised as an important aspect of post-event information. Following the Oklahoma bombing, for which Timothy McVeigh was executed by lethal injection in the summer of 2001, psychologists had the opportunity to study memory conformity. Memon and Wright (1999) identified incidents in the follow-up to the bombing. In one such instance a witness reported seeing McVeigh with a second man renting the truck that was used in the bombing. Although other witnesses had not reported this second man, following the publicity over 'John Doe 2', as he became known, they later came to believe that they had in fact seen him. Memory conformity has also been demonstrated in the laboratory. In an extension to the study, Wright et al. (2000) attempted to replicate the 'John Doe 2' phenomenon by setting up an experiment in which pairs of participants looked at a picture-story in which a woman stole men's wallets from a pool hall. In each pair, one participant saw pictures in which a man entered the pool hall with the thief; the other saw an identical sequence of pictures except that there was no male accomplice. They were asked to recount the story together then fill in a questionnaire individually. One of the questions asked whether the thief had an accomplice. About half the participants who had not seen pictures showing the accomplice conformed to their partner's account and reported an accomplice.

Much recent research has also focused on reconstruction in child witnesses, since Ceci and Bruck (1995) brought to light instances of distortion of children's memories by biased questioning by police and social workers regarding alleged sexual abuse. One such case was reported by Tavris and Wade (1997); that of Kelly Michaels, a primary school teacher who was jailed for 47 years for multiple counts of sexual abuse of children in her class. The conviction was overturned after five years because the interrogation techniques used with the children contained such severely biased questioning. In one recent experimental study Peterson et al. (1999) staged an accident in a craft lesson for 3–5-year-old pupils and interviewed them a week later about their memory of the event. It was found that children's memories were most inaccurate when they were asked yes/no questions, especially when the correct answer was 'no.' It appears that when young children hear of an aspect of the situation which they do not remember in questioning they tend to reconstruct the event incorporating this new information.

# Further Reading

GROSS, R. (2001) *Psychology*. London, Hodder and Stoughton.

JARVIS, M., RUSSELL, J., FLANAGAN, C. AND DOLAN, L. (2000) *Angles on psychology*. Cheltenham, Nelson Thornes.

MEMON, A., VRIJ, A. AND BULL, R. (1998) *Psychology and law*. London, McGraw-Hill.

TAVRIS, C. AND WADE, C. (1997) *Psychology in perspective*. New York, Longman.

# *Social constructionism*

❧

## The Idea

THE BIRTH OF SOCIAL CONSTRUCTIONISM AS A PSYCHOLOGICAL APPROACH CAME WITH
the publication of a paper by Gergens (1973), in which he argued that all psychological research is specific to a culture and a historical period, and that there is no point
in looking for universal rules about human nature because society is constantly
changing. This was a highly radical view at the time because psychologists tended to
believe in the *positivist* view of knowledge, the idea that there is a single truth and that
the job of a scientist is to make unbiased observations of the world and discover this
truth. Gergens argued that there is no way of making unbiased observations because
we are limited by our cultural beliefs. There are now a number of psychological
approaches that fall under the umbrella term of 'social constructionist,' but they all
share the assumption that there is no single version of the 'truth' or the possibility of
unbiased observation. They also share an emphasis on the ways in which we construct
a view of the world by the ways in which we use language.

❀ The importance of culture and language

❀ The politics of language

❀ Discourse and discourse analysis

❀ Discourse and reality

❀ Critical psychology

## The importance of culture and language

THE way we understand the world is determined by our culture. Because we find it very difficult to step aside from our cultural beliefs and practices we are not able to make objective and unbiased observations of people. Rather than a world of 'facts' to be discovered, social constructionists see a world of *social constructs*. Psychological concepts like childhood, intelligence and mental illness are said to be social constructs because they are not fixed in reality, but are whatever we as a culture agree them to be. Language is extremely important to social constructionists, because the type of language we use to describe something influences our perception of it. An example of a social construct is 'intelligence.' Although we certainly have cognitive abilities, and although some people are better at some cognitive tasks than others, this does not mean that what we usually call intelligence truly exists. A social constructionist might argue that the idea of intelligence as a *thing* that can be measured, and of which one person can have more of than another, is simply a social construct.

## The politics of language

UNLIKE other branches of psychology, social constructionists are often intentionally political. Whereas most psychologists would see their work as discovering scientific facts, social constructionists prefer to see their role as to uncover and challenge social inequality and injustice. Social constructionist explanations of psychological phenomena focus on the social and historical reasons why ideas might have emerged, with particular regard to power relationships between groups. An example of this social inequality is between genders. Traditional assumptions about gender include the idea of women as submissive, passive and caring. A social constructionist would probably say that femininity has been constructed in this way, because it means that women will be able to serve the needs of men without challenging the male-dominated society. Similarly, constructs like intelligence can be said to serve the interests of the White middle classes. IQ tests tend to define this group as 'more intelligent' than other people, by virtue of the fact that they tend to score more highly on standard IQ tests (which are of course biased towards the knowledge and skills of White middle-class people). Thus White middle-class Americans and Europeans strengthen their own power relative to other groups in society.

## Discourse and discourse analysis

A central idea in social constructionism is that we construct meanings through our use of language, or *discourse*. The term 'discourse' literally means anything that people say or otherwise communicate, for example in writing or music. There can be several alternative discourses around a single subject, each of which gives that subject a different meaning. This is similar to Moscovici's idea that there can be several social representations of a single subject (see p.145 for a discussion). The difference, however, is that the emphasis in social representations theory is on the nature of the idea as it exists in the mind of the individual and the emphasis in discourse analysis is on the language used in communication. Therefore the type of research conducted by discourse analysts tends to be rather different from that carried out by social representations researchers.

The major research method of social constructionism is called *discourse analysis*. By looking at discourse in the form of conversation, writing and music, discourse analysts can 'unpack' some of the assumptions we have about the world. This is sometimes called *deconstruction* of the material. Discourse analysis is a qualitative research method. It does not generate numbers but describes in detail the possible hidden meanings present in discourse. For example, analyses of some love-songs have revealed hidden assumptions about relationships, and analyses of items such as cereal packets have revealed assumptions about family life. According to social constructionists it is important to reveal these hidden meanings because we construct our view of the world during discourse. When we regularly encounter a stereotyped account of something like family life in discourse, we start to see alternative family structures such as those with gay parents as abnormal.

## Discourse and reality

IF discourse analysis allows us to see different versions of reality, we are left with an awkward question. Is there really such a thing as reality? There is a term in psychology for 'real' or 'true' reality, unaffected by social, cultural or historical factors. We call this the *veridical*. However, whether the veridical really exists and whether people will ever be able to access it are controversies within social constructionism. The most extreme constructionists would deny that there is any reality at all, and say that we construct the world entirely through discourse. Most social constructionists, however, consider the idea that there is *no* reality extreme, and believe that there *is* reality but that our perceptions of it are inevitably distorted by language and culture.

## Critical psychology

SOME social constructionists, known as *critical psychologists*, have focused their efforts on deconstructing other branches of psychology. We have already seen some critical psychology in action when we looked at the psychological construct of 'intelligence.' Psychologists have been forced to step back and reconsider many such concepts as a result of the work of social constructionists. One of the most controversial social constructs in psychology is 'race.' We use the term *race* rather like we do the word 'species' to mean a distinct group but, unlike *species*, which has a precise scientific definition, the term 'race' is scientifically meaningless. There is far more variation, both genetic and behavioural, between the members of any 'race' than there is between any two 'races', and to classify people as different on the basis of their 'race' is actually just as arbitrary as dividing the world into people with blue or brown eyes, or short and tall people. By using the term 'race' we are *socially constructing* a way of classifying people that exaggerates differences between different groups and minimises similarities. Critical psychologists have shown that psychological research that looks at so-called racial differences is constructing a false distinction between different human societies.

D ISCOURSE ANALYSIS HAS NOW BEEN CARRIED OUT ON A WIDE VARIETY OF SUBJECTS AND in many media. Most studies are of discourse already in the public domain but a few have been set up artificially – such as that of Doherty and Anderson (1998). They gave pairs of participants a description of a hypothetical rape and recorded their conversations. The content of these conversations was then 'unpacked'. The participants focused on the dangers of being out alone at night and, through phrases like 'taking a shortcut' and 'it's too dangerous' they constructed a view of the event in which responsibility was attributed to the victim. The researchers suggested that this construction of rape as the result of foolishness of the part of the victim contributes to the phenomenon of *secondary victimisation*, in which victims of rape suffer the additional problem of blame.

Most discourse analyses are of naturally occurring rather than set-up discourse. A very wide range of material can be subject to discourse analysis. Burns (1998) deconstructed the song 'Barbie Girl' which reached no. 1 in the UK singles chart in 1997 and revealed some worrying assumptions about male–female relationships. By saying 'I'm a blonde bimbo girl in a fantasy world' and 'your dolly' Barbie is constructing herself – and by extension all women in relationships with men – as less than human and the property of her partner. She offers sexual services 'you can touch, you can play' provided Ken offers commitment in return ('if you say I'm always yours'). Songs like this may, according to a social constructionist approach, perpetuate this sad and stereotypical construction of what men and women want from relationships.

Psychology textbooks have been deconstructed in a similar fashion. Concerned about the coverage of psychoanalysis (see p.64) in general psychology texts, Jarvis (2000) deconstructed the coverage of Freud and psychoanalysis in a leading American undergraduate textbook, and found numerous examples of the ways in which language can be used to bias a reader against a theory. For example the sentence 'Although Freud's current influence in psychological science is slight, his notoriety continues to colour people's perceptions of psychology, and his influence lingers in literary interpretation, psychiatry and pop-psychology' may be unpacked in a number of ways. Freud is being associated here with three out-groups: a rival discipline (psychiatry), an inferior discipline (pop-psychology) and an irrelevant discipline (literary interpretation). The terms 'notoriety' and 'lingers' are also significant in constructing Freud as an unwelcome and perhaps even criminal influence on psychology. The term 'psychological science' (not used elsewhere in the book) further serves to remind the reader that psychology is a science, and that Freud does not live up to the standards of science.

## Current status of the idea

SOCIAL constructionism has grown enormously in importance in recent years, and discourse analysis is now a major research method. Many psychologists have found it helpful to step back from their traditional assumptions about reality, science and psychology, as we are forced to do by critical psychology, but others point to the sheer waste of abandoning more traditional research. To many psychologists, debating the nature of reality is self-indulgent and a waste of time. That said, there are clearly practical applications of social constructionism. It is difficult therefore to say whether the approach will continue to grow in importance or turn out to have been a brief trend.

# The Idea in Action

THE MAJOR APPLICATION OF SOCIAL CONSTRUCTIONISM HAS BEEN IN IDENTIFYING AND eliminating language that perpetuates inequality and discrimination. Writers in the social sciences now stick to a code of conduct that bans the use of sexist and racist language. Sexist language includes terms like 'spokesman' because this constructs men as able or fit to speak for others but women as unable or unfit to do so. Words like 'tribe' are considered racist, because the term can refer both to humans and animals, but when referring to humans is always used to refer to Black rather than White people. It thus constructs Black people as closer to animals than to White people (Howitt and Owusu-Bempah, 1994). If the social constructionists are correct that we construct our representation of the world through language, then eliminating words like 'spokesman' and 'tribe' should help reduce racism and sexism.

Racism can be embedded in discourse in other ways. An analysis of the 1987 Conservative Party manifesto by Condor (1988, cited in Wetherall, 1997) revealed that the subheading 'race' appeared next to 'the fight against crime and 'tackling drug abuse' under a general heading of 'Freedom, law and responsibility'. This constructs minority ethnic groups as a problem equivalent to, and perhaps even associated with, crime and drugs.

Discourse analysis has also helped us to uncover inequalities in the mental health system. Stowell-Smith and McKeown (1999) analysed the psychiatric reports of Black and White men admitted to psychiatric hospitals with a diagnosis of psychopathy. They found that the psychiatrists' accounts of White patients tended to focus on their emotional state and fantasies. Direct links were made between traumatic childhood events and adult mental states. No such links were made in the reports of Black psychopaths and there were very few references to the emotional state of the patients before offending. What was more apparent in the reports on black patients was an emphasis on an escalating cycle of dangerous behaviour. This disparity in the content of psychiatric reports constructs the White patients as victims of their circumstances, but the Black patients as unemotional and inherently dangerous.

# Further Reading

BURR, V. (1995) *An introduction to social constructionism*. London, Routledge.

GROSS, R., HUMPHREYS, P. AND PETKOVA, B. (1997) *Challenges in psychology*. London, Hodder and Stoughton.

PARKER, I. (1998) (ed.) *Social constructionism, discourse and realism*. London, Sage.

# Social identity theory

❖

## The Idea

E ARLY ATTEMPTS TO EXPLAIN RELATIONS BETWEEN GROUPS FOCUSED ON PERSONALITY
differences in people who showed extreme attitudes towards those identifiably
different from themselves. By the 1970s there was a shift in emphasis towards studying
the *social processes* involved in the interactions between members of groups. Before
Tajfel's work, social psychologists had identified conflict between groups as being due
to competition for resources. Tajfel's great contribution was to point out that problems
in relations between groups could be understood by reference to a set of social
processes that operated even when groups were not in direct competition. Tajfel's ideas
are best known for helping us understand negative prejudices, in which members of
one group (for example an ethnic, religious, political or sexually oriented group) adopt
extreme and harsh attitudes towards members of groups other than their own.
However, social identity theory is broader than merely an explanation for prejudice,
and has been used to explain interactions between groups in a number of contexts, for
example how different teams cooperate in the workplace.

- ❀ Minimal group studies
- ❀ Social categorisation
- ❀ Social identification
- ❀ Social comparison and self-esteem

## Minimal group studies

PREVIOUS studies had demonstrated clearly that when two groups are established as being in competition with one another, each group tends to display negative prejudice towards the other. The aim of the minimal group studies was to establish groups that were readily identifiable as being different from one another, but who could not be perceived as in competition. Tajfel (1970) conducted studies using 14–15-year-old British schoolboys. In one of the studies participants were told that the researchers were investigating vision. They were shown clusters of dots and asked to estimate the number of dots. They were then split into two groups and told that one group had underestimated whilst the other had overestimated the number of dots. Actually they were divided at random. Pairs of participants, two 'overestimators,' two 'underestimators' or one of each, were then selected. The other participants were asked to give points to the members of each pair, based on the accuracy of their estimates. The boys favoured the members of the pairs that had been in their group – 'underestimators' allocated more points to 'underestimators' and 'overestimators' favoured 'overestimators.' Even when group membership was based on something so irrelevant as the tendency to under- or overestimate dots on a screen people showed a powerful in-group favouritism. Although there are now a number of ways of investigating social identity in real-world situations minimal group designs remain a popular research method.

## Social categorisation

TAJFEL and Turner (1979) proposed that many types of group interactions, in particular prejudice, can be explained by our natural tendency to identify ourselves as part of a group, and then to classify other people as either within or outside that group. This means that we tend to make immediate judgements of people we encounter as either 'us' or 'them'. This is called *social categorisation*. Whatever group we identify ourselves as belonging to becomes the 'in-group' and any group we can identify as an alternative to the in-group is identified as an 'out-group.' We tend to favour members of the in-group over those of the out-group (this is called *in-group favouritism*). The precise nature of the groups we see ourselves as belonging to can vary widely according to our individual experience. We all tend to subscribe to categories involving gender, race and socio-economic group; others are particularly relevant to some people as a result of their culture or individual interests (many people, for example, categorise themselves as supporters of a particular football team). According to social identity theory, our tendency to think of ourselves as belonging to one or more groups is a fundamental part of human nature, and takes place irrespective of whether we are in competition with the out-group or whether we have good relations with individuals belonging to the out-group.

## Social identification

SOME psychologists believe that social categorisation is sufficient to explain some aspects of intergroup interaction such as prejudice. This view is known as *social categorisation theory*. Social identity theory differs from social categorisation theory by emphasising the importance of *social identification*. Once we have categorised ourselves as part of a group we adopt the identity of this group and behave as we believe members of the group act, possibly adopting visual symbols of membership. If, for example, you have categorised yourself as a football supporter, the chances are you will adopt the identity of a supporter and begin to act in the ways you believe football supporters act. You might wear a scarf in your team's colours and go to watch matches. You are likely to seek out information that is particularly salient to supporters, for example the scores of recent matches and the current league position of your team. There is an emotional significance to identification with a group, and our self-esteem becomes bound up with our group membership. People can thus experience fierce pride in the groups with which they identify.

## Social comparison and self-esteem

ONCE we have categorised ourselves as part of a group and identified emotionally with that group, we have a strong tendency to compare 'our' group with other groups. If an individual's self-esteem is to be maintained then their group needs to compare favourably to others. This is critical to understanding hostility between groups, because once two groups identify themselves as rivals they may be forced to compete if the members are to maintain their self-esteem. To stick with the example of football teams, if your identity is tied up intimately with being a supporter then it can be hard to maintain self-esteem if your team is continually being beaten by other teams. However, groups of football supporters develop identities based on other criteria than winning teams. For example crews of football hooligans establish reputations for fighting ability quite independent of the team they are associated with. Other groups of supporters maintain their self-esteem by being particularly loyal or more good-natured than fans of other teams.

CONTEMPORARY RESEARCH HAS EXTENDED OUR KNOWLEDGE OF SOCIAL IDENTITY phenomena. The original minimal group experiments suggested that the mere existence of in-groups and out-groups is sufficient to produce in-group favouritism. However, recent studies have questioned this. Dobbs and Crano (2001) conducted a minimal group study with different conditions, some of which involved having to explain *why* fewer points were allocated to out-group members. In the condition where the person allocating the points was in the majority group and had to justify their decision, there was much less in-group favouritism than in the control condition. However, when the allocator was in the minority and had to justify discriminating against the majority out-group, in-group favouritism increased. This suggests that in-group favouritism is actually a more complex business than indicated by the original studies.

Two important questions concern the age from which children will show in-group favouritism and the extent to which in-group favouritism overrides status differences between groups. To test both these questions Nesdale and Flesser (2001) performed a minimal group study, randomly assigning children aged 5–8 to teams, telling them that the teams were of different drawing ability. Some children were given the opportunity to change to a different group. The children were asked to rate their liking for their own and other groups. As expected, they showed a bias towards their own group, rating them more highly than others of the same 'ability'. They were, however, sensitive to the status of their group and were more likely to opt to move if offered a place in a higher-status group. Studies like this have enhanced our understanding of social identity because they show that although in-group favouritism exists, even in children as young as 5 years, it is a limited effect and where people can boost their self-esteem by moving to a higher-status group they sometimes do so.

A recent survey of 15–18-year-old adolescents (Poppe and Linssen, 1999) found a similar mixture of in-group favouritism and assessment of other groups based on other factors. They questioned 1000 adolescents from Russia, Bulgaria, Belarus, Hungary, Poland and the Czech republic concerning their beliefs about the morality and competence of people from a range of European countries. As expected, the young people rated their own country as more moral and competent than other Eastern European countries. They also displayed stereotyped views of Western Europeans – the English were rated as the most moral people in Europe and the Germans as the most competent. Studies like this show that whilst in-group favouritism is one factor affecting people's responses to other groups, there are other important factors, like group stereotypes.

## Current status of the idea

THERE is large volume of contemporary research into social identity, involving minimal group experiments, simulations of real-life group situations, the analysis of in- and out-group media representations of events and survey studies. Despite the artificial nature of the minimal group studies, social identity theory has numerous practical applications and has proved to be reasonably effective for understanding social behaviour in real-life situations. This is not to say, however, that social identity theory is without its critics. One problem is its limited ability to explain individual differences in affiliation to groups. Whilst it is true that people have a general tendency to identify with groups and to display in-group favouritism there are variations in just how prone we are to this. For example, highly competitive people show greater in-group favouritism than more cooperative individuals (Platow et al., 1990). Social identity theory is thus an important (although incomplete) way of understanding group behaviour.

The Idea in Action

SOCIAL IDENTITY THEORY IS BEST KNOWN AS AN EXPLANATION OF PREJUDICE, AND IT CAN be applied to understanding popular strategies for reducing prejudice. Thus *collective action* (Kelly and Breinlinger, 1996), in which minority groups combine forces and take action against discrimination, can be seen as working because of the strengthening of the in-group identity. The *common in-group identity model* (Gaertner, 1993) works on precisely the opposite principle, by breaking down the boundaries between in-groups and out-groups. Hergovich and Olbrich (1996) have gone further and designed a computer simulation of intergroup conflict based partly on social identity theory research. The program was given data for the backgrounds to 49 conflicts involving Britain, USA and the former Soviet Union, and it often correctly predicted when armed conflict took place most (87.5% of the time for USA, 70% for the Soviet Union and 62.5% for Britain). This is highly significant as it means that social identity theory can help us predict wars.

Of course, social identity theory has a variety of other applications. One of these is in advertising. Using a questionnaire, Madrigal (2000) tested the relationship between identification of sports fans with their team and the likelihood of their buying products from the sponsor of that team. The more strongly fans identified with their team the more likely they were to buy products. This has clear applications for sponsors, in choosing teams that have the most involved and loyal fans rather than the most successful teams. Politicians can also make use of social identity phenomena. In a study by Matthews and Dietz-Uhler (1998) students with different political affiliations evaluated the advertisements of their own (the in-group) and other parties (the out-groups). The most positively evaluated adverts were those from their own party that were positive towards the party. However, adverts from the participants' own party that were negative towards the party were even more disliked than adverts negative to the party produced by a rival party. This suggests that it is essential that advertisements from political parties do not contain any ambiguous or overly modest messages, as these will have a negative impact on their own supporters.

Social identity theory is also important in understanding the behaviour of people within organisations. Worchel et al. (1998) investigated ways in which social identity could be used to improve the performance of work groups. They set up a number of experimental situations involving groups of students working together on tasks. Productivity was higher when the groups anticipated working together in the future, when they shared a uniform and when they shared a reward for group productivity rather than receiving individual rewards. What these three variables have in common is that they lead to greater identification with the work group.

 Further Reading

HAYES, N. (2000) *Foundations of psychology*. London, ITP.

WETHERALL, M. (ed.) (1997) *Identities, groups and social issues*. Milton Keynes, Open University Press.

# Social representations theory

SOCIAL REPRESENTATIONS THEORY IS A SOCIAL THEORY OF KNOWLEDGE. ITS ROOTS LIE in sociological theory (Farr, 1998). The functionalist sociologist Emil Durkheim proposed that people develop a shared understanding of reality, which effectively becomes the 'truth' for those that share this interpretation. Durkheim was interested primarily in shared understandings of reality in whole societies, but the French psychologist Serge Moscovici has applied the idea to understand the social influences that affect *individuals'* understanding of the world. Social representations are beliefs about the world, acquired from and shared by the members of a group.

 Social representations

 Individual and consensual beliefs

 Social identification

 Anchoring and objectification

## Social representations

WE can define a social representation as a belief shared with other members of a group about one aspect of the world. This sharing of beliefs helps us organise our view of the world, and allows us to communicate more effectively with other group members. Different groups can have very different social representations of the same idea. For example, everyone in Britain knows about foxhunting, but we might have very different social representations of it depending on whether we live in the town or country and according to our social and political views. One social representation of foxhunting is as a time-honoured traditional rural pastime that keeps the fox population under control and provides jobs and shared social activities for rural communities – a view associated with people who live in the country and those who hold more conservative political views. An alternative social representation of foxhunting, more commonly held in towns and amongst those with left-wing politics, is that it is a cruel and outdated pastime of the idle rich that serves no useful purpose. It is easy for people who fall into one of these camps to communicate on the subject with others in the same group because they share a social representation of foxhunting. However, foxhunting is currently proving a headache for politicians because it is extremely difficult for those with different social representations of the same subject to have any meaningful communication about it because they are effectively not talking about the same idea.

Social representations are acquired through interaction with other people. To stick with our foxhunting example, people living in rural communities that practice hunting will acquire their representation of foxhunting through hearing their families, friends and neighbours talk about it, and by reading the sort of publications normally read in those communities. By contrast, people outside hunting communities tend to hear a very different account in discussions and in the media.

## Individual and consensual beliefs

WE all have slightly different perceptions or representations of the world. This is self-evident as there is almost never complete agreement on issues within groups. An individual's social representations of the world are a mixture of *consensual* and *individual* beliefs. Consensual beliefs are those that are generally shared by members of a group, individual beliefs are influenced by consensual beliefs evaluated from the perspective of our own experience. As well as acquiring social representations by responding to consensual beliefs we contribute to them. Whenever we respond to a consensual belief, we modify it slightly in the mind of the person we are addressing, and this new representation is passed on. Thus social representations are constantly changing. However, social representations have two aspects, and only one of these is modified as it is passed on. *Peripheral elements* can be defined as those aspects of a social representation that vary between individuals with the same fundamental representation, and which are modified as they are passed between people. However, the *figurative nucleus* of a social representation is not negotiable. We can illustrate the distinction between the figurative nucleus of a representation and its peripheral elements by looking at the issue of people seeking political asylum in Britain. There is a popular social representation of asylum seekers as dishonest scroungers who are simply seeking a better standard of living than that available in their native country. The idea that allowing asylum seekers to settle in Britain is a bad thing forms a figurative nucleus of this social representation. However, amongst people who hold this representation, the extent to which violence against asylum seekers is justified is very much negotiable and in this there is a wide spectrum of individual belief. The issue of violence to asylum seekers can thus be said to be a peripheral element of the social representation.

## Social identification

WE respond differently to social representations that we receive from members of our in-group and members of out-groups (see p.141 for a more detailed discussion of in- and out-groups). There is a tendency for individual beliefs to be more strongly affected by the consensual beliefs of in-groups, particularly those with which we identify strongly. One of the aims of social representations theory was to explain the Holocaust, and Moscovici has pointed to the role of powerfully negative social representations of Jewish people amongst those who identified with the Nazi movement in allowing the Holocaust.

Social identification explains why people with particular social and political affiliations have a tendency to reach a consensus on issues that are not particularly connected to the core beliefs of their social or political ideology. For example, at the time of writing there is much debate about Britain joining the European currency, the Euro. Although there is nothing intrinsically left or right wing about sharing a currency with other countries the debate has become polarised along political lines, with more left-wing politicians favouring joining the Euro and right-wingers favouring keeping the Pound. From a social representations perspective, this is because people have identified with the political group that normally represents their views and taken on their representation of the issue.

## Anchoring and objectification

MOSCOVICI proposed that we form social representations by two processes, anchoring and objectification, which are both ways of making ideas easier to think about (Moscovici, 1977, 2000). *Anchoring* takes place when we set a new social representation in the context of something familiar, making it more familiar. A recent example of anchoring took place in the 2000 fuel protests, when protesters drew parallels between their action and that of marchers in the great depression of the 1930s. They even started a procession from Jarrow, in Newcastle, calling it the 'second Jarrow march' (the first having been made by starving people during the Depression). By anchoring their action in the familiar (and clearly justified) protests of the 1930s the protesters were establishing a social representation of extreme but justified action.

*Objectification* takes place when we make abstract ideas concrete. Moscovici identified two ways in which objectification takes place: personification and figuration.

- *Personification* involves associating an idea with a particular person. Thus when we speak of a 'free market economy' or 'union bashing', we often think in terms of *Thatcherism*; when we think about the importance of psychodynamics in psychology we think about adopting a *Freudian* perspective. Although it is easier to think of complex ideas when we can 'hang' them on to a particular individual, personification distorts the meaning of the idea we are representing – it is, for example, quite possible to subscribe to some of Margaret Thatcher's or Sigmund Freud's ideas but not others, yet once we label someone a Thatcherite or Freudian we quickly lose sight of this and form a stereotyped representation of them.

- A similar problem arises when we use *figuration*. Figuration involves 'hanging' ideas onto mental images and metaphors. For example, Moscovici and Hewstone (1983) found a consensual belief amongst participants that the left and right halves of the human brain had entirely different functions, that personality could be explained by left or right brain dominance – and that in fact social problems could be explained by society's bias towards left-brain dominant people. In reality the split-brain research on which this understanding is based merely showed that the left brain plays a greater role in language and the right brain in spatial tasks like drawing. By using the metaphor of left and right brain dominance as a figurative way to understand personality, people formed a misleading consensual belief about the brain, personality and social issues.

The Idea Today

CONTEMPORARY RESEARCH HAS SUPPORTED THE EXISTENCE OF PROCESSES LIKE objectification in the way people come to understand the world, particularly when the layperson needs to understand scientific ideas. A recent study by Bangerter (2000) used a serial reproduction method to investigate people's understanding of conception. Serial reproduction involves people passing on information to the next one in a line. In this case the information passed down the line was from a textbook account of the process of conception and took place over a period of 2 weeks. The version of conception passed on at each stage was recorded and analysed. Two types of change were noted as the account of conception was passed on. Firstly, accounts of the sperm and egg became progressively less abstract and more centred on the human-like behaviour of the sperm and egg (personification). Secondly the accounts of the egg and sperm became more gender-stereotyped, with the sperm behaving a forceful, aggressive (masculine) manner and the egg becoming more passive (feminine).

An interesting development in social representations theory in the last few years has been in its relationship with another social psychological theory, that of *social impact* (Latane, 1981) Latane's law of social impact suggests that the extent to which other people influence an individual depends on their numbers, closeness and importance. Schaller and Latane (1996) proposed that social impact could complement social representations theory by explaining how and when people will absorb social representations from others. Evidence to support this idea comes from Huguet et al. (1998): they had 10 groups of 24 students exchange messages regarding 6 social issues over a period of 1–2 weeks and found that, as would be expected according to social impact theory, people who had interacted the most had the most similar views.

Extensive discussion of issues has helped to develop similar social representations even when the people involved start out having directly opposing views. Echebarria et al. (1996) gave 100 people a questionnaire designed to assess their social representation of smoking. They placed them in discussion groups of 10 people, each group containing people with opposing views. After discussions, the representations of the group members were assessed again, and their views had become much less extreme. However, this dilution of social representations does not always occur where different groups are merged. For example, when an immigrant community becomes acculturated into the mainstream, keeping distinctive social representations can be a powerful means of maintaining a distinctive cultural identity. Thus when Jovchelovitch and Gervais (1999) examined the social representations of health and illness amongst Chinese communities in Britain by a series of interviews and focus groups, they found that respondents had tended to maintain their representation of health and illness in terms of 'balance' and 'harmony' even though they varied in the extent to which they had supplemented these beliefs with Western medical ideas.

## Current status of the idea

SOCIAL representations theory, in conjunction with social identity theory, underlies much of the work in social psychology currently being undertaken in Britain and the rest of Europe. As we have seen, examining social representations enhances our understanding of a range of social processes ranging from acculturation of immigrant communities to the ways in which the layperson takes on board scientific ideas. It also has clear practical applications in tackling unhealthy behaviours and prejudice. In spite of these strengths social representations theory has not been accepted in the same way in the USA. One critic (Jahoda, 1988) has described it as 'fuzzy' and criticised the difficulty in generating testable predictions that might validate the approach.

SOCIAL REPRESENTATIONS THEORY HAS BEEN USED IN A NUMBER OF APPLIED SETTINGS, IN particular health psychology. Social representations of health-related behaviour such as smoking and drinking have helped us understand people's motives in adopting unhealthy behaviours. In a survey study Lloyd et al. (1997) examined the social representations of smoking of 125 girls aged 11–16. Both smokers and non-smokers placed an emphasis on being cool, grown-up and popular. However, the smokers had social representations of smoking that included these qualities whereas non-smokers did not. This suggests that efforts to reduce smoking in teenagers should be targeted at changing social representations. Similar results have been found with regard to drinking. Demers et al. (1996) assessed the social representations of drinking and the frequency and volume of drinking of 2000 Canadian drinkers. There was a strong relationship between social representations of drinking and both the volume consumed and the frequency of drinking. The researchers calculated that social representations of drinking accounted for about a third of the variance between individuals' drinking habits.

Social representations theory has other applications within health psychology. Studies have found that health workers spend less time with AIDS patients than with others with comparable care needs (Hunter and Ross, 1991). This can be understood using a social representations approach. Mannetti and Pierro (1994) assessed the social representations of AIDS held by 345 Italian healthcare workers by asking them to write the first thing that came to their minds when thinking of AIDS and its sufferers. Positive or negative attitudes to AIDS patients were not associated with levels of scientific understanding of AIDS, but they were associated with social representations. Negative attitudes to patients were associated with particular social representations. People whose representations focused on the transmission of HIV rather than its effects, on the dangers to the other people posed by people carrying HIV rather than the ways in which this danger has been exaggerated, and on their personal rather than medical response tended to have more negative attitudes to patients. Studies like this suggest that effective strategies to tackle prejudices, for example against AIDS patients, should focus on social representations.

 **Further Reading**

HAYES, N. (2000) *Foundations of psychology*. London, ITP.

MCILVEEN, R. AND GROSS, R. (1998) *Social psychology*. London, Hodder and Stoughton.

MOSCOVICI, S. (2000) (ed) *Social representations*. Cambridge, Polity.

# *Stroop effect*

❋

## The Idea

P EOPLE ARE SURPRISINGLY SKILLED AT MULTI-TASKING – DOING MORE THAN ONE THING at once. We seem to be much better at it when the tasks are quite different (such as walking and talking) than when they are similar (such as tapping out one rhythm while singing another). Clearly some types of tasks interfere more with one another than others. In an attempt to investigate how interference occurs between two competing responses (colour naming and colour-word reading), J. Ridley Stroop conducted a series of elegant experimental studies.

❋ The Stroop effect

❋ The effects of training and gender

❋ Explaining the Stroop effect

❋ Variations on the Stroop task

## The Stroop effect

STROOP (1935) compared the relative effect of colour presence on the reading and naming of coloured stimuli. A list of words that were names of colours (red, blue, green, brown and purple) was prepared in two formats: in one, all the words were printed in black; in the other, the words appeared in every colour except their own (for instance, the word 'blue' was printed in red, green, brown and purple). Two further versions consisted of the same order of colours but presented as either solid squares of colour or as swastikas (then a relatively meaningless shape that allowed some white to show through the pattern as it would in the letters of a word, thereby matching the colour intensity with that of lettering).

The difference in time taken to read the word list printed in black and in colours is a measure of the interference of colour stimuli upon the reading of words (a semantic task). The difference in time taken to name colours when presented as colour-words or as squares (or swastikas) is a measure of the interference of conflicting word stimuli upon colour naming (a physical task). The interference of conflicting *colour stimuli* upon the time to read 100 words was only slight, causing an increase of only 2.3 seconds (5.6%) over the time taken to read the list in black. However, the interference of conflicting *word stimuli* on the time to name 100 colours caused a 74.3% increase compared to the time for naming coloured squares.

## The effects of training and gender

STROOP concluded that, since the effect of interference caused by the presence of words, but not colours, was significant, the associations formed between word stimuli and the reading response were stronger than those formed between coloured stimuli and the naming response. He suggested that these differences were the product of differences in training as he had previously shown that training affected the interference response. Word stimuli are associated only with reading whereas colours many be associated with actions such as admiring (a red rose), reaching for (a ripe tomato) or avoiding (a hot coal) as well as naming. Furthermore, Stroop found gender differences in the responses of his participants (in favour of females). Such differences had, in previous studies, been attributed to the greater verbal facility in women but Stroop proposed that they might be the product of gender-specific differences in education: 'Education of colour is more intense for girls than for boys as observing, naming, and discussing colours relative to dress is much more common among girls than among boys' (Stroop, 1935). Stroop concludes that for girls the colour naming process might be a product of training.

## Explaining the Stroop effect

THE results described above rapidly became known as the *Stroop effect* and have generated a vast amount of research (MacLeod, 1991). The Stroop effect offers an opportunity for investigating cognitive conflict and the automatic processing of information. So, did Stroop's participants really attend to words more readily because reading is a more highly trained, automatic process that interferes with the less practised process of colour naming? Treisman and Fearnley (1969) investigated three possible explanations:

1 Automaticity of reading compared with naming.
2 Response competition due to interference during articulation.
3 Response competition due to the relative speed of the processes.

To test these possibilities, Treisman and Fearnley developed a new Stroop-type task in which participants were required to sort cards into sets on the basis of colour or word. The tasks could be varied such that matching was either within attribute (e.g. matching colour to colour) or across attribute (e.g. matching colour to word). As with the original task, these tests were compared across situations in which a *colour stimulus* appeared as a word or patch and a *word stimulus* appeared in black or coloured ink.

The ink colours and words were either matching (congruent) – for example, 'red' written in red ink – or non-matching (non-congruent) – for example, 'red' written in blue ink.

Treisman and Fearnley discovered that the word stimulus effect was absent – when words were the source of interference there was no effect on sorting time, which contradicted the effect predicted by Stroop's notion of reading as a more 'trained' response. Competition at the level of articulation could not explain the results, as differences still occurred despite the absence of a spoken response. Instead, the results supported the third explanation: in tests where matching occurred across attributes the processing of the two sources of information (word and colour) appeared to occur in parallel but at different speeds. The faster process (of reading) seemed to interfere with the slower process (of colour naming). However, subsequent research provided some evidence for the automaticity hypothesis as well (e.g. La Berge and Samuels 1974).

## Variations on the Stroop task

SIMILAR effects have been demonstrated using matching and non-matching stimuli such as letters (e.g. a large letter H composed of smaller Ss) (Eriksen and Eriksen, 1974) and with rows of digits (in which the numerical value of the digit is either equivalent to or different from the number of digits in the row (e.g. 333, 2222) (Flowers et al., 1979). In each case, the faster, semantic process seems to interfere with the slower, physical process. Further studies have been conducted with matching and non-matching tones (responding *low* to the word 'low' presented in a high or a low tone) and spatial locations (responding with *left* or *right* to words or the location of the stimulus on a screen).

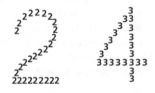

The Idea Today

COHEN AT AL (1990) PROPOSED A *CONNECTIONIST* MODEL TO EXPLAIN THE STROOP effect, and developed a computer simulation that placed different weights on connections between hypothetical cognitive units in the processes of colour naming and colour-word reading. In the developmental stages, the simulation program was given more training in word identification than colour naming, thus simulating the relatively more practised task of reading rather than colour naming. The program was then used to measure the speed with which it could identify colours and colour words under conditions of congruency and non-congruency. The findings were almost identical to those of human participants on a Stroop task; identification of colour words was the faster process and was relatively unaffected by the presence of matching or non-matching colours. The speed of colour naming, however, was inhibited by non-matching words and slightly enhanced by matching words.

The findings of Cohen et al.'s model were explained in the following way. Colour congruency does not affect reading because it is a practised task (represented in the model by stronger input and output connections) and is activated by the task demand (the goal of reading). Word congruency *does* affect colour naming because words are more practised (have stronger input units) than colours. Because the input activation from words (during the naming task) is not as strong as the task activation for naming, the naming process continues but the effects of greater input activation from words than from colours does affect the speed of the colour naming process. Where word and colour do not match this slows the naming process, and the effect is great because there is scope to delay the process. Where word and colour match, the naming process is only slightly faster than in the control condition because the system is approaching a ceiling of activation – it cannot become 'more activated'.

Since the results from the computer simulation so closely resemble those of people under similar circumstances, this connectionist approach seems to offer a good explanation of Stroop's original findings. However, there are a number of criticisms of the simulation, for instance that it cannot account for the errors people make in word naming. Besner et al. (1997) and Monsell et al. (2001) suggest that the task of reading provides a source of interference in addition to response competition. Recent evidence does, however, support the connectionist explanation. DeSoto et al. (2001) used event-related optical signals to measure brain activity during conflict situations on a spatial Stroop task (e.g. where the participant has to identify that the word 'above' lies *below* a central location). They found that response activation occurred for both possible responses in non-matching situations but only for the appropriate response in matching trials. This supports parallel-processing models such as that of Cohen et al. (1990), which suggest that in non-matching situations response activation arises for the more practised task (in this case the semantic task, reading, rather than the physical task of identifying spatial location).

Borzoni and Hines (1996) tested the response times of trained proof-readers and non-proof-readers on a Stroop colour-word task. The participants in the control group showed significantly more interference on the task than did the proof-readers. It would seem that either proof-reading trains people to treat words as physical as well as semantic stimuli, equating the two tasks, or perhaps that an individual who readily attends to all aspects of words (e.g. spelling as well as meaning) is more likely to end up in a career as a proof-reader.

Recent research has replicated Stroop's findings with regard to gender differences. Mekarski et al. (1996) found that men were consistently slower than women on a Stroop task whether a verbal or manual response was required (although their error rates did not differ significantly). They ascribed the differences to the greater verbal ability and fine motor control of women.

The Stroop paradigm has been extended to other situations of interference. Zbrodoff and Logan (2000) investigated a Stroop-like phenomenon in mental arithmetic. Participants asked to complete simple addition sums were slower to respond if an incorrect solution was provided (e.g. $3 + 4 = 9$) than if a letter, a symbol, no answer or the correct answer were given. It appeared that participants were unable to ignore the answer provided and that this interfered with their own verification of the sum much as participants in a colour-word task cannot not attend to one aspect of the stimulus.

## Current status of the idea

THERE appear to be ever-diversifying investigations and applications for the Stroop effect, with large numbers of papers being published every year. It still remains an unresolved problem for cognitive psychologists seeking to further our understanding of the ways we process information, yet it offers a useful tool for clinical research. Techniques such as PET and fMRI are being used to determine the location in the brain of cognitive activity specific to Stroop-type tasks and to use this to help to resolve the dilemma between response conflict and interference explanations (e.g. Zysset, 2001).

THERE ARE MANY CLINICAL APPLICATIONS OF THE STROOP PARADIGM, INCLUDING WORK with phobic patients and clients with post-traumatic stress disorder or eating disorders. Jones-Chesters et al. (1998) tested patients with eating disorders on a modified Stroop task where coloured words from experimental categories of food/eating, weight/shape, emotion or neutral were given. Participants with anorexia took longer to colour name food/eating and weight/shape words than neutral words; those with bulimia were also slower to read emotion-related words. These patterns were not seen in the control group. The interference effects seen in the Stroop task correlated with depression and anxiety reported by the patients with eating disorders, thus the paradigm may offer a useful diagnostic measure for eating disorders.

People with phobias exhibit similar patterns in emotional Stroop tasks. Lundh et al. (1999) and Kindt and Brosschot (1997), working with agoraphobic patients and people with spider-phobia respectively, have found phobia-related processing biases in Stroop tasks. In the agoraphobics, like those with eating disorders, bias was also related to the severity of anxiety and depression. Lundh and Oest (2001) used a Stroop task to measure the attentional bias exhibited by social phobics before and after cognitive-behavioural therapy. Following therapy, the treatment group showed significantly lower attentional bias for social threat words than the non-treatment group. This appeared to be a valid measure of recovery as it paralleled an increase in self-confidence and decrease in perfectionism.

The results of experiments using emotional Stroop tasks as a tool are not, however, always clear cut. Freeman and Beck (2000) compared the cognitive processing of fear-related words by sexually abused adolescent girls with post-traumatic stress disorder and non-abused controls. Responses to words from abuse-related threat, developmentally relevant (e.g. trust, secrecy, intimacy), general threat, positive and neutral categories were measured in a modified Stroop procedure. Although overall colour naming was slower in the traumatised girls, both groups, contrary to expectations, demonstrated interference for trauma-related words.

In an alternative approach, Osimani et al. (1997) have explored the use of a computerised version of the Stroop phenomenon as a diagnostic tool for malingering. A comparison of performance in groups of participants showed that the deficits in performance of patients with genuine brain damage were different from those exhibited by participants naïve to the test who had been asked to simulate cognitive impairment. The genuine patients showed longer reaction times, but those feigning impairment differed from controls as they had longer reaction times, increased errors and an inverted or absent Stroop effect. Such an alternation of the Stroop effect is not seen in those with real impairments – thus may offer a means to detect individuals who are malingering.

 **Further Reading**

ELLIS, R. AND HUMPHREYS, G. (1999) *Connectionist Psychology: A text with readings.* Hove: Psychology Press.

MACLEOD (1991) Half a century of research on the Stroop effect: An integrative review. *Psychological Bulletin* 109, 163–203.

# Theory of mind

TRADITIONAL THEORIES OF COGNITIVE DEVELOPMENT, LIKE THAT OF PIAGET (SEE P.122), are described as 'domain-general' theories because they aim to explain all aspects or *domains* of cognitive development by the same developmental processes. However, an alternative way of looking at cognitive development has evolved in recent years. This is the *domain-specific* approach, in which different domains of cognitive development are seen as developing separately, and in which theories just aim to explain a single aspect of cognitive development. A domain of cognitive development that has received particular attention is *theory of mind*. Theory of mind is not a theory itself, but refers to the ability to understand what other people think, believe and know. A child is said to have a theory of mind when they have an understanding (i.e. a theory) of other people's minds.

- ❋ False belief tasks
- ❋ Intentional reasoning in toddlers
- ❋ Modularity and the development of theory of mind
- ❋ Representational understanding of mind
- ❋ Advanced theory of mind

## False belief tasks

WIMMER and Perner (1983) developed what has become one of the major ways of studying theory of mind, the *false belief task*. They presented children with a story in which a boy called Maxi had left his chocolate in a green container in the kitchen. Maxi's mother had taken some of the chocolate for cooking and put the rest in a blue container. The child's task was to say which container Maxi would look in when he returned. Of course the correct answer is the green container, because Maxi wouldn't know his mother had moved it. However, this task requires an understanding of Maxi's mind, and Wimmer and Perner found that very few 3-year-old children gave the correct answer, although most 4-year-olds did. This is called a false belief task because for children to get the answer correct they need to understand that Maxi had a false belief about the location of the chocolate.

A limitation of Wimmer and Perner's procedure was the length of the story. It may have been that younger children found the task difficult because they had to think about quite a lot of information. To get around this, Baron-Cohen et al. (1985) developed a similar false belief task known as the Sally-Anne task. This involves telling children the shorter story of two dolls, Sally and Anne. Sally has a basket and Anne a box. Sally puts a marble in her basket, but when she isn't looking Anne takes the marble and puts it in her box. The task for participants is to say where Sally will look for her marble. Results were similar to those of the Wimmer and Perner study: most 4-year-olds realised that Sally would look in her own basket, but most 3-year-olds did not.

## Intentional reasoning in toddlers

CHILDREN generally do badly at false belief tasks until the age of 4 years, when they appear to suddenly acquire the ability. However, there may be other ways of assessing theory of mind, and on some tasks surprisingly young children seem to show an understanding of the intentions of adults. This is called *intentional reasoning*. If children can understand the intentions underlying people's actions, then they must have some appreciation of their state of mind. Meltzoff (1988) demonstrated that 18-month-old children could understand the intentions of adults when performing simple tasks. The toddlers watched adults perform tasks such as putting beads in a container. In one condition the adult succeeded in the task but in another condition failed, for example by dropping the beads on the floor. When given the chance to imitate the procedure there was no difference in the actions of the children – they attempted to fulfil tasks like getting the beads in the container. The children must have understood what the adult was intending to do rather than merely imitating them, otherwise those who saw the adult drop the beads or otherwise fail in the task should have similarly dropped the beads.

## Modularity and the development of theory of mind

THE best-known explanation for the development of children's theory of mind comes from Leslie's theory (Leslie, 1994), which is part of the innatist modular approach to cognitive development. *Modular* theories propose that for each of our cognitive abilities – such as theory of mind – there is a corresponding module – a neural mechanism in the brain (not necessarily localised in one brain region). *Innatist* theories emphasise the development of the brain through genetically determined processes of maturation, and minimise the role of environment. According to innatist modular theories, each module become active at a particular age, and so children become capable of particular cognitive tasks at specific ages.

Leslie (1994) proposed that two modules are necessary for the ability to perform intentional reasoning and false belief tasks. The first module is activated in infancy, and is concerned with understanding the causes of mechanical actions. The second is activated at around 4 years and is concerned with theory of mind proper. Leslie proposed that in Meltzoff's studies the children understood that the adults' actions were leading towards outcomes like getting the beads in the container, but did not understand the adult's *intention* to perform the task. Leslie's theory neatly explains why children suddenly acquire the ability to perform false belief tasks at 4 years as their theory of mind module is activated at this point.

## Representational understanding of mind

PERNER (1991) has proposed that children develop theory of mind at around 4 years, when they gain the ability of *metarepresentation* (an appreciation of the distinction between representations such as words or pictures and the thing they represent). This means, for example, that children understand that 'rabbit' and 'bunny' mean the same thing, and that the same object will look different if viewed from a different angle.

According to Perner, metarepresentation is necessary for false belief tasks because the child needs to distinguish between the actual location of an object and the representation of that location in the mind of a person (e.g. Maxi or Sally) of where it is. Unlike Leslie, Perner proposed that children under the age of 4 do have some understanding of minds, but that their understanding improves vastly when they acquire metarepresentation and thus they can perform false belief tasks.

## Advanced theory of mind

A limitation of research using false belief tasks like those used by Wimmer and Perner (1983) is that they are too easy to differentiate between different levels of theory of mind. Actually, older children and adults who can easily perform false belief tasks vary widely in their ability to recognise and understand complex emotions in others. This understanding of complex emotions is an aspect of theory of mind, but at a much more advanced level than merely being aware of false beliefs. It is thus termed *advanced theory of mind*. Baron-Cohen et al. (1997) have devised a way of assessing advanced theory of mind. The *Eyes Test* comprises 30 photographs of pairs of eyes taken from faces expressing particular emotions. The task is to identify the emotion from the limited information in the eyes and without the normal cues from the rest of the face. Poor scores on the *Eyes Test* are associated with poor social skills and some mental disorders.

The Idea Today

THERE IS AN ENORMOUS BODY OF CONTEMPORARY RESEARCH LOOKING AT THE development of theory of mind. One line of research with implications for Leslie's theory concerns the universality of acquisition of theory of mind. If the age at which children acquire the ability to perform false belief tasks remains constant across a variety of cultures, this would support Leslie's innatist modular explanation. Avis and Harris (1991) replicated the study with children of the Baka people, who live in a remote part of the Cameroon, suggesting that the sudden appearance of theory of mind at 4 years is universal. However, more recent studies have called this into question. Vinden (1996) tested the Quecha children of Peru on a range of theory of mind tasks and found that they had great difficulty, scoring below levels expected by chance. For instance, Vinden noted that the Quecha language did not contain words for mental states, and suggested that her findings indicate that theory of mind is cultural in origin rather than a result of predetermined activation of a brain module.

Another line of research that has cast serious doubt on Leslie's views concerns the profound effects of the early social environment on the development of theory of mind. Astington (1998) has suggested that children internalise a theory of mind during their early interactions. This idea is supported by studies that have shown that theory of mind is superior in children who have secure attachments and whose primary carers display high levels of sensitivity. For example, Symons and Clark (2000) measured both sensitive responsiveness and security of attachment in 2-year-old children and followed them up to 5 years, when they were tested on false belief tasks. It was found that the children assessed as securely attached and those whose mothers were rated as the most sensitive at 2 years (these were usually the same children) generally had a superior theory of mind at 5 years.

Contemporary studies have supported a link between the development of theory of mind and Perner's theory of representational understanding of mind. In one study Doherty and Perner (1998) assessed 3 and 4-year-old children on false belief tasks and a synonyms task, in which children were taught that rabbit and bunny mean the same thing and then given the task of saying 'rabbit' every time a puppet said 'bunny' and vice versa. There was a very strong correspondence between the abilities of the children to perform the two tasks, with older children performing better on each. This relationship between a measure of theory of mind and a task that requires metarepresentation (because children need to understand that rabbits can be represented by two different words) supports Perner's theory.

## Current status of the idea

OF the articles in the *British Journal of Developmental Psychology* in the year 2000 24% concerned theory of mind. This makes it currently the most researched area in British developmental psychology. Debate continues between people emphasising early theory of mind abilities and those emphasising the dramatic shift that occurs at around 4 years. Debate also continues on the importance of environmental factors such as attachment and the role of modularity in development of theory of mind. There is also a growing interest in advanced theory of mind and its role in social competence.

## The Idea in Action

THE BEST-KNOWN APPLICATION OF THEORY OF MIND RESEARCH IS IN UNDERSTANDING autism. Autism is a disorder first apparent in childhood, characterised by difficulty in relating to other people, difficulty in communication and restricted, repetitive behaviour. Although autism is usually associated with below average IQ autistic individuals often display average or better than average abilities in some tasks, such as rote-learning and spatial tasks. In a classic study Baron-Cohen et al. (1985) compared autistic children, children with Down's syndrome and children without any learning difficulties on the Sally-Anne task. Over 80% of the children in the two non-autistic groups got the answer right, but less than 20% of the autistic children did so. Baron-Cohen et al. proposed that a lack of ability in theory of mind may the cause of autism. The extent to which autism can be explained by a deficit in theory of mind is an ongoing controversy (see Chandler, 2001 for a review), but the realisation that theory of mind is a major deficit in autism has greatly enriched the understanding of those researching and working with people with autism.

Theory of mind research is also important in understanding children with poor social skills. Bosacki and Astington (1999) have established a link between theory of mind and social competence as rated by peers and teachers. Dunn et al. (2000) have identified poor development of theory of mind in 'hard-to-manage' children, suggesting that children who have a poor appreciation of the mental states of others tend to have difficulty in interacting with adults. Sutton et al. (2000) report a significant correlation between advanced theory of mind and avoidance of responsibility (measured by denial of responsibility and lack of remorse for failure to take responsibility), suggesting that children with poor theory of mind development may experience particular difficulty in taking responsibility in working with others.

## Further Reading

BARON-COHEN, S., TAGER-FLUSBERG, H. AND COHEN, D.J. (2000) (eds) *Understanding other minds*. Oxford, Oxford University Press.

CHANDLER, E. (2001) Autism. In Jarvis, M. (ed.) *Angles on child psychology*. Cheltenham, Nelson Thornes.

# References

ABRAMS, M. AND ELIS, A. (1996) Rational emotive behaviour therapy in the treatment of stress. In Palmer, S. and Dryden, W. (eds) *Stress management and counselling*. London, Cassell.

ADAMS, H.E., WRIGHT, L.W. AND LOHR, B.A. (1996) Is homophobia associated with homosexual arousal? *Journal of Abnormal Psychology* 105 (3), 440–445.

ADLER, A. (1927) *What life should mean to you*. London, George, Allen and Unwin.

ADLER, A. (1939) *Social interest: a challenge for mankind*. London, Faber and Faber.

ADORNO, T.W., FRENKEL-BRUNSWICK, E., LEVINSON, J.D. AND SANFORD, R.N. (1950) *The authoritarian personality*. New York, Harper and Row.

AGGLETON, J.P. AND WASKETT, L. (1999) The ability of odours to serve as state-dependent cues for real-world memories. Can Viking smells aid the recall of Viking experiences? *British Journal of Psychology* 90 (1), 1–18.

AINSWORTH, M.D.S. (1967) *Infancy in Uganda: Infant care and the growth of love*. Baltimore, Johns Hopkins University Press.

AINSWORTH, M.D.S. AND WITTIG, B.A. (1969) Attachment theory and the exploratory behaviour of one-year-olds in a strange situation. In Foss, B.M. (ed.) *Determinants of infant behaviour vol 4*. London, Methuen.

AINSWORTH, M.D.S., BLEHAR, M.C., WATERS, E. AND WALL, E. (1978) *Patterns of attachment*. Hillsdale, Erlbaum.

AL-ABOOD, S.A., DAVIDS, K. AND BENNETT, S.J. (2001) Specificity of task constraint and effects of visual demonstrations and verbal instructions in directing learners' search during skill acquisition. *Journal of Motor Behaviour* 33, 295–305.

ALCOCK, J. (1998) *Animal behavior, An evolutionary approach*. Sunderland, MA: Sinauer.

ALEIXO, P.A. AND NORRIS, C.E. (2000) Personality and moral reasoning in young offenders. *Personality and Individual Differences* 28, 609–623.

ALLPORT, G.W. AND POSTMAN, L. (1947) *The psychology of rumour*. New York, Henry Holt.

ALTEMEYER, B. (1988) *The enemies of freedom: understanding right-wing authoritarians*. San Fransisco, Jossey-Bass.

ALTSHULER, D.L. AND NUNN, A.M. (2001) Observational learning in humming-birds. *Auk* 118, 795–799.

AMIR, S. AND STEWART, J. (1996) Resetting the circadian clock by a conditioned stimulus. *Nature* 397, 542–545.

ANBAR, R.D. (2001) Self-hypnosis for the treatment of functional abdominal pain in childhood. *Clinical Pediatrics* 40, 447–451.

ANDREANI, O.D. (1995) Knowledge and intrinsic motivation. *European Journal for High Ability* 6, 220–225.

ANDREWS, G., SLADE, T. AND PETERS, L. (1999) Classification in psychiatry: ICD-10 vs DSM-IV. *British Journal of Psychiatry* 174, 3–5.

ASTINGTON, J.W. (1998) Theory of mind, Humpty Dumpty and the ice box. *Human Development* 41, 30–39.

AVIS, J.S. AND HARRIS, P.L. (1991) Belief-desire reasoning among Baka children: evidence for a universal conception of mind. *Child Development* 62, 460–467.

BAILLARGEON, R. AND DeVOS (1991) Object permanence in young infants: further evidence. *Child Development* 62, 1227–1246.

BANDURA, A. (1989) Human agency in social cognitive theory. *American Psychologist* 44, 1175–1184.

BANDURA, A. (1977) *Social learning theory*. Englewood Cliffs, New Jersey, Prentice-Hall.

BANGERTER, A. (2000) Transformations between scientific and social representations of conception: the method of serial reproduction. *British Journal of Social Psychology* 39, 521–535.

BARBER, J. (2001) Freedom from smoking: Integrating hypnotic methods and rapid smoking to facilitate smoking cessation. *International Journal of Clinical and Experimental Hypnosis* 49, 257–266.

BARON-COHEN, S., LESLIE, A.M. AND FRITH, U. (1985) Does the autistic child have a theory of mind? *Cognition* 21, 37–46.

BARON-COHEN, S., JOLIFFE, T., MORTIMORE, C. AND ROBERTSON, M. (1997) Another advanced test of theory of mind: evidence from very high-functioning adults with autism or Asperger syndrome. *Journal of Child Psychiatry and Psychology* 38, 813–822.

BARRETT, P.M., DUFFY, A.L., DADDS, M.R. AND RAPEE, R.M. (2001) Cognitive-behavioural treatment of anxiety disorders in children: long-term (6–year) follow-up. *Journal of Consulting and Clinical Psychology* 69, 135–141.

BARTLETT, F.C. (1932) *Remembering*. Cambridge, Cambridge University Press.

BATEMAN, A. AND FONAGY, P. (1999) Effectiveness of partial hospitalisation in the treatment of borderline personality disorder: a randomised control trial. *American Journal of Psychiatry* 156, 1563–1569.

BECK, A. (1976) *Cognitive therapy and the emotional disorders*. New York, International Universities Press.

BELOFF, J. (1993) *Parapsychology: a concise history*. London, Athlone.

BEM, D.J. AND HONORTON, C. (1994) Does psi exist? Replicable evidence for an anomalous process of information transfer. *Psychological Bulletin* 115, 4–18.

BENJAMIN, J., LI, L., PATTERSON, C., GREENBERG, B.D., MURPHY, D.L. AND HAMER, D.H. (1996) Population and familial association between the D4 dopamine receptor gene and novelty seeking. *Nature Genetics* 12, 81–84.

BENTLEY, E. (1999) *Awareness*. London, Routledge.

BERGIN, A.E. AND GARFIELD, S.L. (1994) *Handbook of psychotherapy and behaviour change*. New York, Wiley.

BESNER, D., STOLZ, J.A. AND BOUTILIER, C. (1997) The Stroop effect and the myth of automaticity. *Psychonomic Bulletin and Review* 4, 221–225.

BLASS, T. (1996a) Attribution of responsibility and trust in the Milgram obedience experiment. *Journal of Applied Social Psychology* 26, 1529–1535.

BLASS, T. (1996b) The Milgram obedience experiment: support for a cognitive view of defensive attribution. *Journal of Social Psychology* 136, 407–410.

BLUNDELL, P., HALL, G. AND KILCROSS, S. (2001) Lesions of the basolateral amygdala disrupt selective aspects of reinforcer representation in rats. *Journal of Neuroscience* 21, 9018–9026.

BORZONI, S. AND HINES, T. (1996) Proofreaders' decreased Stroop interference. *Perceptual and Motor Skills* 83(3, part 2), 1104–1106.

BOSACKI, S. AND ASTINGTON, J.W. (1999) Theory of mind in preadolescence: relations between social understanding and social competence. *Social Development* 8, 237–255.

BOWEN, A.M. AND BOURGEOUIS, M.J. (2001) Attitudes towards lesbian, gay and bisexual college students: the contribution of pluralistic ignorance, dynamic social impact and contact theories. *Journal of American College Health* 50, 91–96.

BOWLBY, J. (1951) *Maternal care and mental health*. Geneva, World Health Organization.

BOWLBY, J. (1969) *Attachment and loss vol I*. London, Pimlico.

BRADMETZ, J. (1999) Precursors of formal thought: a longitudinal study. *British Journal of Developmental Psychology* 17, 61–81.

BRANDENBERGER, G., EHRHART, J., PIQUARD, F. AND SIMON, C. (2001) Inverse coupling between ultradian oscillations in delta wave activity and heart rate variability during sleep. *Clinical Neuropsychology* 112, 992–996.

BRAUD, W., SHAFER, D., MCNEILL, K. AND GUERRA, V. (1995) Attention focusing facilitated through remote mental interaction. *Journal of the American Society for Psychical Research* 89, 103–115.

BRAZLETON, T.B., TRONICK, E., ADAMSON, L., ALS, H. AND WISE, S. (1975) Early mother-infant reciprocity. Parent–infant interaction. *Ciba Symposium* 33, 137–154.

BREUER, J. AND FREUD, S. (1895) *Studies on hysteria*. London, Hogarth.

BROWN, G.W. AND HARRIS, T.O. (1978) *The social origins of depression: a study of psychiatric disorder in women*. London, Tavistock.

BROWN, R. AND MCNEILL, D. (1966) The 'tip of the tongue' phenomenon. *Journal of Verbal Learning and Verbal Behaviour* 5, 325–337.

BURMAN, E. (1994) *Deconstructing developmental psychology*. London, Routledge.

BURN, S.M. (2000) Heterosexuals' use of 'fag' and 'queer' to deride one another: a contributor to heterosexism and stigma. *Journal of Homosexuality* 40, 1–11.

BURNETT, P.C. (1999) Children's self-talk and academic self-concepts. *Educational Psychology in Practice* 15, 195–200.

BURNS, A. (1998) Pop psychology or Ken behaving badly. *The Psychologist* 11 (7), 360.

BUSS, D.M. (1999) *Evolutionary psychology*. Boston, MA: Allyn and Bacon.

BUSS, D.M. AND SCHMITT, D.P. (1993) Sexual strategies theory: An evolutionary perspective on human mating. *Psychological Review* 100, 204–232.

CAHILL, L., VAZDARJANOVA, A. AND SETLOW, B. (2000) The basolateral amygdala is involved with, but not necessary for, rapid acquisition of Pavlovian 'fear conditioning'. *European Journal of Neuroscience* 12, 3044–3050.

CAMPBELL, S.J. AND MURPHY, P.J. (1998) Extraocular circadian phototransduction in humans. *Science*, 279: 396.

CARLI, L.L. (1999) Cognitive reconstruction, hindsight and reactions to victims and perpetrators. *Personality and Social Psychology Bulletin* 25, 966–979.

CARLO, G., ROESCH, S.C. AND MELTBY, J. (1998) The multiplicative relations of parenting and temperament to prosocial and antisocial behaviours in adolescence. *Journal of Early Adolescence* 18, 266–290.

CARTWRIGHT, J. (2000) *Evolution and human behaviour.* London, Macmillan.

CAVE, S. (1999) *Therapeutic approaches*. London, Routledge.

CECI, S.J. AND BRUCK, M. (1995) *Jeopardy in the courtroom: A scientific analysis of children's testimony*. Washington DC, American Psychological Association.

CHADWICK, P., SAMBROOKE, S., RASCH, S. AND DAVIES, E. (2000) Challenging the omnipotence of voices: group cognitive behaviour therapy for voices. *Behaviour Research and Therapy* 38, 993–1003.

CHANDLER, E. (2001) Autism. In Jarvis, M. *Angles on child psychology*. Cheltenham, Nelson Thornes.

CHORNEY, M.J., SEESE, K., OWEN, M.J. ET AL. (1998) A quantitative trait locus (QTL) associated with cognitive ability in children. *Psychological Science* 9, 159–166.

CLAMP, A. (2001) *Evolutionary psychology*. London, Hodder and Stoughton.

CLAMP, A.G. AND RUSSELL, J. (1998) *Comparative Psychology*. London, Hodder and Stoughton.

COHEN, J.D., DUNBAR, K. AND MCCLELLAND, J.L. (1990) On the control of automatic processes: A parallel distributed processing account of the Stroop effect. *Psychological Review* 97, 332–361.

CONDOR, S. (1988) 'Race stereotypes' and racist discourse *Text 8*, 69–91.

COOPER, J.J. AND MASON, G.J. (2000) The use of operant technology to measure behavioural priorities in captive animals. *Behaviour Research Methods, Instruments and Computers* 33, 427–434.

CORRIGAN, P.W., RIVER, L.P., LUNDIN, R.K. ET AL. (2000) Stigmatising attributions about mental illness. *Journal of Community Psychology* 28, 91–102.

CZEISLER, C.A. AND BROWN, E.N. (1999) Commentary: models of the effect of light on the human circadian system: current state of the art. *Journal of Biological Rhythms* 14(6), 538–543.

DALKVIST, J. AND WESTERLUND, J. (1998) Five experiments on telepathic communication of emotions. *Journal of Parapsychology* 62, 219–253.

DARWIN, C. (1859) *The Origin of Species by Means of Natural Selection*. London, John Murray.

DAVIES, R. (1995) Selfish altruism. *Psychology Review* 1, 2–9.

DAWKINS, R. AND KREBS, J.R. (1979) Arms races between and within species. *Proceedings of the Royal Society of London, Series B* 205, 489–511.

DEAKIN, J.M. AND PROTEAU, L. (2000) The role of scheduling in learning through observation. *Journal of Motor Behavior* 32, 268–276.

DE CASTRO, J.M. AND PEARCEY, S.M. (1995) Lunar rhythms of the meal and alcohol intake of humans. *Physiology and Behavior* 57, 439–444.

DELANOY, D.L. AND MORRIS, R.L. (1999) A DMILS training study utilising two shielded environments. *European Journal of Parapsychology* 14, 52–67.

DEMERS, A., KISHCHUK, N., BOURGAULT, C. AND BISSON, C. (1996) When anthropology meets epidemiology: using social representations to predict drinking patterns. *Substance Use and Misuse* 31, 847–871.

DE PASCALIS, V., MAGURANO, M.R., BELLUSCI, A. AND CHEN, C.A.N. (2001) Somatosensory event-related and autonomic activity to varying pain reduction cognitive strategies in hypnosis. *Clinical Neuropsychology* 112, 1475–1485.

DESOTO, M.C., FABINI, M., GEARY, D.C. AND GRATTON, G. (2001) When in doubt, do it both ways: Brain evidence of the simultaneous activation of conflicting motor responses in a spatial Stroop task. *Journal of Cognitive Neuroscience*, 13 (4): 523–536.

DOBBS, M. AND CRANO, W.D. (2001) Outgroup accountability in the minimal group paradigm: implications for aversive discrimination and social identity theory. *Personality and Social Psychology Bulletin* 27, 355–364.

DOHERTY, K. AND ANDERSON, I. (1998) Perpetuating rape-supportive culture. *The Psychologist* 11 (12) 583–587.

DOWNEY, D. (1995) When bigger is not better: family-size, parental resources and children's educational performance. *American Sociological Review* 60, 746–761.

DUCK, J.M. (1990) Children's ideals: the role of real life versus media figures. *Australian Journal of Psychology* 42, 19–29.

DUKA, T., WEISSENBORN, R. AND DIENES, Z. (2001) State-dependent effects of alcohol on recollective experience, familiaruty and awareness on memories. *Psychopharmacology* 153, 295–306.

DUKER, P.C. AND SEYS, D.M. (2000) A quasi-experimental study on the effect of electrical aversion treatment on imposed mechanical restraint for severe self-injurious behaviour. *Research in Developmental Disabilities* 21, 235–242.

DUNN, J., CUTTING, A.L. AND DEMETRIOUS, H. (2000) Moral sensibility, understanding others and children's friendship interactions in the preschool period. *British Journal of Developmental Psychology* 18, 159–178.

DUTTON, D.G. AND HOLTZWORTH-MUNROE, A. (1997) The role of early trauma in males who assault their wives. In Cicchetti, D. and Toth, S.L. (eds) *Developmental perspectives on trauma: theory, research and intervention*. Rochester, University of Rochester Press.

EBSTEIN, R.P., NOVICK, O., UMANSKY, R., PRIEL, B., OSHER, Y. AND BLAINE, D. (1995) Dopamine receptor D4exon III polymorphism associated with the human personality trait of novelty seeking. *Nature Genetics* 12, 78–80.

ECHEBARRIA, E., GONZALES, C.J.L. AND FDEZ, G.E. (1996) Arguing about tobacco and its effects on social representations. *European Journal of Social Psychology* 26, 265–276.

ELEY, T.C. AND STEVENSON, J. (2000) Specific life-events and chronic experiences differentially associated with depression and anxiety in young twins. *Journal of Abnormal Child Psychology* 28, 383–394.

ELLIS, A. (1977) The basic clinical theory of rational emotive therapy. In Ellis, A. and Grieger, R. (eds) *Handbook of rational emotive therapy*. Monterey, Brooks/Cole.

ELLIS, R. AND HUMPHREYS, G. (1999) *Connectionist psychology: A text with readings*. Hove: Psychology Press.

ELLIS, J. AND FOX, P. (2001) The effect of self-identified sexual orientation on helping behaviour in a British sample: are gay men and lesbians treated differently? *Journal of Applied Social Psychology* 31, 1238–1247.

ERIKSEN, B.A. AND ERIKSEN, C.W. (1974) Effects of noise letters upon identification of a target letter in a nonsearch task. *Perception and Psychophysics* 16, 143–149.

EZELL, H.K. AND JUSTICE, L.M. (2000) Increasing the print focus of adult-child shared book-reading through observational learning. *American Journal of Speech Language Pathology* 9, 36–47.

FARR, R. (1998) From collective to social representations: aller et retour. *Culture and Psychology* 4, 275–296.

FAVA, G.A., RAFANELLI, C., GRANDI, S., CONTI, S. AND BELLUARDO, P. (1998) Prevention of recurrent depression with cognitive behavioural therapy: preliminary findings. *Archives of General Psychiatry* 55, 816–820.

FEATHER, N.T. AND OBERDAN, D. (2000) Reactions to penalties for an offence in relation to ethnic identity, responsibility and authoritarianism. *Australian Journal of Psychology* 52, 9–16.

FEATHER, N.T., BOECKMAN, R.J. AND MCKEE, I.R. (2001) Reactions to an offence inrelation to authoritarianism, knowledge of risk and freedom of action. *European Journal of Social Psychology* 31, 109–126.

FERGUSON, E. AND CASSADAY, H.J. (1999) The Gulf War and illness by association. *British Journal of Psychology* 90, 459–475.

FERENCZI, M. (1997) Seasonal depression and light therapy. http://nimnet51.nimr.mrc.ac.uk/mhe97/sad.htm [accessed 14/05/98]

FISHER, R.P. AND GEISELMAN, R.E. (1988) Enhancing eyewitness testimony with the cognitive interview. In Gruneberg, M.M. and Morris, P.E. and Sykes, R.N. (eds) *Practical aspects of memory: research and issues* vol 1, Chichester, Wiley.

FLANAGAN, C. (1996) *Applying Psychology to Early Childhood Development*. London, Hodder and Stoughton.

FLETT, G.L., HEWITT, P.L. AND SINGER, A. (1995) Perfectionism and parental authority styles. *Individual Psychology: Journal of Adlerian Theory, Research and Practice* 51, 50–60.

FLOWERS, J.H., WARNER, J.L. AND POLANSKY, M.L. (1979) Response and encoding factors in ignoring irrelevant information. *Memory and Cognition* 7, 86–94.

FLOYD, F.J., STEIN, T.S., HARTER, K.S.M., ALLISON, A. AND NYE, C.L. (1999) Gay, lesbian and bisexual youths: separation-individuation, parental attitudes, identity consolidation and well-being. *Journal of Youth and Adolescence* 28, 719–739.

FONAGY, P., STEELE, M., MORAN, G., STEELE, H. AND HIGGITT, A. (1993) Measuring the ghost in the nursery: an empirical study of the relation between parents' mental representations of childhood experiences and their infants' security of attachment. *Journal of the American Psychoanalytic Association* 41, 957–989.

FOX, N.J., JOESBURY, H. AND HANNAY, D.R. (1991) Family attachments and medical sociology: a valuable partnership for student learning. *Medical Education* 25, 155–159.

FREEMAN, J.B. AND BECK, J.G. (2000) Cognitive interference for trauma cases in sexually abused adolescent girls with posttraumatic stress disorder. *Journal of Clinical Child Psychology* 29(2), 245–256.

FREESE, J., POWELL, B. AND STEELMAN, L.C. (1999) Rebel without a cause or effect: birth order and social attitudes. *American Sociological Review* 64, 207–231.

FREUD, A. (1936) *The ego and the mechanisms of defence*. London, Hogarth Press.

FREUD, S. (1894) The defence neuropsychoses. *Collected Papers* vol I, 59–75. London, Hogarth Press.

FREUD, S. (1899) Screen memories. *Standard Edition III*. London, Hogarth.

FREUD, S. (1900) *The interpretation of dreams*. London, Hogarth.

FREUD, S. (1905) *Three essays on sexuality*. London, Hogarth.

FREUD, S. (1914) *Psychopathology of everyday life*. London, Benn.

FREUD, S. (1924) The passing of the Oedipus complex. *Collected Papers* vol II. London, Hogarth.

FREUD, S. (1933) *New introductory lectures on psychoanalysis*. London, Hogarth.

FRITZ, J. AND KOTRSCHAL, K. (1999) Social learning in common ravens, *Corvus corax*. *Animal Behaviour* 57 785–793.

GAERTNER, S.L., RUST, M.C., DIVISIO, J.C., BACHMAN, B.A. AND ANASTASIO, P. (1993) The contact hypothesis: the role of a common in-group identity on reducing intergroup bias. *Small Business Research*.

GARMON, L.C., BASINGER, K.S., GREGG, V.R. AND GIBBS, J.C. (1996) Gender differences in stage and expression of moral judgement. *Merrill-Palmer Quarterly* 42, 418–437.

GERGENS, K. (1973) Social psychology as history. *Journal of Personality and Social Psychology* 26, 309–320.

GHOSH, S. AND CHATTOPADHYAY, P.K. (1993) Application of behaviour modification techniues in treatment of attention deficit hyperactivity disorder: A case report. *Indian Journal of Clinical Psychology* 20, 124–129.

GIBSON, H.B. AND HEAP, M. (1991) *Hypnosis in therapy*. London, Lawrence Erlbaum Associates.

GILBERT, D.T., PELHAM, B.W. AND KRULL, D.S. (1988) On cognitive business: when person perceivers meet persons perceived. *Journal of Personality and Social Psychology* 54, 733–740.

GILLIGAN, C. (1977) In a different voice: women's perspectives on self and morality. *Harvard Educational Review* 47, 481–517.

GILLIGAN, C. (1982) *In a different voice: psychological theory and women's development*. Cambridge MA, Harvard University Press.

GILLIGAN, C. AND ATTANUCCI, J. (1988) Two moral orientations. In Gilligan, C., Ward, J.V. and Taylor, J. (eds) *Mapping the moral domain: a contribution of women's thinking to psychological theory and education*. Cambridge MA, Harvard University Press.

GLANZMAN, D.L. (1995) The cellular basis of classical conditioning in *Aplysia californica* – it's less simple than you think. *Trends in Neurosciences* 18, 30–36.

GODDEN, D.R. AND BADDELEY, A. (1975) Context-dependent memory in two natural environments: on land and under water. *British Journal of Psychology* 66, 325–331.

GODDEN, D.R. AND BADDELEY, A. (1980) When does context influence recognition memory? *British Journal of Psychology* 71, 99–104.

GOLDSMITH, H.H. AND ALANSKY, J. (1987) Maternal and infant temperamental predictors of attachment: a meta-analytic review. *Journal of Consulting and Clinical Psychology* 55, 805–816.

GOODMAN, J.F. (2000) Moral education in early childhood: the limits of constructivism. *Early Education and Development* 11, 37–54.

GOODWIN, D.W., POWELL, B., BREMER, D., HOINE, H. AND STERN, J. (1969) Alcohol and recall: state dependent effects in man. *Science* 163, 1358.

GRAHAM, K. AND WELLS, S. (2000) 'Somebody's gonna get their head kicked in tonight!' Aggression among young males in bars; A question of values? *Paper presented at XIV World Meeting of the International Society for Research on Aggression*, 9–14 July, Valencia, Spain.

GRANT, H.M., BREDAHL, L.C., CLAY, J. ET AL. (1998) Context-dependent memory for meaningful material: information for students. *Applied Cognitive Psychology* 12, 617–623.

GRAZIOLI, R. AND TERRY, D.J. (2000) The role of cognitive vulnerability and stress in the prediction of postpartum depressive symptomatology. *British Journal of Clinical Psychology* 39, 329–347.

GREENBERG, L.S., ELLIOTT, R.K. AND LIAETER, G. (1994) Research on experiential therapies. In Bergin, A.E. and Garfield, S.L. (eds) *Handbook of psychotherapy and behaviour change*. New York, Wiley.

GRICE, G.R. (1948) The relation of secondary reinforcement to delayed reward in visual discrimination learning. *Journal of Experimental Psychology* 38, 1–16.

GRIGORENKO, E.L. AND CARTER, A.S. (1996) Co-twin, peer and mother-child relationships and IQ in a Russian adolescent twin sample. *Journal of Russian and East European Psychology* 34, 59–87.

GROTH-MARNAT, G. AND SUMMERS, R. (1998) Altered beliefs, attitudes and behaviours following near-death experiences. *Journal of Humanistic Psychology* 38, 110–125.

HAMILTON, V.L. AND SANDERS, J. (1995) Crimes of obedience and conformity in the workplace: surveys of Americans, Russians and Japanese. *Journal of Social Issues* 51, 67–88.

HARRINGTON, R., CAMPBELL, F., SHOEBRIDGE, P. AND WHITTAKER, J. (1998) Meta-analysis of CBT for depression in adolescents. *Journal of the Academy of Child and Adolescent Psychiatry* 37, 1005–1006.

HARRIS, K. AND CAMPBELL, E.A. (1999) The plans in unplanned pregnancy: secondary gain and the partnership. *British Journal of Medical Psychology* 72 (1), 105–120.

HAYES, N. (2000) *Foundations of psychology*. London, ITP.

HEAP, M. (1996) The nature of hypnosis. *The Psychologist* 9, 498–501.

HEIDER, F. (1958) *The psychology of personal interpersonal relationships*. New York, Wiley.

HENRIQUES, J.B. AND DAVIDSON, R.J. (2000) Decreased responsiveness to reward in depression. *Cognition and Emotion* 14(5), 711–724.

HERGOVICH, A. AND OLBRICH, A. (1996) The expert system for peacefare: a new approach to peace and conflict research. *Review of Psychology* 3, 11–21.

HEREK, G.M. AND BERRILL, K.T. (1992) *Hate crimes: confronting violence against lesbians and gay men*. London, Sage.

HERZ, R.S. (1997) The effects of cue distinctiveness on odour-based context-dependent memory. *Memory and Cognition* 25, 375–380.

HILGARD, E.R. (1977) *Divided consciousness: Multiple controls in human thought and action*. New York, Wiley.

HINSZ, V.B., MATZ, D.C. AND PATIENCE, R.A. (2001) Does women's hair signal reproductive potential? *Journal of Experimental Social Psychology* 37, 166–172.

HIRATA, S. AND MORIMURA, N. (2000) Naïve chimpanzees' (*Pan troglodytes*) observation of experienced conspecifics in a tool-using task. *Journal of Comparative Psychology* 114, 291–296.

HOLLEMAN, M.C., THORNBY, J.I. AND MERRILL, J.M. (2000) Substance abusers: role of personal and professional role traits in caregivers' causal attributions. *Psychological Reports* 86, 407–413.

HOLM-HADULLA, R., KIEFER, L. AND SESSAR, W. (1997) Effectiveness of psychoanalytically founded brief and dynamic psychotherapy. *Psychotherapy and Psychosomatic Medicine* 47 (8), 271–278.

HOLTZWORTH-MUNROE, A., BATES, L., SMUTZLER, N. AND SANDIN, E. (1997) A brief review of the research on husband violence: 1. Maritally violent vs non-violent men. *Aggression and Violent Behaviour* 2, 65–99.

HONORTON, C. (1974) Psi-mediated imagery and ideation in an experimental procedure for regulating perceptual input. *Journal of the American Society for Psychical Research* 68, 156–168.

HONORTON, C., BERGER, R.E., VARVOGLIS, M.P. ET AL. (1990) Psi communication in the ganzfield: experiments with an automated testing system and a comparison with a meta-analysis of earlier studies. *Journal of Parapsychology* 54, 99–139.

HORNER, S.L. (2000) The effects of observational learning on pre-schoolers' book-related behaviors and alphabet knowledge. *Child Study Journal* 31, 1–11.

HOWITT, D. AND OWUSU-BEMPAH, K. (1994) *The racism of psychology: time for change*. Hemel Hempstead, Harvester Wheatsheaf.

HUNTER, C.E. AND ROSS, M.W. (1991) Determinants of health-care workers' attitudes towards people with AIDS. *Journal of Applied Social Psychology* 21, 947–956.

HUGUET, P., LATANE, B. AND BOURGEOIS, M. (1998) The emergence of a social representation of human rights via international communication: empirical evidence for the convergence of two theories. *European Journal of Social Psychology* 28, 831–846.

HUSTON, A.C. AND WRIGHT, J.C. (1998) Mass media and children's development. In Damon W (ed.) *Handbook of child psychology: volume 4. Child psychology in practice*. New York, Wiley.

ISAACSON, S.S. (2001) The influence of sex, age, and personality on mate-age preferences: An evolutionary perspective. *Dissertation Abstracts International: Section B: The Sciences and Engineering*, 61(7–B), 3901.

JAHODA, G. (1988) Critical notes and reflections on social representations. *European Journal of Social Psychology* 18, 195–209.

JARVIS, M. (2000) Teaching psychodynamic psychology: from discourse analysis towards a model of reflective practice. *Psychology Teaching* 8, 13–21.

JARVIS, M., RUSSELL, J., FLANAGAN, C. AND DOLAN, L. (2000) *Angles on psychology*. Cheltenham: Nelson Thornes.

JENSEN, S.M., BARABASZ, A., BARABASZ, M. AND WARNER, D. (2001) EEG P300 event-related markers of hypnosis. *American Journal of Clinical Hypnosis* 44, 127–139.

JERABEK, I. AND STANDING, L. (1992) Imagined test situations produce contextual memory enhancement. *Perceptual and Motor Skills* 75, 400.

JONES, E.E. AND DAVIS, K.E. (1965) From acts to dispositions: the attribution process in person perception. In Berkowitz, L. (ed.) *Advances in experimental social psychology*, vol 2. New York, Academic Press.

JONES-CHESTERS, M.H., MONSELL, S. AND COOPER, P.J. (1998) The disorder-salient Stroop effect as a measure of psychopathology in eating disorders.

JOVCHELOVITCH, S. AND GERVAIS, M. (1999) Social representations of health and illness: the case of the Chinese community in England. *Journal of Community and Applied Social Psychology* 9, 247–260.

JUFFER, F., HOKSBERGEN, R.A.C., RENE, A.C., RIKSEN-WALRAVEN, J.M. AND KOHNSTAMM, G.A. (1997) Early intervention in adoptive families: supporting maternal sensitive responsiveness, infant-mother attachment and infant competence. *Journal of Child Psychology and Psychiatry and Allied Disciplines* 38, 1039–1050.

KATZ, S., SHEMESH, T. AND BIZMAN, A. (2000) Attitudes of university students toward the sexuality of persons with mental retardation and persons with paraplegia. *British Journal of Developmental Disabilities* 46, 109–117.

KEEL, M., SLATON, D.B. AND BLACKHURST, A.E. (2001) Acquisition of content area vocabulary for students with learning difficulties. *Education and Training of Children* 24, 46–71.

KELLEY, H.H. (1967) Attribution theory in social psychology. In Levine, D. (ed.) *Nebraska Symposium on Motivation*, vol 15. Lincoln, Nebraska University Press.

KELLEY, H.H. (1972) Causal schemata and the attribution process. In Jones, E.E., Kanouse, D., Kelley, H.H., Valins, B. and Weiner, B. (eds) *Attribution: perceiving the causes of behaviour.* Morristown, General Learning Press.

KELLY, C. AND BREINLINGER, S. (1996) *The social psychology of collective action: identity, injustuce and gender.* London, Taylor and Francis.

KINDT, M. AND BROSSCHOT, J.F. (1997) Phobia-related cognitive bias for pictorial and linguistic stimuli. *Journal of Abnormal Psychology* 106(4), 644–648.

KIPPIN, T.E. (2000) Olfactory-conditioned ejaculatory preference in the male rat: implications for the role of learning in sexual partner preferences. *Dissertation Abstracts International: Section B: The Sciences and Engineering* 61 (3–B), 1678.

KIRACOFE, N.M. (1992) Child-centred parental favouritism and self-reported personal characteristics. *Individual Psychology* 48, 349–356.

KIRBY, K.N. AND HERRNSTEIN, R.J. (1995) Preference reversals sue to myopic discounting of rewards. *Psychological Science* 6, 83–89.

KIRSCH, I., MONTGOMERY, G. AND SAPIRSTEIN, G. (1995) Hypnosis as an adjunct to cognitive-behavioural psychotherapy: A meta-analysis. *Journal of Counselling and Clinical Psychology* 63, 214–220.

KITAYAMA, S. AND MARKUS, H.R. (1992) Construal of self as cultured frame: implications for internationalising psychology. *Symposium of Internationalism and Higher Education.* Ann Arbor.

KITZINGER, C., COYLE, A., WILKINSON, S. AND MILTON, M. (1998) Towards lesbian and gay psychology. *The Psychologist* 11, 529–534.

KOENKHEN, G., MILNE, R., MEMON, A. AND BULL, R. (1999) The cognitive interview: a meta-analysis. *Psychology, Crime and Law* 5, 3–27.

KOHLBERG, L. (1963) The development of children's orientations towards a moral order: I Sequence in the development of moral thought. *Vita Humana* 6, 11–33.

KOHLBERG, L. (1969) Stage and sequence: the cognitive developmental approach to socialisation. In Goslin, D.A. (ed.) *Handbook of socialisation theory and research.* Chicago, Rand-McNally.

KRAEPLIN, E. (1883) *Clinical psychiatry.* Delmar, New York.

KRACKOW, A. AND BLASS, T. (1995) When nurses obey or defy inappropriate physician orders: atributional differences. *Journal of Social behaviour and Personality* 10, 585–594.

KURDEK, L.A. (2001) Differences between heterosexual non-parent couples and gay, lesbian and heterosexual-parent couples. *Journal of Family Issues* 22, 727–754.

LA BERGE, D. AND SAMUELS, S.J. (1974) Toward a theory of automatic information processing in reading. *Cognitive Psychology,* 6, 293–323.

LANGENFELD, M.C. (2000) The effects of hypnosis on pain-control with people living with HIV-AIDS. *Dissertation Abstracts International: Section B: The Sciences and Engineering* 60(11–B), 5780.

LATANE, B. (1981) The psychology of social impact. *American Psychologist* 36, 343–356.

LATTAL, A.K. AND GLEESON, S. (1990) Response acquisition with delayed reinforcement. *Journal of Experimental Psychology: Animal Behavior Processes* 16, 27–39.

LAU, S. AND PUN, K. (1999) Parental evaluations and their agreement: relationship with children's self-concepts. *Social behaviour and Personality* 27, 639–650.

LAZARUS, R.S. AND FOLKMAN, S. (1984) *Stress, appraisal and coping.* New York, Springer.

LEIBERMAN, D.A. (2000) *Learning: behavior and cognition.* London: Wadsworth.

LESLIE, A. (1994) ToMM, ToBy and agency: core architecture and domain specificity. In Hirschfield, L. and Gelman, S. (eds) *Mapping the mind: domain specificity in cognition and culture.* Cambridge, Cambridge University Press.

LEVI, A.M. (1998) Are defendants guilty if they were chosen in a line-up? *Law and Human Behaviour* 22, 389–407.

LI, C.N., NUTTALL, R.L. AND ZHAO, S. (1999) A test of the Piagetian water-level task with Chinese students. *Journal of Genetic Psychology* 160, 369–380.

LICHTENBERG, I.D. (2000) Voluntary consent or obedience to authority: an inquiry into the consensual police-citizen encounter. *Dissertation Abstracts International* 60, 3802.

LIPPINCOTT, B.M. (2001) Owls and larks in hypnosis: An experimental assessment of the ultradian theory of therapeutic suggestion. *Dissertation Abstracts International: Section B: The Sciences and Engineering* 62(1–B), 554.

LLOYD, B., LUCAS, K. AND FERNBACH, M. (1997) Adolescent girls' constructions of smoking identities: implications for health promotion. *Journal of Adolescence* 20, 43–56.

LOFTUS, E.F. (1975) Leading questions and the eyewitness report. *Cognitive Psychology* 7, 560–572.

LOFTUS, E.F. AND PALMER, J.C. (1974) Reconstruction of an automobile destruction: an example of the interaction between language and memory. *Journal of Verbal Learning and Verbal Behaviour* 13, 585–589.

LOW, B.S. AND HEINEN, J.T. (1993) Population, resources, and environment: Implications of human behavioral ecology for conservation. *Population and Environment* 15, 7–41.

LUNDH, L.G. AND OEST, L.G. (2001) Attentional bias, self-consciousness and perfectionism in social phobia before and after cognitive-behaviour therapy. *Scandinavian Journal of Behaviour Therapy* 30(1), 4–16.

LUNDH, L.G., WIKSTROM, J., WESTERLUND, J. AND OST, L.G. (1999) Preattentive bias for emotional information in panic disorder with agoraphobia. *Journal of Abnormal Psychology* 108(2), 222–232.

MACDONALD, J. AND MORLEY, I. (2001) Shame and non-disclosure: a study of the emotional isolation of people referred for psychotherapy. *British Journal of Medical Psychology* 74, 1–22.

MACLEOD (1991) Half a century of research on the Stroop effect: An integrative review. *Psychological Bulletin* 109, 163–203.

MADRIGAL, R. (2000) The influence of social alliances with sports teams on intentions to purchase corporate sponsors' products. *Journal of Advertising* 29, 13–24.

MANDLER, G., PEARLSTONE, Z. AND KOOPMANS, H.S. (1969) Effects of organisation and semantic similarity on recall and similarity. *Journal of Verbal Learning and Verbal Behaviour* 8, 410–423.

MANNETTI, L. AND PIERRO, A. (1994) Social representations of AIDS among Italian health care workers. *Revista de Psicologia Social* 9, 31–42.

MATTHEWS, D. AND DIETZ-UHLER, B. (1998) The black-sheep effect: how positive and negative advertisements affect voters' perceptions of the sponsor of the advertisement. *Journal of Applied Social Psychology* 28, 1903–1915.

MATUTE, H. (1996) Illusion of control: detecting response-outcome independence in analytic but not in naturalistic conditions. *Pscyhological Science* 7, 289–293.

MCADAMS, D.P., DIAMOND, A. AND ST AUBIN, A. (1997) Stories of commitment: the psychosocial construction of generative lives. *Journal of Personality and Social Psychology* 72, 678–694.

MCADAMS, D.P. AND ST AUBIN, A. (1992) A theory of generativity and its assessment through self-report, behavioural acts and narrative themes in autobiography. *Journal of Personality and Social Psychology* 62, 1003–1015.

MCCARTHY, G. (1999) Attachment style and adult love relationships and friendships: a study of a group of women at risk of experiencing relationship difficulties. *British Journal of Medical Psychology* 72, 305–321.

MCCOURT, K., BOUCHARD, T.J., LYKKEN, D.T., TELLEGEN, A. AND KEYES, M. (1999) Authoritarianism revisited: genetic and environmental influences on twins reared apart and together. *Personality and Individual Differences* 27, 985–1014.

MCFARLAND, S.G., AGEYEV, V.S. AND DJINTCHARADE, N. (1996) Russian authoritarianism two years after communism. *Personality and Social Psychology Bulletin* 22, 210–217.

MASLOW, A. (1954) *Personality and motivation.* Boston, Houghton-Mifflin.

MEINS, E. (1997) *Security of attachment and the development of social cognition.* Hove, Psychology Press.

MEKARSKI, J.E., CUTMORE, T.R.H. AND SUBOSKI, W. (1996) Gender differences during processing of the Stroop task. *Perceptual and Motor Skills* 83, 563–568.

MEMON, A. AND WRIGHT, D.B. (1999) Eyewitness testimony and the Oklahoma bombing. *The Psychologist* 12, 389–295.

MEVARECH, Z., SILBER, O. AND FINE, D. (1991) Learning with computers in small groups: cognitive and affective outcomes. *Journal of Educational Computing Research* 7 (2), 233–243.

MILES, C. AND HARDMAN, E. (1998) State-dependent memory produced by aerobic exercise. *Ergonomics* 41, 20–28.

MILGRAM, S. (1963) Behavioural study of obedience. *Journal of Abnormal and Social Psychology* 67, 371–378.

MILGRAM, S. (1974) *Obedience to authority.* New York, Harper and Row.

MILLIS, L.A. (1999) Contextual effects on the development of children's sociomoral judgements: a comparison of public school and non-school dilemma contexts. *Dissertation Abstracts International* 60, 1923.

MONSELL, S., TAYLOR, T.J. AND MURPHY, K. (2001) Naming the color of a word: Is it responses or task sets that compete? *Memory and Cognition* 29(1), 137–151.

MOORE, B.R. (1992) Avian imitation and a new form of mimicry: tracing the evolution of complex learning. *Behavior* 122, 231–263.

MORGAN, S. (2001) Hypnosis and simple phobia. *Australian Journal of Clinical and Experimental Hypnosis* 29, 17–25.

MORRIS, R.L., DALTON, K., DELANOY, D. AND WATT, C. (1995) Comparison of the sender/no sender condition in the Ganzfield. *Paper delivered at the 38th Convention of the Parapsychological Association*, Canada.

MORRIS, R. (2000) Parapsychology and teaching critical thinking. *Paper presented at the Annual Conference of the Association for the Teaching of Psychology,* Edinburgh University.

MORROW, C. (1999) Family values/valued families: storytelling and community formation among LBG families with children. *Journal of Gay, Lesbian and Bisexual Identity* 4, 345–356.

MOSCOVICI, S. (1977) *Essai sur l'histoire humaine de la nature.* Paris, Flammarion.

MOSCOVICI, S. (ed.) (2000) *Social representations: explorations in social psychology.* Cambridge, Polity.

MOSCOVICI, S. AND HEWSTONE, M. (1983) Social representations and social explanations: from the naive to the amateur scientist. In Hewstone, M. (ed.) *Attribution theory: social and functional extensions.* Oxford, Blackwell.

MOSS, G.J. AND OAKLEY, D.A. (1997) Stuttering modification using hypnosis: An experimental single-case study. *Contemporary Hypnosis* 14, 126–131.

MYRON-WILSON, P. AND SMITH, P.K. (1998) Attachment relationships and influences on bullying. *Proceedings of the British Psychological Society* 6 (2), 89–90.

NESDALE, D. AND FLESSER, D. (2001) Social identity and the development of children's group attitudes. *Child Development* 72, 506–517.

NEUBAUER, A.C. AND FREUDENTHALER, H.H. (1995) Ultradian rhythms in cognitive performance: no evidence for a 1.5 h rhthym. *Biological Psychology* 40, 281–298.

NIAZ, M. AND CARAUCAN, E. (1998) Learning to learn: a neo-Piagetian interpretation of the potential for learning. *Perceptual and Motor Skills* 86, 1291–1298.

NICHOLLS, D., CHATER, R. AND LASK, B. (2000) Children into DSM don't go: a comparison of classification systems for eating disorders in childhood and early adulthood. *International Journal of Eating Disorders* 28, 317–324.

NICOL, C.J. AND POPE, S.J. (1999) The effects of demonstrator social status and prior foraging success on social learning in laying hens. *Animal Behaviour* 57, 163–171.

NTOUMANIS, N. AND BIDDLE, S. (1998) The relationship of coping and its perceived effectiveness to positive and negative affect in sport. *Personality and Individual Differences* 24, 773–788.

OAKLEY, D., ALDEN, P. AND DEGUN MATHER, M. (1996) The use of hypnosis in therapy with adults. *The Psychologist* 9, 502–505.

OAKLEY, D. (1998) Emptying the habit: A case of trichtillomania. *Contemporary Hypnosis* 15, 109–117.

OAKLEY, D. (1999) Hypnosis and consciousness: A structural model. *Contemporary Hypnosis* 16, 215–223.

OIE, T.P.S. AND FREE, M.L. (1995) Do cognitive behaviour therapies validate cognitive models of mood disorders? A review of the empirical evidence. *International Journal of Psychology* 30, 145–180.

OKWONKO, R. (1997) Moral development and culture in Kohlberg's theory: a Nigerian (Igbo) evidence. *Ife Psychologia: an International Journal* 5, 117–128.

O'NEILL, R.M., GREENBERG, R.P. AND FISHER, S. (1992) Humour and anality. *Humour: International Journal of Humour Research* 5, 283–291.

ONYSKIW, J.E. (2000) Processes underlying children's responses to witnessing physical aggression in their families. *Dissertation Abstracts Internatioinal: Section B: The Sciences and Engineering* 61(3-B), 1620.

ONYSKIW, J.E. AND HAYDUK, L.A. (2001) Process underlying adjustment in families characterized by physical aggression. *Family Relations: Interdisciplinary Journal of Applied Family Studies* 50, 376–385.

OSIMANI, A., ALON, A., BERGER, A. AND ABARBANEL, J.M. (1997) Use of the Stroop phenomenon as a diagnostic tool for malingering. *Journal of Neurology, Neurosurgery and Psychiatry* 62(6), 617–621.

OTTONI, E.B. AND MANNU, M. (2001) Semi-free ranging tufted capuchins spontaneously use tools to crack open nuts. *International Journal of Primatology* 22, 347–358.

PALMER, S. AND DRYDEN, W. (1995) *Counselling for stress problems*. London, Sage.

PARKER, G., MITCHELL, P. AND WILHELM, K. (2000) Twelve month episodes of non-melancholic depressive subjects: refinements of subgroups by examination of trajectories. *Annals of Clinical Psychiatry* 12, 219–225.

PARKINSON, J.A., CROFTS, H.S., MCGUIGAN, M., DAVORKA, T.L., EVERITT, B.J. AND ROBERTS, A.C. (2001) Role of the primate amygdala in conditioned reinforcement. *Journal of Neurosience* 21, 7770–7780.

PATTERSON, C.J. (1997) Children of lesbian and gay parents. *Advances in Clinical Child Psychology* 19, 235–282.

PATTERSON, T.L., SMITH, L.W. AND SMITH, T.L. (1992) Symptoms of illness in late adulthood are related to childhood deprivation and misfortune in men but not in women. *Journal of behavioural Medicine* 15, 113–125.

PAVLOV, I.P. (1927) *Conditioned reflexes*. Oxford: Oxford University Press.

PEARCE, J.M. (1997) *Animal learning and cognition: An Introduction*. Hove, Psychology Press.

PEARCE, J.M. AND HALL, G. (1980) A model for Pavlovian learning: Variations in the effectiveness of conditioned but not of unconditioned stimuli. *Psychological Review* 87, 532–552.

PEPLAU, L.A. (1991) Lesbian and gay relationships. In Gonsiorek, J.C. and Weinrich, J.D. (eds) *Homosexuality: research implications for public policy*. London, Sage.

PEREZ, M.G., RIVERA, R.M., BANOS, F. AND AMPARO, B. (1999) Attentional bias and vulnerability to depression. *Spanish Journal of Psychology* 2, 11–19.

PERNER, J. (1991) *Understanding the representational mind*. Cambridge, Bradford Books.

PERSONS, J.B. (1989) *Cognitive therapy in practice: a case formulation approach*. New York, Norton.

PETERS, K. AND RICHARDS, P. (1998) 'Why we fight:' Voices of youth combatants in Sierra Leone. *Africa* 68, 183–210.

PETERSON, C., DOWDEN, C. AND TOBIN, J. (1999) Interviewing preschoolers: comparisons of yes/no and wh-questions. *Law and Human Behaviour* 23, 539–555.

PFEFFER, K., COLE, BANKOLE, AND DADA, M.K. (1998) Attributions for youth crime among British and Nigerian primary school children. *Journal of Social Psychology* 138, 251–253.

PHILO, G., SECKER, J., PLATT, S., HENDERSON, L., McLAUGHLIN, G. AND BURNSIDE, J. (1994) The impact of the mass media on public images of mental illness: media content and audience belief. *Health Education Journal* 53, 271–281.

PHILLIPS, C.J.C. AND MORRIS, I.D. (2001) A novel operant conditioning test to determine whether dairy cows dislike passageways that are dark or covered with excreta. *Animal Welfare* 10, 65–72.

PIAGET, J. (1952) Logic and psychology. Series of lectures at Manchester University, published by Basic Books, New York, 1957.

PIAGET, J. AND INHELDER, B. (1956) *The child's conception of space*. London, Routledge and Kegan Paul.

PLATOW, M.J., McCLINTOCK, AND LIEBRAND, W.B. (1990) Predicting intergroup fairness and in-group bias in the minimal group paradigm. *European Journal of Social Psychology* 20, 221–239.

PLAUTZ, J.D., KANEKO, M., HALL, J.C. AND KAY, S. (1997) Independent photoreceptive circadian clocks throughout *Drosophila*. *Science* 278, 1632.

POINTER, S.C. AND BOND, N.W. (1998) Context-dependent memory: colour vs odour. *Chemical Senses* 23, 359–362.

POPPE, E. AND LINSSEN, H. (1999) In-group favouritism and the reflection of realistic dimensions of difference between national states in Central and Eastern European nationality stereotypes. *British Journal of Social Psychology* 38, 85–102.

PUTNAM, D.E. (2000) Initiation and maintenance of online sexual compulsivity: Implications for assessment and treatment. *CyberPsychology and Behavior* 3, 553–563.

RABOW, J., STEIN, J.M. AND CONLEY, T.D. (1999) Teaching social justice and encountering society: the pink triangle experiment. *Youth and Society* 30, 483–514.

RADEN, D. (1999) Is anti-Semitism currently part of an authoritarian attitude syndrome? *Political Psychology* 20, 323–343.

RADIN, D.I. (1997) *The conscious universe: the scientific truth of psychic phenomena*. New York, Harper Edge.

RADIN, D.I. AND FERRARI, D.C. (1991) Effects of consciousness on the fall of dice: a meta-analysis. *Journal of Scientific Exploration* 5, 61–84.

RALPH, M.R., FOSTER, T.G., DAVIS, F.C. AND MENAKER, M. (1990) Transplanted suprachiasmatic nucleus determines circadian period. *Science* 247, 975–978.

RESCORLA, R.A. (1966) Predictability and number of pairings in Pavlovian fear conditioning. *Psychonomic Science* 4, 383–384.

RHINE, J.B. (1934) *Extra-sensory perception*. Boston, Boston SPR.

ROGERS, C. (1959) *On becoming a person*. London, Constable.

ROGERS, C. (1961) *Client-centred therapy*. Boston, Houghton-Mifflin.

ROGNER, J. (1994) One year after the end of an analytical Adlerian psychotherapy: changes in symptomatology *Zeitschift fuer Individualpsychologie* 19, 191–202.

ROSE, S. AND ZAND, D. (2000) Lesbian dating and courtship from young adulthood to midlife. *Journal of Gay and Lesbian Social Services* 11, 77–104.

ROUSSY, F., CAMIRAND, C., FOULKES, F., DEKONICK, J., LOFTIS, M. AND KERR, N. (1996) Does early night REM content reliably reflect pre-sleep state of mind? *Dreaming* 6, 121–130.

RUBINSTEIN, G. (1995) Right-wing authoritarianism, political affiliation, religiosity and their relation to psychological androgyny. *Sex Roles* 33, 569–586.

SANDAHL, C., HERLITZ, K. AND AHLIN, G. (1998) Time-limited group psychotherapy for moderately alcohol dependent patients: a randomised controlled clinical trial. *Psychotherapy Research* 8, 361–378.

SANDELL, R. (1999) Long-term findings of the Stockholm Outcome of Psychotherapy and Psychoanalysis Project (STOPP). *Paper presented at the Psychoanalytic long-term treatments: a challenge for clinical and empirical research in psychoanalysis meeting*, Hamburg.

SCHACHTER, D.L., EICH, J.E. AND TULVING, E. (1978) Richard Semon's theory of memory. *Journal of Verbal Learning and Verbal Behaviour* 17, 721–743.

SCHALLER, M. AND LATANE, B. (1996) Dynamic social impact and the evolution of social representations: a natural history of stereotypes. *Journal of Communication* 46, 64–77.

SCHLOZMAN (2000) Vampires and those who slay them: using the television program Buffy the Vampire Slayer in adolescent therapy and psychodynamic education. *Academic Psychiatry* 24, 49–54.

SENEVIRATNE, H. AND SAUNDERS, B. (2000) An investigation of alcohol dependent respondents' attributions for their own and others relapses. *Addiction Research* 8, 439–453.

SHELDON, K.M. AND KASSER, T. (2001) Goals, congruence and positive well-being: new empirical support for humanistic theories. *Journal of Humanistic Psychology* 41, 30–50.

SHELDRAKE, R. (2000) Telepathic telephone calls: two surveys. *Journal of the Society for Psychical Research* 64, 224–232.

SHERMAN, J.W. AND BESSENOFF, G.R. (1999) Stereotypes as source-monitoring cues: on the interaction between episodic and semantic memory. *Psychological Science* 10, 106–110.

SIEBERT, A. (2000) How non-diagnostic listening led to a rapid recovery from paranoid schizophrenia: what is wrong with psychiatry? *Journal of Humanistic Psychology* 40, 34–58.

SKINNER, B.F. (1948) Superstition in the pigeon. *Journal of Experimental Psychology* 38, 168–172.

SKINNER, B.F. (1974) *About behaviourism*. London, Jonathan Cape.

SKINNER, B.F. (1938) *The behavior of organisms: an experimental analysis*. New York: Appleton-Century-Croft.

SKINNER, B.F. (1953) *Science and human behaviour*. New York: Macmillan.

SMITH, P.K., COWIE, H. AND BLADES, M. (1998) *Understanding children's development*. London, Blackwell.

SMITH, P.B. AND BOND, M.H. (1998) *Social psychology across cultures*. Hemel Hempstead, Prentice Hall.

SNAREY, J.R., REIMER, R. AND KOHLBERG, L. (1985) Development of moral reasoning among Kibbutz adolescents: a longitudinal, cross-cultural study. *Developmental Psychology* 21, 3–17.

SOLMS, M. (2000) Freudian dream theory today. *The Psychologist* 13, 618–619.

SROUFE, L.A. (1985) Attachment classification from the perspective of infant-caregiver relationships and infant temperament. *Child Development* 56, 1–14.

STANDER, V.A., HSIUNG, P. AND MACDERMID, S. (2001) The relationship of attributions to marital distress: a comparison of mainland Chinese and US couples. *Journal of Family Psychology* 15, 124–134.

STEINKAMP, F., MILTON, J. AND MORRIS, R.L. (1998) A meta-analysis of forced-choice experiments comparing clairvoyance and precognition. *Journal of Parapsychology* 62, 193–218.

STEVENS, P. (1999) Remote psychokinesis. *European Journal of Parapsychology* 14, 68–79.

STOWELL-SMITH, M. AND MCKEOWN, M. (1999) Race, psychopathy and the self: a discourse analytic study. *British Journal of Medical Psychology* 72, 459–470.

STROGANOVA, T.A., TSETLIN, M.M., MALYKH, S.B. AND MALAKHOVSKAYA, E.V. (2000) Biological principles of individual differences of children of the second half-year of life: communication II. The nature of individual differences in temperamental features. *Human Physiology* 26, 281–289.

STROOP, J.R. (1935) Studies of interference in serial verbal reactions. *Journal of Experimental Psychology* 18(6), 643–662.

SUTTON, J., REEVES, M. AND KEOGH, E. (2000) Disruptive behaviour, avoidance of responsibility and theory of mind. *British Journal of Developmental Psychology* 18, 1–12.

SYMONS, D.K. AND CLARK, S.E. (2000) A longitudinal study of mother-child relationships and theory of mind in the preschool period. *Social Development* 9, 3–23.

TAJFEL, H. (1970) Experiments in intergroup discrimination. *Scientific American* 223, 96–102.

TAJFEL, H. AND TURNER, J.C. (1979) An integrative theory of intergroup conflict. In Austin, W.G. and Worchel, S. (eds) *The social psychology of intergroup relations*. Cambridge, Cambridge University Press.

TARG, R. AND PUTHOFF, H. (1974) Information transfer under conditions of sensory shielding. *Nature* 251, 602–607.

TARRIER, N., KINNEY, C., MCCARTHY, E. ET AL. (2001) Are some types of psychotic symptoms more responsive to cognitive-behaviour therapy. *Behavioural and Cognitive Psychotherapy* 29, 45–55.

TASKER, S.L. AND GOLOMBOK, F. (1997) *Growing up in a lesbian family*. London, Guildford Press.

TARNOW, E. (2000) Self-destructive obedience in the airplane cockpit and the concept of obedience optimisation. In Blass, T. (ed.) *Obedience to authority*. Mahwah, Lawrence Erlbaum.

TAVRIS, C. AND WADE, C. (1997) *Psychology in perspective*. New York, Longman.

TERMAN, M., AMIRA, L., TERMAN, J.S. AND ROSS, D.C. (1996) Predictors of response and nonresponse to light treatment for winter depression. *American Journal of Psychiatry* 153, 1423–1429.

THORNDIKE, E.L. (1905) *Elements of psychology*. New York: AG Seiler.

THORNHILL, R. AND THORNHILL, N.W. (1983) Human rape: An evolutionary analysis. *Ethology and Sociobiology* 4, 137–173.

TOTTERDELL, P. (1995) Effects of depressed affect on diurnal and ultradian variations in mood in a healthy sample. *Chronobiology International* 12, 278–289.

TRACY, R. AND AINSWORTH, M.D.S. (1981) Maternal affectionate behaviour and infant-mother attachment patterns. *Child Development* 52, 1341–1343.

TREISMAN, A. AND FEARNLEY, S. (1969) The Stroop Test: Selective attention to colours and words. *Nature* 22, 437–439.

TULVING, E. (1974) Cue dependent forgetting. *American Scientist* 62, 74–82.

TULVING, E. (1976) In Brown, J. (ed.) *Recall and recognition.* London, Wiley.

TULVING, E. (1983) *Elements of episodic memory.* Oxford, Oxford University Press.

TULVING, E. AND PEARLSTONE, Z. (1966) Availability vs accessibility of information in memory for words. *Journal of Verbal Learning and Verbal Behaviour* 5, 389–391.

UTTS, J. (1996) An assessment of the evidence for psychic functioning. *Journal of Scientific Exploration* 10, 3–30.

VAN DEN BOOM, D.C. (1994) The influence of temperament and mothering on attachment and exploration: an experimental manipulation of sensitive responsiveness among lower-class mothers with irritable babies. *Child Development* 65, 1457–1477.

VINDEN, P.G. (1996) Junin Quechua children's understanding of theory of mind. *Child Development* 67, 1701–1716.

VISWESVARAN, C. AND SCHMIDT, F.L. (1992) A meta-analytic comparison of the effectiveness of smoking cessation methods. *Journal of Applied Psychology* 77, 554–561.

VITARO, F., BRENGDEN, M. AND TREMBLAY, R.E. (2000) Influence of deviant friends on delinquency: searching for moderator variables. *Journal of Abnormal Child Psychology* 28, 313–325.

VONDRA, J.I., SHAW, D.S. AND KEVENIDES, M.C. (1995) Predicting infant attachment classification from multiple contemporaneous measures of maternal care. *Infant Behaviour and Development* 18, 415–425.

VONK, R. AND KONST, D. (1998) Intergroup bias and correspondent inference bias: people engage in situational correction when it suits them. *British Journal of Social Psychology* 37, 379–385.

WAGSTAFF, G.F. (1986) Hypnosis as compliance and belief: a socio-cognitive view. In Naish, P.L.N. (ed.) *What is hypnosis: Current theories and research.* Milton Keynes: Open University Press.

WAHLBERG, K.E., WYNNE, L.C., OJA, H. ET AL. (1997) Gene-environment interaction in vulnerability to schizophrenia: findings from the Finnish adoptive family study of schizophrenia. *American Journal of Psychiatry* 154, 355–362.

WALDNER, L.K. AND MAGRUDER, B. (1999) Coming out to parents: perceptions of family relations, perceived resources and identity expression as predictors of identity disclosure for gay and lesbian adolescents. *Journal of Homosexuality* 37, 83–100.

WALKER, W.R., VOGL, R.J. AND THOMPSON, C.P. (1997) Autobiographical memory: unpleasantness fades faster than pleasantness over time. *Applied Cognitive Psychology* 11, 399–413.

WALL, T.N. AND HAYES, J.A. (2000) Depressed patients' attributions of responsibility for the causes of and solutions to their problems. *Journal of Counselling and Development* 78, 81–86.

WEINROTT, M.R., RIGGAN, M. AND FROTHINGHAM, S. (1997) Reducing deviant arousal in juvenile sex offenders using vicarious sensitization. *Journal of Interpersonal Violence* 12, 704–728.

WENINGER, M.S. (1999) Cerebellar deep nuclei contributions to the learned eye-blink response in the rabbit. *Dissertation Abstracts International: Section B: The Sciences and Engineering* 59 (8–B), 4451.

WETHERALL, M. (1997) *Identities, groups and social issues.* London, Sage.

WHITBOURNE, S.K., ZUSCHLAG, M.K., ELLIOT, L.B. AND WATERMAN, A.S. (1992) Psychosocial development in adulthood: a 22–year sequential study. *Journal of Personality and Social Psychology* 63, 260–271.

WHITLEY, B.E. AND LEE, S.E. (2000) The relationship of authoritarianism and related constructs to attitudes toward homosexuality. *Journal of Applied Social Psychology* 30, 144–170.

WILLIAMS, J.D. AND GRUZELIER, J.H. (2001) Differentiation of hypnosis and relaxation by analysis of narrow band theta and alpha frequencies. *International Journal of Clinical and Experimental Hypnosis* 49, 185–206.

WILLIN, M.J. (1996) A ganzfield experiment using musical targets with previous high scorers from the general population. *Journal of the Society for Psychical Research* 61, 103–108.

WIMMER, H. AND PERNER, J. (1983) Beliefs about beliefs: representation and constraining function of wrong beliefs in young children's understanding of deception. *Cognition* 13, 103–128.

WITTENBAUM, G.W. AND STASSER, G. (1995) The role of prior expectancy and group discussion in the attribution of attitudes. *Journal of Experimental Social Psychology* 31, 82–105.

WORCHEL, S., ROTHGERBER, H., DAY, E.A., HART, D. AND BUTEMEYER, J. (1998) Social identity and individual productivity within groups. *British Journal of Social Psychology* 37, 389–413.

WORKMAN, J.E. AND FREEBURG, E.W. (1999) An examination of date rape, victim distress and perceiver variables within the context of attribution theory. *Sex Roles* 41, 261–277.

WRIGHT, D.B., SELF, G. AND JUSTICE, C. (2000) Memory conformity: exploring misinformation effects when presented by another person. *British Journal of Psychology* 91, 189–202.

WYNN, V.E. AND LOGIE, R.H. (1998) The veracity of long-term memories: did Bartlett get it right? *Applied Cognitive Psychology* 12, 1–20.

YAPKO, M.D. (1995) *Essentials of Hypnosis.* New York: Brunner/Mazel.

YOST, J.H. AND WEARY, G. (1996) Depression and correspondent inference bias: evidence for more effortful processing. *Personality and Social Psychology* 22, 192–200.

YOUNG, J. (1990) *Cognitive therapy for personality disorders: a schema-focussed approach.* Sarasota, Professional Resource Exchange.

ZBRODOFF, N.J. AND LOGAN, G.D. (2000) When it hurts to be misled: A Stroop-like effect in a simple addition production task. *Memory and Cognition,* 28(1): 1–7.

ZINBARG, R.E. AND MINEKA, S. (2001) Understanding, treating, and preventing anxiety, phobias, and anxiety disorders. In Carroll, M.E. and Overmier, J.B. (eds) *Animal research and human health: Advancing human welfare through behavioral science.* Washington DC: American Psychological Association.

ZWEIGENHAFT, R.L. AND VON AMMON, J. (2000) Birth order and civil disobedience: a test of Sulloway's born to rebel hypothesis. *Journal of Social Psychology* 140, 624–627.

ZYSSET, S., MÜLLER, K., LOHMANN, G. AND YVES VON CRAMON (2001) Color-word matching Stroop task: separating interference and response conflict. *NeuroImage* 13, 29–36.

# Index